BEST BIRDWATCHING SITES IN NORFOLK

by Neil Glenn

Dedicated to my wife Jackie, for her
endless support.

BUCKINGHAM PRESS

Published in 2002 by:
Buckingham Press
55 Thorpe Park Road, Peterborough
Cambridgeshire PE3 6LJ
United Kingdom

01733 561739
e-mail: buck.press@btinternet.com

© Buckingham Press 2002

ISBN 0 9533840 47
ISSN 0144-364 X

Editor: David Cromack
Design and maps: Hilary Cromack
Publisher: Hilary Cromack

Black and white illustrations: Alan Harris
Alan has been a freelance bird illustrator since graduating with a BA in Graphic Design in 1980. His illustrations have been published in many books and field guides, including *A Field Guide to the Birds of Britain and Europe* by John Gooders and the recent ground-breaking work on Sylvia Warblers by Hadoram Shirihai. He has also had many illustrations published in magazines and a number of identification papers published in *British Birds*. Alan accepts commissions.
Address: 60 East Park, Harlow, Essex CM17 0SE.

Cover illustration: *Marsh Harrier at Cley Marshes* - by Jan Wilczur
Jan has been a keen birder and artist for 25 years but only became a fulltime freelance illustrator in 1994. He has provided artwork for the *Handbook of Birds of the World, Concise Birds of the Western Palearctic, Birds of SE Asia* and other field guides.
Jan accepts commissions.
Further examples of his work can be seen on www.birdillustrators.com
Address: 30 Dover House Road, London SW15 5AV. 0208 878 8925

Printed and bound in Great Britain by:
Biddles Ltd, Book Manufacturers, Guildford, Surrey.

CONTENTS

CONTENTS

ACCESS INFORMATION   **200**
(Each site is assessed for its suitability for wheelchair users
and availability of public transport. Boat mooring information
is also given for Broadland sites).

THE NORFOLK BIRD LIST   **205**
(Status report on all species ever recorded in Norfolk.
Can be used as a checklist).

DEFINITIONS OF BIRD GROUPS   **216**
(An explanation of collective terms used in this publication).

GLOSSARY/BIRDSPEAK   **217**
(An explanation of acronyms, birdwatching terms and jargon words
used in this publication).

BIBLIOGRAPHY   **219**

USEFUL CONTACTS   **220**

INDEX   **221**
(All target species listed, plus alternative site names).

INTRODUCTION

MY FIRST MEMORIES of Norfolk are non-birding ones. As a child, my family's annual holidays were all spent in a static caravan at East Runton, just outside Cromer. This was not the most exotic of venues, I'll grant you, but we loved it all the same.

In those days, it seemed like a major logistical operation by my mother to get us there from Nottingham. The journey used to take five to six hours, including at least three toilet stops, a meal break and the inevitable hour's tailback on the Old Clenchwarton Road. However, this was nothing compared to my father's efforts to join us – he used to cycle all the way overnight, a distance of some 120 miles. Mind you, he couldn't move for a day or so afterwards but each to his own! The same drive now takes me 90 minutes and I don't stop for *anything*, as many an unfortunate passenger will testify.

When I reached my teens, my mate 'Gnome' would join us for two weeks of chips, sandcastles and bingo. Occasionally, my mum would drop us off at Cley on her way to help my Great Aunt Cissie move house (yes, she did move house *every* year, amazingly always coinciding with our two weeks with an estate car). Gnome and I would roam the reserve with our Boots binoculars and have absolutely no idea what we were looking at, but hey, we enjoyed it immensely. The birdwatching seeds were sown.

Though I cannot remember, nor have any record of, the birds we saw on these trips to Cley, I do know that I fell in love with the place which some – including my wife Jackie – describe as bleak. I still get a thrill when walking along the sea wall as I look across the expanse of reeds to see the famous windmill in the distance.

I do have two Norfolk bird memories from these holidays. The first is of a chap walking into the hide and declaring that there was a Purple Sandpiper in front of the hide and asking Gnome and I if we have seen the Bean Goose on the scrape. We looked goggle-eyed at the gent, amazed at his identification prowess. Now, bear in mind this was the beginning of August, and you can see that this chap was a complete nutter, but two 14-year-olds were impressed at the time.

The second memory is of walking from Runton to Cromer across the large grass car park on the cliff top, which is still there to this day. We came across a small wader in the grass, not moving as we approached. As self-proclaimed experts, we immediately identified the exhausted bird as a Dunlin, as all waders were at this time. We continued on to the heady attractions of the big metropolis known as Cromer without a second thought for the bird. I now wonder what that wader was; it had obviously just landed in an exhausted state, the time of year was prime rare wader time (White-rumped Sandpiper, Baird's Sandpiper, Stilt Sandpiper, etc). What did I miss? Probably a Dunlin.

Sadly, I have now lost touch with Gnome in the way one tends to lose track of best friends from schooldays. He was last seen calling himself Steven, with wife, three kids and two dogs in tow, but I hope he would be proud to know that I am trying to instil into others – including my wife – our love of a fantastic county by way of this book.

DEDICATION

And so I dedicate this book to my parents, who love Norfolk as much as I do; Gnome, with whom I spent so many happy hours trying to identify little brown birds in my formative years; and most of all to my wife Jackie who has been the model of patience and understanding throughout, as she uncovers more of my obsessions (birding is just one!) as our years together whizz by.

ACKNOWLEDGEMENTS

I WOULD like to acknowledge the following people, without whom this book would not have been possible:

Firstly, the hard-working staff at Buckingham Press for their excellent maps and page-layouts, and for asking me to write this tome in the first place;

Secondly, many friends, too numerous to mention, who have shown boundless support and enthusiasm for this project from the outset;

Thirdly, Brian of Essex for his comments on disabled access at some of the sites listed;

Fourthly, the many hard-working wardens and regional office staff of the various management bodies, who have been extremely helpful in verifying the accuracy of the site information.

Fifthly, the many birding folk I have met on my travels who have, in the main, been friendly, helpful and contributed towards many a fantastic day in the field;

Finally, and most importantly, my long-suffering wife who has been unconditionally supportive throughout the writing of this book, and long-before I ever started work on it! She has also borne the brunt of most of the proof-reading. Maybe, after reading this material, she will have learned what a wonderful place Norfolk is!

My thanks must also go to you, the reader, for purchasing the book. If you find any mistakes within its pages, I apologise profusely. Please let me know so I may alter the details in forthcoming editions. Also let me know if this book has enhanced your visit to Norfolk.

Neil Glenn, c/o Buckingham Press, 55 Thorpe Park Road, Peterborough, PE3 6LJ

WHY NORFOLK IS THE TOP COUNTY FOR BIRDWATCHING

FOR the bulk of the British population, Norfolk is a sleepy tucked-away county with little to make it noteworthy, but among birdwatchers it enjoys a reputation second to none. Why is this so? Until I began to research this book, I freely admit that I'd been content to watch the diverse bounty of birds without being particularly bothered why they were attracted to the county. However, on further reflection, this question demands some answers.

A quick glance at a map of Britain gives a simple clue to the county's importance to birds. East Anglia (of which Norfolk is the northern half) is a bulky land-mass that juts out into the North Sea, pointing towards Europe and Scandinavia and for any off-course birds migrating from these continental areas, making landfall here could be the difference between life and death.

This explains why so many rarities are discovered, but many other commoner species actively choose this county as their preferred wintering or summering grounds. There must be some other attraction other than geographical positioning and that can be summed up in one word: habitat.

Many birdwatchers in Norfolk concentrate along the north coast, dominated by The Wash and large tracts of salt marsh, because this is the area with the greatest concentration of birds. The Wash is a huge estuary of mud, super-abundant in invertebrates – a crucial food supply for thousands of wintering wading birds. The 2,000 hectares of salt marsh – stretching from Holme to Salthouse – is internationally important for many breeding species and over-wintering wildfowl. For instance, up to a third of the world's population of Pink-footed Goose choose to spend the Winter on these marshes. Norfolk is lucky in that most of its salt marsh has been protected from development. Similar habitat in Essex and Kent, which once supported large bird communities, has been reclaimed for housing and industrial use. As other areas of marsh disappear under housing, so the Norfolk marshes become even more important for birds.

However, it is important to remember that the interior of Norfolk contains other valuable habitats. Further south are the Norfolk Broads, a bird-rich habitat created in medieval times by people digging for peat. These waters, so beloved of boating enthusiasts, spread inland from Great Yarmouth to Wroxham and Norwich. The pure waters of The Broads attract many species of wildfowl, and many more species of insect and plant. Ironically, the activities of man are now threatening this delicate habitat through pollution, though this is being addressed by numerous conservation organisations. Most Broadland reed beds and wet woodlands (carrs) are being restored and preserved by hard-working organisations such as Norfolk Wildlife Trust, The Broads Authority and the RSPB.

WHY NORFOLK IS BEST

Breckland is yet another important area for birds. This is an area of some 94,000 hectares, originally of sandy heathland, located around Thetford. This nutrient-poor soil was extensively planted with Scots pines in the 1940s and these are still being harvested to this day by Forest Enterprise. This harvesting creates many clearings inhabited by Wood Larks and Nightjars. The other important resident of The Brecks is the humble Rabbit: constant nibbling of vegetation ensures the continued presence of ground-nesting species such as Stone Curlew, Wheatear and Wood Lark.

The Fens of East Anglia have mostly been drained and reclaimed for agricultural use, though some areas remain, most notably around The Ouse Washes. In Norfolk, this means WWT Welney and its famous wintering herds of wild swans and huge numbers of wildfowl, which find the combination of rivers, flood plains and grazing marsh to their liking. The RSPB is creating the largest wetland reserve in Britain on the Fens of Lakenheath, hoping to attract Bitterns, Bearded Tits and Marsh Harriers back to the area.

We must not forget farmland in our equation. The majority of land in Norfolk is intensively farmed and is thus inaccessible to visitors. However, it is this inaccessibility that protects some species from disturbance on farms managed sympathetically with wildlife in mind. Many of Norfolk's 100 pairs of Stone Curlews nest on farmland, free from the pressures of egg-collectors and birdwatchers. The same can be said for winter flocks of Tree Sparrows and Corn Buntings. Of course, some farmers motivated largely by EC subsidies have much to answer for, as many farms these days are completely devoid of life, but I feel the tide is turning.

Add gravel workings, small tracts of ancient woodland, extensive dune systems, former Victorian estates and the North Sea into the equation and the wide range of habitats in Norfolk becomes evident. There are even a couple of sea-cliffs, recently colonised by Fulmars; not bad for a "boring, flat county"!

One final thought: as Norfolk's attraction for birds became evident, more and more birdwatchers congregated in the county. Norfolk now has a large, resident population of birders, plus many more who spend their holidays there. This means that new and interesting birds are always likely to be discovered, fuelling the county's reputation as the bird capital of Britain, thus attracting more birdwatchers, and so on and so forth...

WHY THIS SITE GUIDE?

THERE are several guides to Norfolk bird and wildlife sites available for you to buy, so why choose this one? I shall explain.

When I visit a bird site, particularly one I haven't visited before, I want to know:
  i) **Exactly what I am likely to see at the time of year I am visiting.**
  ii) **The likelihood of seeing the birds listed in the site guide.**

For instance, how many times have you been to a reserve in Winter and seen Merlin on the sightings board? Lots. And how many Merlins have you seen? Not many, I bet! In this guide you will find Merlin listed for many reserves, but you will also be given an idea of how likely you are to see one. This is expressed by a percentage score after the name of each target bird for each site.

The fact that Merlins zip through Titchwell once a day in Winter doesn't mean you will see one, and this guide makes that obvious. In this way, the visiting birdwatcher will not let their hopes rise too high, but will know which birds are most likely to be encountered.

A major feature of this guide is that **sites are listed in alphabetical order**: no more struggling to find site 3.14, or reading through reams of text to find the site you want. Sites are also cross-referenced on pages for **Disabled Access, Partly Disabled Access, Public Transport Access**, and **Broadland Boat Access**. If you are visiting Norfolk for a Norfolk Broads boating holiday, for instance, this feature makes it easy to look up which sites are accessible for you. You then simply turn to the site guide page for more details.

Another bugbear is that many site guides hide the most important information in masses of text. **This guide displays the most relevant facts prominently** (when to visit, grid reference of parking area, target species, likelihood of seeing your targets). More detailed background information is given in the adjoining text, but the important stuff is right there up front.

Another important feature of this book is that it is up to date. I visited every site listed in 2001 (and several in 2002) and noted any changes to previous visits. Of course, things may have changed since I last visited, and some sites I frequented in 2001 altered from one visit to the next, which was quite frustrating at times.

On my travels, I have also learned of two new reserves opening in 2002, too late to be included in this book. The Norfolk Ornithologists' Association is opening its newly-purchased Hempton Marsh reserve, near Fakenham, while a wildlife-friendly farm reserve is opening in Summer near Glandford. The birding scene in Norfolk is, quite literally, changing day by day! **This makes the Contacts section for each site an essential feature**, enabling visitors to check details of opening times, entrance fee, etc before their trip.

Complete beginners will find the **Calendar section details the seasonal comings and goings of birds in Norfolk**, and a list of birdwatching sites recommended according to the season. More experienced birders may wish to visit somewhere they have heard about but not yet visited. In either case the reader can easily locate the relevant page, as sites are arranged in alphabetical order.

WHY THIS SITE GUIDE?

The layout for each site is designed to help you make the most of your visit. As stated above, important information (e.g. parking) is easy to find but this guide comes into its own as **the background text takes you on the walk itself.** The best areas for certain target species are described, as are tips on fieldcraft, enabling the birdwatcher to make the most of their visit.

In a nutshell, this book is designed to enable any birdwatcher visiting Norfolk to confidently plan a day, weekend, or holiday seeing exactly what they want to see, when they want to see it (within reason!), no matter how experienced or inexperienced they may be.

Finally, every effort has been made to check, check and check again the details for each site. If you find that this guide is incorrect in any way, please let me know so that I can amend the details in future editions. Also, I would be extremely happy to hear from you if you have enjoyed a day out at one of the sites mentioned: it would make all my hard work worthwhile!

The Birdwatcher's Code of Conduct

1. Welfare of birds must come first
Whether your particular interest is photography, ringing, sound recording, scientific study or just birdwatching, remember that the welfare of birds must always come first.

2. Habitat protection
A birds's habitat is vital to its survival and therefore we must ensure that our activities do not cause damage.

3. Keep disturbance to a minimum
Birds' tolerance of disturbance varies between species and seasons. Therefore, it is safer to keep all disturbance to a minimum. No birds should be disturbed from the nest in case the opportunities for predators to take eggs or young are increased. In very cold weather, disturbance to birds may cause them to use vital energy at a time when food is difficult to find. Wildfowlers impose bans during cold weather: birdwatchers should exercise similar discretion.

4. Rare breeding birds
If you discover a rare breeding bird and feel that protection is necessary, inform the appropriate RSPB Regional Officer, or the Species Protection Department at the RSPB, The Lodge, Sandy, Beds SG19 2DL. Otherwise, it is best in almost all circumstances to keep the record strictly secret to avoid disturbance by other birdwatchers and attacks by egg-collectors. Never visit known sites of rare breeding birds unless they are adequately protected. Even your presence may give away the site to others and cause so many other visitors that the birds may fail to breed successfully. Disturbance at or near the nest of species listed on the First Schedule of the Wildlife and Countryside Act 1981 is a criminal offence.

5. Rare migrants
Rare migrants or vagrants must not be harassed. If you discover one, consider the circumstances carefully before telling anyone. Will an influx of birdwatchers disturb the bird or others in the area? Will the habitat be damaged? Will problems be caused with the landowner?

6. The law
The bird protection laws, as now embodied in the Wildlife and Countryside Act 1981, are the result of hard campaigning by previous generations of birdwatchers. As birdwatchers, we must abide by them at all times and not allow them to fall into disrepute.

7. Respect the rights of landowners
The wishes of landowners and occupiers of land must be respected. Do not enter land without permission. Comply with permit schemes. If you are leading a group, do give advance notice of the visit, even if a formal permit scheme is not in operation. Always obey the Country Code.

8. Keeping records
Much of today's knowledge about birds is the result of meticulous record keeping by our predecessors. Make sure you help to add to tomorrow's knowledge by sending records to your county bird recorder.

9. Birdwatchng abroad
Behave abroad as you would at home. This code should be firmly adhered to when abroad (whatever the local laws). Well behaved birdwatchers can be important ambassadors for bird protection.

(Reprinted with permisson from the RSPB)

YOUR BIRDING YEAR

THIS PART of the book is aimed at helping you plan your birding trips more effectively. For example, you may wish to observe wild geese: by reading the monthly summaries you will be able to find out which species will be present, the best time of year to visit and which sites to head for. Then simply turn to the site page in the main section to find out how to get to your chosen birding venue.

January's calendar is very comprehensive, covering species which occur throughout the period from October to March, and is intended to be complementary to the calendars for each of those months.

JANUARY

MANY evocative sights and sounds can be experienced without much effort from the enthusiastic birdwatcher in this exciting month. What could be better than starting the day with thousands of Pink-footed Geese flying overhead on the way to their feeding grounds and ending it, by watching Hen Harriers silently drifting in to roost over a reedbed? Pure magic.

Herons and Cranes: If areas of shallow water freeze over on reserves such as Titchwell, Hickling Broad, Cley, etc, keep an eye open for Bitterns in the open, as their usual feeding areas deep in the reeds become inaccessible. One or two Little Egrets should be seen at Titchwell no matter what the weather conditions and head for Stubb Mill to see Cranes coming into roost.

Geese: Huge numbers of wintering wild geese can be seen at various accessible sites. Almost half of all Britain's wintering Pink-footed Geese roost on The Wash at Snettisham. Get there early in the morning for a real avian spectacular but avoid three days either side of a full moon, when the geese will remain in the fields feeding throughout the night. During the day, flocks can be encountered anywhere along the coast and surrounding fields.

Brent Geese visit most of the salt marshes between Salthouse and Holme but try Titchwell and Cley for close views on the ground. Most of the Brents will be of the dark-bellied race (*bernicla*) but it is possible to test your identification skills by trying to pick out a pale-bellied race (*hrota*) or a Black Brant (*branta*) from their commoner cousins. The Black Brant, a vagrant from America, has become an annual visitor to Norfolk, favouring sites such as Cley and Titchwell in the last couple of years. At Burnham, three hybrid young (*branta x bernicla*) were identified in 2001 to further test the keen birder!

White-fronted Geese are best viewed from Lady Anne's Drive at Holkham. Thousands of Pink-footed Geese are usually in the area and mixed in with them might be one or two Barnacle Geese, or a Lesser White-fronted Goose on rare occasions. There should also be one or two Egyptian Geese at this site along with the other two 'plastic' geese, Canada and Greylag.

The other Winter goose to see in the county is the (taiga) Bean, the larger of the two races. There is a wintering flock of around 150 birds, usually to be found on Buckenham

11

YOUR BIRDING YEAR

Marshes. Please call in to Strumpshaw Fen visitor centre for up-to-date sightings. A few individuals of the smaller (tundra) Bean Goose can sometimes be found with the White-fronted Geese at Holkham or the swans at Welney.

Swans: If you are looking for superb views of wild swans, then Welney is the place to head for. Most of the Bewick's and Whoopers spend the day in fields away from the reserve, but return to roost in the early evening. The warden spreads grain out for the swans and ducks and the whole spectacle can be watched from the comfort of a heated hide. A small number of wild swans can sometimes be seen around Haddiscoe Marsh or Halvergate Marsh, and occasionally in the Horsey area.

Wildfowl: Thousands of ducks make Norfolk their home in Winter. These can be split into two categories: seaducks and inland ducks. Species of seaduck such as Long-tailed Duck, Common Scoter, Velvet Scoter and Red-breasted Merganser are usually best found somewhere between Hunstanton and Titchwell, though Holme seems to be the most reliable site for the former species. They can be accompanied by Red-throated, Black-throated and Great Northern Divers, or Red-necked and Slavonian Grebes.

Species such as Wigeon, Pintail, Pochard and Mallard can be found on virtually any marsh or lake, but for the most comfortable viewing try Welney. You can see all of the above species and many more from the comfort of the heated hide.

Also look out for Scaup and Smew around the county: neither can be guaranteed but Snettisham occasionally attracts the former species, while Tottenhill gravel pits has gained a reputation for attracting the latter.

Birds of prey: When I think of Norfolk in Winter, I think of raptor roosts. There is nothing more evocative than ending a cold day's birding by watching Hen and Marsh Harriers drifting in to roost along with a lightning fast Merlin or two. My favourite site to head for is Stubb Mill, where Cranes can also be virtually guaranteed. Other raptor roosts include Roydon Common, Strumpshaw Fen and Titchwell.

Away from the traditional roost sites, raptors during January are usually just passing through. Merlin and Peregrine scour the marshes for unwary waders. If you see a flock of ducks or waders take to the air, always look skyward for a hunting raptor.

Waders: The north Norfolk coast is an internationally important area for wintering waders and a trip to Snettisham at high tide is a must. The sight of thousands of birds coming in to roost in front of the hide is truly awe-inspiring. Never mind trying to identify the individual species, just sit and marvel at the sight and sound of Dunlin, Knot, Oystercatcher, Bar-tailed Godwit, Redshank, Ringed Plover, Sanderling, etc. as they whirl through the air, twisting and turning, seemingly at random, before landing on the beach. Magnificent.

Of course, you can see waders at many other sites in January. Hunstanton, Holme, Titchwell, Cley, etc. can be alive with commoner species, but Purple Sandpipers are scarce Winter visitors usually limited to Hunstanton or Titchwell.

Woodcock and Jack Snipe are by far the most elusive waders. Places to try at dusk for the former species include Titchwell, Holkham Park and Stubb Mill. Jack Snipe are very

WHAT TO LOOK FOR

scarce in the county, the most regular site being an inaccessible area of Roydon Common. Snipe should prove easier to see on any marsh, and one or two Spotted Redshank over-winter at Titchwell.

Cley holds Black-tailed Godwits and maybe even an Avocet or two, and Grey Plovers should grace many of the beaches on the north coast. If you are lucky, Sammy the Black-winged Stilt will brighten your day at Titchwell (August 2001 marked the start of its eighth year on site and he was still present in May 2002). If you feel you have to see Avocets in January, then visit Breydon Water where up to a hundred can be found amongst the large number of commoner wader species.

Owls: One of the lasting memories of a trip to Norfolk in January – indeed any month – should be the sight of a Barn Owl silently hunting over a field or marsh. The places I seem to have most success with this species are Hickling, Holme, Flitcham Abbey Farm, Morston Quay and Cley, though the chances of seeing one whilst travelling between sites are quite good, especially if you are out and about at dawn and dusk. Short-eared Owls may be encountered on any marsh. Breydon Water is a favoured site for this owl, with one or two occasionally roosting along the north side. By day they spend their time hunting over Haddiscoe or Halvergate Marshes. A Little Owl or two is virtually guaranteed at Flitcham Abbey or Choseley Barns.

Passerines: Small birds can seem to take a back seat at this time of year, but there are plenty to see if you have the inclination to seek them out. The main target species include Twite, Snow Bunting, Lapland Bunting and Shore Lark. Numbers vary from year to year and Lapland Buntings are becoming extremely scarce, seemingly due to changes in the way the marshes are grazed. For instance, Burnham Norton used to be a reliable site for Laplands, but they seem to have deserted the place in the last couple of Winters. Halvergate Marsh is another traditional site for this species, but scan any set-aside field or marsh along the coast and you may strike it lucky.

Twite spend Winter on the Norfolk coast, but numbers are declining. Titchwell usually hosts 50 or so, but they can be very elusive. The best place to see them in recent years seems to be Holkham NNR, where 70-plus could be seen daily in 2001 and 2002. This site has, in recent years, also been the best site for Shore Lark (in fact the *only* site in January 2001 and 2002). Titchwell, Cley and Salthouse Beach are also traditional sites for Shore Lark in a good year, but never guaranteed. In addition, Titchwell is a good bet to find Snow Buntings, though Hunstanton, Holme, Salthouse Beach, Blakeney Point and Great Yarmouth Beach are all worth searching for the mobile flocks. Holkham NNR was the best site in 2002.

Cley is virtually guaranteed to produce a handful of Water Pipits in among the Meadow Pipits and Pied Wagtails feeding to the right of the east bank. Large numbers of Rock Pipits spend the Winter in Norfolk, the biggest flocks being on Scolt Head Island and Breydon Water. On a still day, the more colourful Bearded Tits should make an appearance at Cley, Titchwell, Welney, Gypsy Lane and Hickling.

Hawfinches should be in evidence, but their numbers are declining rapidly in the county.

13

YOUR BIRDING YEAR

Holkham Hall used to be a very good site but now it is best to head for Lynford Arboretum or Barnhamcross Common for a better chance of seeing this elusive beauty.

Buntings and finches may form large feeding flocks during the Winter months, with Flitcham Abbey Farm, Choseley Barns and East Wretham Heath being prime sites. Scan any flock carefully, as it may contain one or two Bramblings or Tree Sparrows.

Rarities: Rarity-hunters can have a hard time at this time of year, but during the Winter of 2002, a King Eider was present at Holkham Gap/Wells Harbour. This species has a history of returning to a favoured site, so look out for his return in December 2002. Iceland or Glaucous Gulls may be found around the county (try King's Lynn Docks), Mediterranean Gulls should be encountered on Great Yarmouth Beach and hardy seawatchers may be rewarded with a Pomarine Skua or two.

Waxwings may be seen during irruption years, though no single site can be recommended as they head for the nearest berry bushes, stay for a couple of days to strip them bare, then move on to another area.

A Rough-legged Buzzard is usually to be found wintering in the county, but as with Waxwings, no single site can be recommended. I have found single birds at Titchwell (1998) and Horsey (1999). In the Winters of 2001 and 2002, Haddiscoe Marsh was the venue for this species.

Titchwell has gained a reputation in recent years for attracting a Penduline Tit and any feeding finch flocks encountered on your travels should be scrutinised for Common and Arctic Redpolls (Titchwell in 2002) and Serin.

A day or weekend in Norfolk in January ensures an exciting start to the birding year for the visiting birdwatcher. For a 'sad lister' such as me, it is the ideal county to get your year-list off to a flying start!

FEBRUARY

THOUGH species largely mirror those detailed in January's calendar, Spring migration gets under way during this month. This may seem unlikely as you stand birdwatching, dressed like Sir Ranulph Fiennes at the North Pole, but it is true.

Geese: Many Pink-footed Geese will have moved on by mid-month, but you should still be able to catch up with a few at Holkham NNR or Snettisham. Bean Geese usually leave Buckenham by the second week of February. Egyptian Geese will already be nesting, though few of the first batch of chicks will survive if there is a prolonged freeze.

Wildfowl: Some wintering ducks will move out later in the month, but there are still plenty at the sites mentioned for January.

Birds of prey: All the raptors previously mentioned in January will still be in evidence.

Waders: Avocets will return to their breeding grounds so try Cley, Breydon Water and Titchwell.

WHAT TO LOOK FOR

Owls: Long-eared Owls begin to breed, so listen out for hooting from suitable coniferous woods in the county (e.g. Thetford Forest and Dersingham Bog). It is a good month to call at Holkham Park to see the Tawny Owls in their traditional roost tree around the monument. Also look out for Lesser Spotted Woodpecker in this area.

Passerines: Early breeding species include Crossbill, which start nesting in Lynford Arboretum, Holkham, Sandringham and Dersingham Bog. Bunting and finch flocks will still be around – check out sites such as Flitcham Abbey Farm, East Wretham Heath and Choseley Barns.

Apart from the above species, you should read the calendar notes for January if visiting Norfolk in February.

MARCH

SPRING migration picks up speed in March, but only just. Several early-arriving species will have been recorded by the end of the month, but this is usually only a tantalising taster of the mass arrival of birds in April and May.

Herons and Cranes: It is worth pausing by any large area of reeds to listen for the evocative booming of a Bittern. This is still a rare sound, but is gradually increasing at places such as Strumpshaw Fen, Cley, etc. March could be the last month for a while that you catch a glimpse of Crane around the Horsey area.

Swans: Bewick's and Whooper Swans will be leaving in their droves early in the month, so watch for flying flocks. A handful of both species remain at Welney until the last week of March, but after that, only injured birds unable to fly are seen here.

Geese: Brents will still be much in evidence on the coastal marshes all month. Virtually all the Pink-feet depart, though up to 1,000 can usually be found around Holkham until the end of April. All White-fronted Geese will have departed from their favoured areas (Buckenham Marshes and Holkham NNR) by mid-month.

Wildfowl: Winter ducks remain in impressive numbers with Smew probable at Tottenhill gravel pits and Red-breasted Merganser and Common Scoter on the sea between Hunstanton and Scolt Head Island. Long-tailed Duck records are few and far between in March but Goosanders are usually still present at Barnhamcross Common (the BTO lake), Denver Sluice, etc.

Wigeon in their thousands can be seen at several sites (Welney, Buckenham Marshes, Holkham NNR, Halvergate Marshes, etc.), with numbers of Tufted Duck, Teal and Shoveler remaining stable at suitable sites such as Welney. Pochard and Pintail numbers start to dwindle as birds migrate north, but many hang on to the end of the month.

Just one duck species moves in for the Summer. By the end of the month, a few Garganey will have returned from Africa to breed in Norfolk. The most likely sites to encounter this attractive species are Welney, Cley, Hickling Broad and the flash at Lakenheath, though any marsh or shallow pool should be carefully checked.

15

YOUR BIRDING YEAR

Waders: Another addition to the scene will be Little Ringed Plover, usually appearing during the last third of the month at any suitable wader habitat, (e.g. Titchwell and Holme), but the most likely places are Pentney gravel pits, Welney and Cantley Beet Factory. Other waders to be seen include all species mentioned in January's summary. Titchwell, Cley and Breydon Water are the main breeding centres for Avocets, but you can also check out Welney, Cantley, Hickling Broad, etc. High tides at Snettisham should still produce thousands of waders in the roost. Purple Sandpipers should be in residence at Hunstanton throughout the month.

Ringed Plovers move back to their breeding grounds in March, and Black-tailed Godwits don their striking breeding plumage, thus becoming more conspicuous, at sites such as Cley, Breydon Water and Welney. Stone Curlews return to Norfolk during March, though the only place to see this species without disturbing them, Weeting Heath, remains closed all month to allow the birds to settle.

Birds of prey: Raptor roosts such as Roydon Common and Stubb Mill continue to attract Hen Harrier and Merlin, though numbers dwindle as the month wears on. Wintering Marsh Harriers also continue to appear at their roost sites (mainly Stubb Mill), but their numbers are augmented by migrating birds. Any north coast watchpoint should be watched for an incoming Marsh Harrier, as well as for the odd Goshawk and Buzzard. A trip to Thetford Forest should reveal a displaying Goshawk or two on mild March mornings.

Terns: A welcome reminder that warmer weather is just around the corner comes with the appearance of the first Sandwich Terns of the year, during mid to late March. Any coastal site could be the first to record this species, though Blakeney Point or Scolt Head Island are usually ahead of the rest.

Woodland species: Lesser Spotted Woodpeckers begin to display at the end of the month. Check sites such as Holkham Park, Felbrigg Hall, Upton Fen, etc. to see the fluttering display flight of this otherwise elusive species. Another species typical of a March birdwatching trip is Wood Lark. Any clearing in The Brecks should be alive with their mournful song (try Santon Downham, East Wretham Heath, etc).

Passerines: It is a fun diversion during March to try to spot the first Swallow or House Martin of the year, though Sand Martin is more likely. Spend time at any migration watchpoint for a chance of catching these heralds of Summer. Also keep an eye open for the first Wheatear and Ring Ouzel of the year: Blakeney Point or Holme are prime sites.

Any over-wintering Shore Larks and Water Pipits will be coming into their smart breeding plumage by the end of the month. Try Holkham NNR for the former species and Cley, or Buckenham Marshes, for the latter.

A visit to the Norfolk Broads on a fine, mild day in March should result in a chorus of Cetti's Warblers. They may be easier to see at this time of year, before the leaves have grown on the bushes they favour. Head for Rockland Broad, Cantley Beet Factory, Strumpshaw Fen, etc.

After March, Hawfinches become elusive until December, so visit Lynford Arboretum

WHAT TO LOOK FOR

or Barnhamcross Common before the month is out. Other finches and buntings should still be found in feeding flocks around Flitcham Abbey Farm, Choseley Barns, etc.

APRIL

SPRING is here! By the end of the April, many of Norfolk's Summer visitors will have returned, though the month may start off slowly if poor weather prevails. By poor weather, I mean low pressure over Europe or strong offshore winds.

Throughout April, any site in Norfolk could produce migrants passing through or lingering for a day or two. If the weather charts show high pressure over Europe with a low pressure system over the east coast of Britain, then you should head for Winterton, Holme, Blakeney Point, Weybourne, etc. If it is raining when you arrive, do not complain as you will almost certainly discover many common migrants forced to land by these 'unpleasant' conditions.

Divers and grebes: A late Red-throated moving north at sea will be the only possible diver this month. Likewise, any wintering Red-necked and Slavonian Grebes should have moved on, though Black-necked Grebes may be encountered on any stretch of water: try Welney, the flashes at Lakenheath, or any of the Broads. Great Crested Grebes will be nesting on any suitable pit or lake, though the Broads is their stronghold in the county.

Geese: Of the wintering geese, only Brents will be seen in any sort of number, on any coastal marsh. A few Pink-feet may remain around Holkham but cannot be guaranteed.

Wildfowl: If you wish to catch up with Red-breasted Merganser or Goldeneye, do it early in the month, but those wishing to find Pintail, Long-tailed Duck and Goosander will have to wait until next Winter.

Numbers of Pochard, Gadwall, Teal and Tufted Duck greatly reduce as birds move out of the county to breed, though one or two of each species remain at traditional sites all year (Welney, Snettisham, Titchwell, etc). Eider and Common Scoter may still be found around the north coast. April is probably the best month to see Garganey, with Welney, Cley and Hickling Broad the most likely sites.

Birds of prey: Raptors desert their Winter roost sites in March, so concentrate on watching Marsh Harriers on their breeding grounds (e.g. Hickling Broad, Cley, Titchwell, etc) or trying to find a migrating Osprey on Broadland lakes. Buzzards may also be on the move and Goshawks will still be in display flight on fine mornings in The Brecks. In late April, the first Hobbies will be arriving along with one or two Montagu's Harriers (over any watchpoint).

Gamebirds: April is a good month to locate Golden Pheasants as they are very vocal at this time of year. Visit the Wolferton Triangle, Santon Downham or Wayland Wood to hear their harsh calls.

Waders: The wader scene in Norfolk during April is a confusing mixture of returning breeding birds, lingering Winter visitors and birds dropping in on migration for a quick refuelling stop.

Snettisham continues to be the centre of attraction, though numbers of birds start to dwindle. Purple Sandpipers desert their Winter roost sites by mid-month, but wintering Woodcock numbers begin to be augmented by migrant birds (check any coastal site for tired arrivals).

April is a good month to find species such as Green, Common and Wood Sandpipers, Whimbrel and Greenshank at any suitable marsh, scrape or gravel pit. Golden Plovers leave the county for their northern breeding grounds, while Avocets can be seen nest-building. Other waders settling down to breed include Redshank, Curlew, Snipe and Lapwing on the marshes, Ringed Plover and Oystercatcher on shingle beaches and Little Ringed Plover on scrapes and gravel pits.

Weeting Heath opens its gates to visitors wishing to see Stone Curlew. This species can be particularly vocal at this time of year, especially at dawn and dusk.

Gulls and terns: Mediterranean Gulls can be virtually guaranteed on Great Yarmouth Beach while other species can be found nesting on marshes and scrapes around the county. One or two Little Gulls may be found – try Welney, Hickling Broad, etc.

Activity at tern colonies increases during April and, by the end of the month, most birds will have returned to sites such as Blakeney Point. Common Terns will have also returned to nesting platforms in the Broads. One or two Black Terns may be seen at the end of the month, though they are more likely in May: check out any Broadland lake or Lakenheath.

Migrants: Latest additions to the year list will be Turtle Dove, Cuckoo and Swift, all usually reported during the last week of the month at any migration point (Holme, Blakeney Point, Winterton etc). Also look out for classic Spring scarcities such as Hoopoe, Wryneck and Bluethroat.

Woodpeckers: Lesser Spotted Woodpeckers may still be displaying during the first half of the month at Holkham Park, Felbrigg Hall and Ted Ellis Reserve.

Passerines: Wood Larks should still be singing throughout the month and several Shore Larks may linger at one or two sites (Holkham NNR or Salthouse Beach for instance) with wintering flocks augmented by migrating birds. By now, this attractive species will have moulted into Summer plumage, and be sporting the horns which give it its American name, Horned Lark.

Sand Martin numbers build up during the month (Sparham Pools, Tottenhill and Pentney gravel pits, etc.) with Swallows and House Martins streaming in throughout.

Rock and Water Pipits will desert their Winter quarters by the end of April. Tree Pipits return to their breeding grounds throughout the month, with migrant birds being seen on the coast from early April. This is also an excellent month to find flocks of Yellow Wagtails in any wet field. Try Kelling Quags, Cley or Salthouse Beach. Also keep an eye open for one of the rarer races of Yellow Wagtail - usually Blue-headed – amongst the flocks, or possibly a White Wagtail.

A trip to Norfolk in late April would not be complete without a visit to a Nightingale site such as Foulden Common or Salthouse Heath. Nightingales are easier to see now than later

WHAT TO LOOK FOR

in the season, but you may still have to settle for 'just' hearing their distinctive song.

Black Redstarts can turn up anywhere along the Norfolk coast, as can Redstart. The latter species may also be encountered at inland sites such as Felbrigg Hall and East Wretham Heath. Whinchat, Wheatear and Ring Ouzel should all be looked out for in the dunes along the coast, as well as any suitable field or hedgerow. Also keep an eye open for Fieldfare and Redwing flocks leaving the county on the way to Scandinavia.

April is an excellent month to catch a glimpse of Cetti's Warbler. Try Strumpshaw Fen, Cantley Beet Factory, Rockland Broad, and Ted Ellis Reserve. Other returning warbler species in April include Chiffchaff, Willow Warbler, Blackcap, Sedge and Reed Warblers, Whitethroat, Lesser Whitethroat, Grasshopper Warbler, and maybe Garden and Wood Warbler at the end of the month. The usual migration watchpoints, such as Winterton, Blakeney Point, Holkham NNR, Wells Woods and Holme, will generally be best for warblers. Also keep an eye open at these sites, as well as Felbrigg Hall and Salthouse Heath, etc. for Pied Flycatchers.

Bearded Tits can be quite showy at this time of year, especially on still days, as the males may already be collecting insects to feed to their sitting females. The wintering Twite flocks will mostly be gone, but one or two birds linger all month (Holkham NNR). Brambling may occasionally be seen, with some males sporting their fine breeding plumage.

In coniferous forest, listen out for the '*chip-chip*' calls of Crossbills. This species may already be feeding young and are particularly vocal at this time. Hawfinches become scarcer as the month wears on, though optimistic birders can still try their luck at sites recommended for March.

As well as the species already mentioned, common birds such as Robin, Blackbird, Song Thrush, Goldcrest, etc. can also be found in impressive numbers at migration watchpoints. In suitable weather conditions, hundreds of these common species might be forced down by fog or rain to delight the visiting birdwatcher.

MAY

WHAT a fantastic time to visit Norfolk – migrants will be streaming into all sites to set up breeding territories so enjoy the show at migration watchpoints such as Blakeney Point, Winterton Dunes and Holme.

High pressure over Europe encourages birds to undertake the trip across the channel, only for them to hit the poor weather associated with low pressure. This inclement weather forces the migrants down at the first visible land, hopefully where you will be waiting for them. Repeat after me, "rain and fog are good......rain and fog are good........ rain and..."

By the end of the month, the enthusiastic birdwatcher will be able to watch birds from dawn until dusk. Insomniacs may wish to start the day with a woodland dawn chorus, move on to the marshes during the day, or visit The Brecks, and end the day on a heathland for Nightjar and Woodcock.

Grebes: To see any grebes, venture onto inland pits and lakes where Great Cresteds will

YOUR BIRDING YEAR

be sitting on nests. Broadland lakes sometimes turn up a Black-necked Grebe in May, by now sporting its stunning breeding plumage.

Wildfowl: A few Eider and Common Scoters may linger around the coast all month, usually around Titchwell or Holme. Other than the resident 'plastic' geese, the only species to be seen with any certainty will be Brents (Titchwell, Blakeney harbour, etc).

Terns: Replacing the ducks and divers at sea will be terns. Common, Sandwich and Little Terns will all be busy settling into their colonies (Blakeney Point, Great Yarmouth Beach, etc) and can be seen fishing anywhere along the coast. Common Terns also return to their breeding platforms at inland sites such as Hoveton Great Broad, Breydon Water and Ranworth Broad. Also look out for Arctic and Roseate Terns at Blakeney and Cley.

Black Terns used to breed on Broadland lakes, but sadly they can now only be encountered on passage, May being the prime month. Try Lakenheath, Hardley Flood, etc. The first Manx Shearwaters of the year will be seen off Sheringham, Cley, Titchwell, Holme, etc. by the end of the month.

Birds of prey: Raptor enthusiasts are spoiled in May. It is an excellent time to see Honey Buzzards in the county, as a few pass over on migration. By the 20th, the Great Wood at Swanton Novers should be occupied by this rare breeder, accompanied by Buzzards. Marsh Harriers should be seen over any marsh or reedbed.

May is a good month to scan the skies for migrating Ospreys, some dropping in on Broadland lakes for a brief fishing sortie. Hobbies return during the month, causing chaos among the *hirundine* flocks at Weeting Heath and Hickling Broad, etc. The rarest breeding raptor in the county is Montagu's Harrier, which can sometimes be seen over Snettisham or Cley on passage, so stay alert.

Waders: Snettisham still attracts good numbers of waders to its roost and several attractive species can be seen on breeding grounds. Avocets can be seen on virtually any marsh or pit and stunning Black-tailed Godwits should be sought out at Holme and Welney.

If you are walking on any shingle beach, you should be careful not to disturb Ringed Plovers and Oystercatchers from their nests. Little Ringed Plover can be seen well at Welney, and more distantly at Pentney gravel pits. Stone Curlews will be raising young at Weeting, with Wood Larks also showing well here in front of the hides.

This is a good month to find scarce and rare waders throughout the county. Regular species include Red-necked Phalarope and Temminck's Stint at Cley, with Kentish Plover and Temminck's Stint sometimes at Breydon Water.

Heathland species: From late May you can make a dusk visit to a Nightjar site (Roydon Common, Buxton Heath, Santon Downham, Salthouse Heath, Dersingham Bog). While waiting for the Nightjars to appear, you should see roding Woodcock and hear young Tawny Owls begging for food (listen out for a sound like an asthmatic smoker sprinting for a bus on a smoggy morning). Also keep an ear open for the begging squeaks of young Long-eared Owls.

Passerines: Swifts arrive from early to mid-month, as do most Turtle Doves. Listen for

20

WHAT TO LOOK FOR

the latter's evocative purring calls especially at Flitcham Abbey Farm and Santon Downham. Another species that gives itself away by its song in May is Tree Pipit. Breckland is a stronghold of this species but it can also be heard at Dersingham Bog, Roydon Common and Kelling Heath as well. Wood Larks will also still be singing over any suitable clearing in the Brecks (Barnhamcross Common, Santon Downham, etc).

On the subject of calling birds, every patch of woodland, heath and reedbed in Norfolk will have a Cuckoo in residence by the end of the month, on the lookout for a suitable nest in which to lay its single egg.

May is a good month to scan any suitable wetland for Yellow Wagtails. Cley is a favoured haunt, but also try Buckenham Marsh, Surlingham Church Marsh, Sparham Pools, etc. This is a prime month to find scarce sub-species such as Blue-headed and White among the commoner Yellows and Pieds.

May is a good time to see Bearded Tits in any expanse of reedbed (Hickling Broad, Cley, Titchwell, Gypsy Lane, etc.). From mid-month, I strongly suggest you pay a visit to Lakenheath to try to catch a glimpse of Golden Oriole. You will almost certainly hear them from the poplars, but seeing one might involve much patience!

Migrants: Migrants to watch out for include Bluethroat (Blakeney Point, Holme Dunes, etc), Redstart and Wood Warbler (Salthouse Heath, Felbrigg Hall, East Wretham Heath, etc.) and Pied Flycatcher (Stiffkey, Wells Woods, etc). Black Redstarts should be singing from the power station and industrial units around Great Yarmouth Beach. Wryneck may be found skulking in any suitable dune system (Winterton, Holme Dunes, etc), where you should also keep an eye open for Red-backed Shrike. Early in the month is a good time to listen for Nightingale at such sites as Foulden Common and Salthouse Heath.

May is definitely a warbler month! As the days tick by, Sedge, Reed, Garden and Willow Warblers all arrive en masse, as well as Whitethroat, Lesser Whitethroat, Blackcap, and Chiffchaff. Grasshopper Warblers may well be heard 'reeling' from suitable habitat (Wells Woods, Winterton Dunes, Horsey, etc.) and rarer visitors could include Icterine and Savi's Warblers. A visit to a large wood at dawn is a must during May, try Ken Hill Wood, Sandringham or Santon Downham.

Spotted Flycatcher is one of the latest Summer arrivals, but a handful will be at breeding sites late in the month (Weeting Heath, Holkham NNR).

Rarities: Rarity hunters will find themselves spoiled for choice. Regular visitors include Red-footed falcon, Caspian Tern, Purple Heron and Broad-billed Sandpiper as well as scarcities such as Spoonbill, Wryneck, Bluethroat, Bee-eater, and Savi's Warbler. There should be at least one national rarity to see in Norfolk during the month, so good hunting.

JUNE

THOUGH June is probably the quietest month for birds in Norfolk, there is still plenty to see. As migration is at its lowest level of the year, the main interest is in watching breeding birds go about the business of raising a family.

YOUR BIRDING YEAR

Wildfowl: Any wildfowl in the county will probably be elusive as they tend to hide while sitting on nests. Noisy Egyptian Geese will be waddling around their chosen breeding sites with large young in tow (Flitcham Abbey Farm, Holkham NNR, Pentney gravel pits, Norfolk Broads, etc).

Birds of prey: Many visitors to Norfolk will be enthralled by Marsh Harriers in June, as they drift over any suitable marsh or reedbed. If you are lucky, you will witness the aerobatics of a food-passing manoeuvre by these wonderful birds.

Honey Buzzard and Montagu's Harrier tend to be elusive during June, but Hobbies are regularly seen at Hickling Broad and Weeting Heath throughout the month.

Waders: Wader species will be on nests, the star attractions being Avocets at Titchwell, Cley and Welney. Common waders such as Curlew, Redshank, Lapwing and Snipe nest at a few sites, but can be hard to locate (try Buckenham Marshes and Welney). Little Ringed Plover, a scarce Norfolk breeder, is best viewed from the main hide at Welney. The Stone Curlews at Weeting will have large young by now, but viewing them through the heat-haze can be frustrating!

Terns and seabirds: A few Manx Shearwaters may be seen off seawatching points, but tern activity is usually restricted to colonies such as Blakeney Point and Great Yarmouth Beach. Common Terns will be seen on any suitable river or pit, especially those with breeding platforms or islands. Noisy Black-headed Gulls are not hard to locate but Kelling Quags is the best site for good views of them at the nest.

Heathland species: One species that shows well throughout the month is Nightjar. Balmy June evenings are perfect to watch these moth-like creatures at such places as Dersingham Bog, Winterton Dunes and Sandringham. At Salthouse Heath, you can combine a Nightjar search with a Nightingale chorus, while at Winterton Dunes, you may also listen to the reeling of Grasshopper Warblers and the croaking of Natterjack Toads.

Passerines: Warblers will still be in full song throughout the month, but towards the end of the month many species become more elusive after the initial explosive start to the day, so catch a dawn chorus sooner rather than later.

Bushes around any marsh, river or pit will be alive with the scratchy song of Sedge Warblers, and the grumpy-sounding song of Reed Warblers will be emanating from every patch of reedbed. Cetti's Warblers should still be singing intermittently from deep cover around their Broadland strongholds, but you will probably not see one!

June is the prime month for Marsh Warbler to appear, so pay attention to any strange song you may hear. The last one I saw in Norfolk was singing by a very well used footpath next to a school in King's Lynn, so be alert in any location.

Golden Orioles will still be whistling from poplars around Lakenheath and Fordham during the early part of the month, but then become very difficult to locate until the young are out and about in late August.

WHAT TO LOOK FOR

JULY

WHILE you stand sweating on the footpath at Titchwell, watching Avocet chicks waddle after their parents, it is hard to believe that Winter migration is under way. Many non-breeding waders return to Norfolk from Scandinavia during July, so it can be an interesting diversion at the end of the month to attempt to match the number of wader species to the date (i.e. 28 species of wader on July 28, and so on).

Seabirds: Seawatching picks up slightly during July, with increased numbers of Manx Shearwaters being seen, and maybe one or two Balearic Shearwaters.

Spoonbills: A touch of the exotic may come in the form of a Spoonbill or two, Holkham NNR and Burgh Castle seem to be favoured sites.

Wildfowl: Duck-watching becomes very dull in July, as the drakes moult into their dowdy 'eclipse' plumage.

Birds of prey: Rare breeding raptors such as Montagu's Harrier and Honey Buzzard show more often as the month wears on (Swanton Novers for the latter), but you may still have to wait an awfully long time for a view. Marsh Harriers will be much in evidence over reeds and marshes across the county (Hickling Broad, Titchwell, Cley, etc), making it hard to believe they were faced with extinction as a British breeding bird just a few years ago. Hobbies will become more obvious as they take advantage of new prey, dragonflies.

Quail: While driving around the county, it may be worth stopping at the side of any wheat field to listen for the *'wet-my-lips'* call of Quail. They turn up anywhere, and are almost impossible to see. Remember, it is illegal to tape-lure this species and you should never enter fields to try to flush one into view!

Waders: Young birds will be prominent and many a sigh of 'aahhh' has gone up from admiring birders at the sight of a young Lapwing/Avocet chick trotting along after its parents, only to be followed by gasps of horror as a Herring or Great Black-backed Gull swoops down and swallows the poor thing whole. Life is tough! Visit sites such as Welney, Titchwell and Cley to see nature in all its gory splendour.

By the end of July, waders such as Knot, Dunlin, Sanderling, etc. will be returning from their breeding grounds. The roost at Snettisham once again begins to attract many birds, though not as numerous as in Winter. Female Red-necked Phalaropes sometimes appear at Cley or Titchwell to sun themselves after leaving the hapless males to rear their young in the bleak northern breeding grounds.

Welney is a good place to visit in July to obtain superb views of baby Little Ringed Plovers, complete with tiny yellow eye-rings. Adult and almost fully grown Stone Curlews should be showing well on Weeting Heath.

Gulls and terns: Yellow-legged Gull is a Summer feature of Norfolk, prime sites being Cley, King's Lynn Docks and Hickling Broad. Black-headed Gull colonies become even noisier as the youngsters beg for food from harassed adults.

YOUR BIRDING YEAR

July is the best month to visit a tern colony. A boat trip out to Blakeney Point at this time of year is a real treat. Many a happy hour can be spent at Little Tern colonies (Great Yarmouth Beach, Winterton Dunes, etc.) watching chicks run to their parents as they land close by.

Heathland species: Nightjars will be churring at dusk throughout the month at sites such as Roydon Common, Buxton Heath, Winterton Dunes, Sandringham and Dersingham Bog. Insect repellent may be advisable if waiting any length of time for the Nightjars to appear.

Passerines: The majority of warblers and woodland birds will become more elusive as the month wears on and the heat builds up. Many species will be hiding away, quietly moulting out of the reach of predators. Even more unsportingly, they stop singing, so you can't even locate them that way.

Alternatives: If things appear to be a little quiet on the birding front, don't forget that there are always plenty of plants, butterflies and dragonflies to be seen, making Norfolk an exciting place to be, even during a supposedly quiet month like July.

AUGUST

IN BIRDING terms, August heralds the onset of Winter with many south-bound species stopping off. Lots of young birds can still be seen, most making very unfamiliar noises that often fool even the most ardent bird-call fanatic. Because there are so many youngsters around, this is a bumper time for raptors too.

Seabirds: August is the real start of the seawatching season. Manx Shearwaters pass watchpoints in impressive numbers in some years, often joined by Balearic or Sooty Shearwaters, or maybe something rarer such as Cory's or Great Shearwaters. Many watchpoints, such as Holme Observatory, Cley and Sheringham will be crowded with birders hoping for the 'biggie' to come past, especially if there is a stiff north wind blowing. However, Gannets and Kittiwakes are much more likely. Tern activity will be at a peak at sea, as adults are joined by scruffy-looking juveniles learning how to fish.

All four skua species should be recorded off seawatching points (Holme Observatory, Cley, Sheringham, etc.) throughout the month, but concentrate your efforts if the wind is coming from the north or north-west. Auk species may also pass watchpoints in reasonable numbers.

Wildfowl: Wigeon numbers will be gradually building on the marshes, along with Teal. By the end of the month, the first returning Pintail will have been noted. Garganey begin to show again, after hiding the whole Summer, with juveniles testing the identification skills of birders at Cley, Welney and Hickling Broad among others. The bad news is that male ducks will still be in their dull 'eclipse' plumage.

Birds of prey: Raptors to be seen in Norfolk during August include the first returning Merlin (maybe Blakeney Point) and the pair of Honey Buzzards at Swanton Novers or

WHAT TO LOOK FOR

Great Ryburgh, possibly accompanied by their young: catch them while you can as they usually depart late in the month. Montagu's Harriers roam far and wide during August and may be encountered at any migration watchpoint or marsh. This is probably the best month to see a Hobby as the youngsters are on the wing learning how to catch Swallows, House Martins and dragonflies at sites such as Upton Fen or Weeting Heath. As ever, Marsh Harriers will be seen over any marsh or reedbed, sometimes food-passing in mid-air.

Crakes: August is a prime month to find a Spotted Crake. Any marsh may be graced by this elusive species, though Titchwell and Holme seem favoured areas. Any Quail in the county should still be calling so check bird newslines to find out this year's best location (2001 was a Kelling Quags year).

Waders: A fine selection will be on show. You may wish to visit the Snettisham roost or concentrate on finding passage birds on any suitable pool or marsh. Greenshank, Green Sandpiper, Wood Sandpiper and Common Sandpiper are guaranteed during August, the best sites being Cantley Beet Factory, Cley, Redwell Marsh, Welney and Breydon Water. The latter site also sees a build-up in number of Avocets during the month.

In general, many species of wader (Whimbrel, Ruff, Little Ringed Plover, Spotted Redshank, Little Stint, Temminck's Stint, etc) can turn up anywhere, so check any suitable-looking patch of marsh, wetland or pool and find your own.

Stone Curlews will be gathering in small flocks by the end of the month, with more than 30 being counted at Weeting Heath during 2001.

Gulls and terns: Gull colonies will still be boisterous, and Yellow-legged Gull numbers at King's Lynn Docks or Cley can reach double figures. Terns will show well in good numbers throughout the month. Keep an eye open for migrating Black Terns on any inland water, though most records come from the Broads.

Nightjars: If you want to hear Nightjar in August, visit your chosen site (Winterton, Buxton Heath, Roydon Common, etc.) sooner rather than later. On cooler evenings, Nightjars may not churr at all, and by the end of the month, most visits will be silent.

Migrants: The number of Turtle Doves, Cuckoos, Sand Martins and Swifts reported start to dwindle as the days tick by, but Swallows and House Martins should still be swarming over any area of water, often pursued by a Hobby or two. Listen and look out for Tree Pipits at any migration watchpoint as they begin to move out of their breeding areas.

Heart-rates of migrant hunters begin to rise as August wears on. Common early drop-ins at watchpoints (Winterton Dunes, Blakeney Point, Holme, etc.) include Redstart, Whinchat, Wheatear, Ring Ouzel, Spotted Flycatcher and Pied Flycatcher. By the end of the month, the first Red-backed Shrike and Firecrest should have been reported.

If easterly winds are forecast, it may be worth a walk to Blakeney Point for such classic species as Greenish and Barred Warblers. The trickle of migrants in August is just a taster of things to come in September and October.

YOUR BIRDING YEAR

SEPTEMBER

SEPTEMBER can be an amazing month in Norfolk. If strong winds blow in from the north, seawatchers come out in their droves. If easterly winds prevail, places such as Blakeney Point, Warham Greens and Holme can be full of birders looking for tasty treats such as Barred Warbler and Red-backed Shrike. If conditions are perfect (high pressure over Scandinavia and the east, with low pressure over Britain and strong easterly winds), anything can turn up.

Seabirds: Throughout the month, seawatching enthusiasts will be out and about at such sites as Sheringham and Holme Observatory, searching the swell for shearwaters, skuas and petrels. Common passage birds during the month include Gannet and Kittiwake in good numbers. The fun really starts when a prolonged period of north or north-westerly winds is experienced. If this happens, seawatching can be extremely exciting (yes, trust me, it can)! Spending a whole morning watching hundreds of terns passing your vantage point is exciting enough, but add up to four species of skua occasionally pursuing them, and Manx, Balearic and Sooty Shearwaters gliding just above the surface of the sea, and you have the recipe for an exceptional day's birding.

Wildfowl: Duck numbers build up on marshes and pools, as Winter migration gathers apace. Garganey can still be seen at Cley but still in drab eclipse or immature plumage. Make sure you catch up with this species early in the month. At the very end of September you can expect to find the first Goldeneyes and Red-breasted Mergansers of Winter, though predicting where they will occur is more difficult.

A few Brent Geese will be returning to their regular haunts by mid-month (Blakeney, Brancaster, etc.) as will Pink-footed Geese (Holkham).

Birds of prey: Honey Buzzard, Montagu's Harrier and Hobby all depart for warmer climes during September and can turn up at any migration watchpoint, or indeed over any other site in Norfolk. Osprey may also pass through on the way to Africa. Peregrines arrive at their wintering grounds during early September and reports of Merlin increase as the month progresses.

Waders: September is another exciting wader month in the county. Any area, and I do mean *any* area, of marsh or water with a muddy edge should be scanned thoroughly for passage birds. Common, Wood and Green Sandpipers are classic September birds, with Cantley Beet Factory, Cley and Redwell Marsh being favoured sites.

I feel this is the best month in which to see Curlew Sandpiper. They tend to show particularly well at Titchwell, but don't expect any gaudy red birds, as most will be juveniles. Other species which should be in evidence include Ruff, Whimbrel, Spotted Redshank and Little Stint among the common species. Wader rarities in September can include such goodies as Pectoral and Buff-breasted Sandpipers, and while on the marsh, keep an eye open for a Spotted Crake creeping at the edge of the reeds (try Titchwell).

A feature of September in The Brecks is the flocking of Stone Curlews before they

WHAT TO LOOK FOR

migrate south. Last year, a flock of more than 30 birds was reported at Weeting, but scan any field in the area for the chance of a wonderful discovery. Up to 60 birds together have been reported on Norfolk farmland in some years.

Migrants: The majority of *hirundines* leave the county by the end of the month, but early on, it may be worth watching reedbeds at dusk for roosting birds (Martham Broad, Cley, etc).

September is a superb time to find your own birds. Depending on weather conditions, numbers of migrants at coastal watchpoints can be staggering. Common species such as Robin, Chiffchaff and Goldcrest can be forced down by fog or rain. Summer warblers such as Whitethroat, Lesser Whitethroat, Garden Warbler and Blackcap should all be encountered on the coast, and hiding among them might be something a bit special.

Other common migrants at this time should include Wheatear, Whinchat and maybe a few Ring Ouzel. Redstart and Pied Flycatcher is also recorded in good numbers each September. Scarce species regularly recorded this month include Wryneck, Richard's Pipit, Red-backed Shrike, Common Rosefinch, Firecrest and Barred Warbler (Holme, Winterton, Blakeney Point).

Any site – and any bush! - on the coast should be checked thoroughly, though hot-spots such as Blakeney Point, NWT Holme Dunes, NOA Holme Observatory, Great Yarmouth Cemetery and Warham Greens are the most visited. Migrant-hunters will be hoping for something a bit rarer (such as Lanceolated Warbler and Pechora Pipit) for their efforts.

Passerines: In my experience, September is the best month to see Bearded Tit. Family parties are very noisy and active, and usually show very well at sites such as Titchwell (around the first hide), Hickling Broad, Gypsy Lane and Brancaster Marsh. Instead of the usual fleeting flight glimpse, at this time of year the patient birdwatcher can obtain very close and prolonged views.

OCTOBER

EXCITEMENT among birders remains high this month. Not only do rarities abound, but common Winter visitors arrive seemingly unnoticed. Swans, geese and ducks return in decent numbers and raptor roosts begin to attract Hen Harriers once more. Winter has arrived!

Seabirds: As in September, keep an eye on weather forecasts for northerly winds. Head for seawatching watchpoints in these conditions as skuas, shearwaters, Gannets and Kittiwakes should be seen in reasonable numbers.

October seems to be the most likely month to encounter the exquisite Sabine's Gull off the Norfolk coast, but beware of confusion with immature Kittiwake (a common error). Numbers of divers, grebes and seaduck build during the month, adding to the excitement of any seawatch.

Wildfowl: Wild swans gradually return to their traditional wintering grounds during the middle of the month. Pink-footed and Brent Goose numbers also build up throughout

27

YOUR BIRDING YEAR

October (Holkham NNR, Snettisham) and one or two White-fronted Geese may have been recorded by the end of the month, though most return in November. The steady influx of wintering ducks which began in September continues throughout October. Welney and other wetland sites will hold thousands of Wigeon, Teal, Pintail, Pochard, etc, by the end of the month.

Birds of prey: As mentioned before, Hen Harriers return to their traditional roosts, as do Merlins. Numbers may be small, but birds should be present during the second half of the month. Peregrines slowly return to their wintering grounds and migration watchpoints may record Buzzard and Marsh Harrier, as they leave the county for the Winter. Some Marsh Harriers do remain in Norfolk, and can be seen over any marsh or reedbed (Cley, Horsey, etc).

Waders: Many passage waders such as Greenshank, Little Stint, Ruff, Green Sandpiper and Curlew Sandpiper will remain on muddy-edged pools and pits such as Pentney, Sparham, Redwell Marsh and Cantley Beet Factory.

Thousands of common wader continue to arrive for the Winter, augmenting the earlier arrivals. The roost at Snettisham attract thousands of birds at high tide. Any beach or marsh, such as Holme Dunes, Titchwell and Cley, can hold common wader species. Any Spotted Crakes that turned up in late Summer may still be in residence (try Titchwell).

Terns: Numbers drop to a trickle by the end of October, but Sandwich, Common, Little and Arctic Terns are all reported regularly. Black Terns sometimes drift across Broadland lakes during the month, and look out for the dark saddles of juvenile White-winged Black Tern among them.

Migrants: October is a fantastic month for finding your own migrant birds in Norfolk. Handfuls of Swallows, Swifts, Sand and House Martins pass over watchpoints all month, and Winter thrushes begin to trickle in. This trickle may become a flood if a high pressure system over Scandinavia combines with strong easterly winds and rain or fog over East Anglia. Sites such as Blakeney Point and Holme should be visited if these conditions prevail.

Experienced birdwatchers will expect something more exciting to turn up in these conditions, with such classic species as Short-toed Lark, Barred Warbler, Richard's Pipit, Ortolan Bunting, Wryneck and Red-backed Shrike all possibilities. Dune systems along the coast (Holme, Winterton, etc.) may also hide exhausted Short or Long-eared Owls, Woodcock or Corncrake.

Warbler numbers at migration watchpoints can be impressive in October, as birds pause on the coast to feed up or await perfect conditions before heading south. Wells Woods, Holkham NNR, Warham Greens and Stiffkey can produce many species, including Garden Warbler, Willow Warbler, Lesser Whitethroat, Whitethroat, Chiffchaff and Blackcap. Among these commoner species may be Firecrest, Red-breasted Flycatcher, Yellow-browed Warbler or Barred Warbler. Any feeding flock should be scanned thoroughly, as scarce and rare birds often latch onto such flocks: every bird should be scrutinised.

28

WHAT TO LOOK FOR

Reed Warblers can sometimes turn up in strange habitat at this time, occasionally confusing unwary birders. Many a time I have witnessed over-eager rarity hunters mistake a Reed Warbler for some unlikely species (for instance, Red-breasted Flycatcher!), simply because it was hopping about in a tree or bush and not in reeds.

Expect to see Whinchat, Wheatear, Pied Flycatcher and Redstart, with common species such as Robin, Song Thrush and Goldcrest, sometimes appearing in their hundreds. Though Lapland Bunting is now a scarce over-wintering species in the county, one or two usually drop in at Salthouse Beach (Little Eye) or Cley (Eye Field) in October.

NOVEMBER

MANY birdwatchers regard November migration as quieter than that of September and October, usually because rare species can be thin on the ground. However, common Summer visitors often linger until the first half of the month, and at the same time Winter visitors stream in from Scandinavia and further north to settle until next Spring. And the rarities that do show up are usually very sought-after species indeed. You cannot afford to relax just yet.

Seabirds: Divers, grebes and Winter seaduck return to the seas of Norfolk during the month as Winter takes a hold. Red-throated Diver is common off such places as Titchwell, Holme and Cley. Long-tailed Duck should be seen off Holme and Winterton, though numbers are small (usually only up to 30). November also seems a good month to connect with Red-necked Grebe (try Titchwell).

The tiny Little Auk should be seen on most days if conditions are favourable, with strong northerly winds. Any flock of Starlings coming in off the sea should be scrutinised thoroughly, as Little Auks sometimes tag on to the end of such flocks and follow them inland. Sometimes exhausted Little Auk are discovered on inland waters. Recent sites have included Snettisham and Wells boating lake.

Wildfowl: Inland duck species return in force, with Wigeon being the most obvious arrival on most coastal marshes. The only wildfowl species leaving us, Garganey, will be gone by the second week of the month.

Bewick's and Whooper Swan numbers build up at Welney along with those of common ducks, while White-fronted Geese return to Holkham and Buckenham Marshes. If visiting Buckenham, I recommend you wait until the latter half of the month by which time the (taiga) Bean Geese should have arrived, though they sometimes don't turn up until December.

Birds of prey: Hen Harrier numbers increase at their traditional roost sites (Stubb Mill, etc.) as do Merlin records. Marsh Harriers become scarcer, though a few remain in the county during Winter (Stubb Mill, Horsey, etc). Short-eared Owl and Peregrine are recorded daily, though can turn up on any marsh at any time (try Haddiscoe Marsh).

Waders: The majority of Winter waders have returned to the county by now, including the small flock of Purple Sandpipers at Hunstanton. Breydon Water supports up to 100

YOUR BIRDING YEAR

Avocets throughout the Winter, the only place to see them during this time.

Snettisham is well worth a visit at high tide for the spectacular wader roost. Common species present include thousands of Dunlin, Golden Plover, Knot, Bar-tailed Godwit, Turnstone, Ringed Plover and Oystercatcher along with smaller numbers of Grey Plover, Snipe, Sanderling, etc.

Most of the passage waders (Green Sandpiper, Greenshank, Little Stint, etc.) will have departed, though a few linger throughout the month (Cantley Beet Factory, etc.). November seems to be a good month to see Grey Phalarope, usually from seawatching sites such as Sheringham during northerly winds.

Please read January's Calendar for a more detailed run-down of waders in the county in November.

Passerines: A tiny number of Swallows and House Martins continue to be recorded throughout November, usually at coastal sites. Any Swift seen should be studied very carefully indeed, as recent Novembers have turned up about ten Pallid Swifts, and Chimney Swift is not out of the question either.

Similarly, any November Wheatear should be scrutinised to make sure it is not of the Desert or Black-eared variety. November is the prime month for records of Pallas's and Dusky Warblers and Olive-backed Pipit, with Wells Woods being as good a place as any to find one.

Shore Larks, Snow Buntings and Twite return in force to the marshes and saltings of Norfolk during the month, and usually remain until April. Please do not harass these birds at this time (or ever) as they need time to settle down into their chosen Winter home.
Woodland birds now become easier to see as the trees lose their leaves: a trip to Holkham Park, Ken Hill Wood or Sandringham may prove to be very productive. The former site should provide you with good views of Tawny Owls in their traditional roost tree by the monument.

By the end of the month, Winter will have arrived. Read January's Calendar section for further details of birds to be seen.

DECEMBER

THIS MONTH'S calendar is basically the same as January's, with one or two minor alterations. In my experience, December is the best month to catch up with Hawfinch. Lynford Arboretum seemed to be the prime site in the Winter of 2002, with up to nine birds being reported in the meadow trees. Barnhamcross Common is another favoured site for this elusive beauty.

All in all, December provides the opportunity to catch up with Winter species you may have missed earlier in the year. Also, there are plenty of bracing walks to help you walk-off your Christmas Turkey dinner.

HOW TO USE THIS BOOK

HERE is a typical layout of the site guide pages. Once familiar with the layout, you will be able to extract the information you need quickly and painlessly.

Title of site. Sites are listed in alphabetical order and numbered.

Key points: Opening times, terrain, suitability for wheelchair users and other useful tips. ALWAYS check opening times before you visit.

Target species and likelihood of seeing them: Lists the species for which the reserve is most famous. The percentage figure gives a rough idea – based on my experiences at the site – of how likely you are to see the target species, provided you visit the site at the correct time and stay for a reasonable amount of time. Where you see 'Winter raptors (25%)' this means that you have a 25% chance of seeing each species of raptor at the site

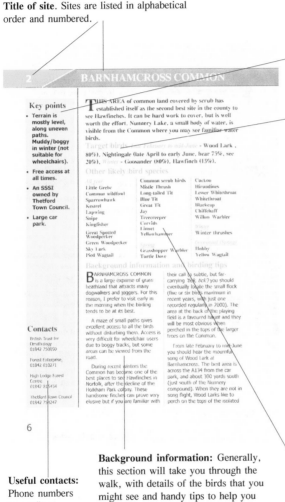

Other likely species: Lists the commoner species you are likely to see. Phrases such as 'Winter thrushes', 'common woodland birds', 'common waterfowl' are used to save space but please see pages 216-217 for a more detailed explanation of what is included. Occasionally, 'good' species are included in this section instead of the Target section if the chance of seeing that species is low.

Background information: Generally, this section will take you through the walk, with details of the birds that you might see and handy tips to help you see them. It might contain more information on points which have been briefly mentioned in previous sections, e.g. more extensive bird lists, more detailed information about terrain etc.

Useful contacts: Phone numbers to confirm access details etc.

HOW TO USE THIS BOOK

Best time of year to visit. There may be things to see at other times of year but this season is likely to produce the best results.

OS Landranger map number

Grid reference(s) of parking area(s) giving easiest access to site.

 WINTER/SPRING   OS MAP 144   TL 867817

Site facility symbols: (see key to symbols below)

bushes and trees dotted around the Common.

Nightingales return to the Common in late April and sing from thick cover adjacent to the playing field. They can be extremely difficult to see here – even more so than at other sites, if that is possible! Bear in mind that they stay very close to the ground most of the time and you might stand a chance.

Other birds include Jays and Green Woodpeckers which will usually be heard first before you pick them out, normally flying from bush to bush. In winter, thrushes are readily seen including Redwings and Fieldfares. Finch flocks will feed noisily in the bushes.

From the east side of the Common you can look into the compound of The Nunnery, headquarters of the British Trust for Ornithology. The small lake in winter is possibly the most reliable site for Goosander in Norfolk. Common ducks, grebes and geese should also be seen on the lake.

Lapwings are present all year round and maybe a Snipe or two in winter. Also on the east side of the Common, behind Nunnery Lake, is the Little Ouse River that usually holds a Kingfisher somewhere along its length.

In summer, the resident birds are joined by several warbler species including Whitethroat, Lesser Whitethroat, Blackcap, Garden Warbler, Willow Warbler, and Chiffchaff. Cuckoos can also show well here in early May. The telephone wires on the south-west side are a favoured perch of Turtle Doves from the end of April

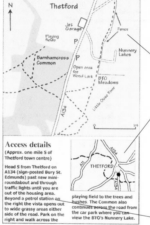

Access details
(Approx. one mile S of Thetford town centre)

Head S from Thetford on A134 (sign-posted Bury St. Edmunds) past new mini-roundabout and through traffic lights until you are out of the housing area. Beyond a petrol station on the right the vista opens out to wide grassy areas either side of the road. Park on the right and walk across the

until July, given away by their gentle purring call.

Barnhamcross Common provides an hour or so's gentle birding, especially useful if you have made Thetford your base for a birding break.

Maps: The small thumbnail map shows the reserve's position within Norfolk. The larger, more detailed map shows trails, hides and other key features for the reserve.

Access: Detailed directions to the parking area(s) or reserve entrance (the harder a site is to find, the more detailed the description). For some sites I have detailed the most straightforward route for those unfamiliar with the area, and not necessarily the quickest.

playing field to the trees and bushes. The Common also continues across the road from the car park where you can view the BTO's Nunnery Lake.

Other nearby sites

East Wretham Heath, Fordham, Foulden Common, Lakenheath RSPB, Lynford Arboretum, Santon Downham, Wayland Wood, Weeting Heath, etc.

7

Other nearby sites: Not comprehensive, but a selection of ideas for sites to visit in the general area of the reserve you have chosen. Refer to the Norfolk map for a complete list of sites in the area.

Key to symbols

 £ Payment required

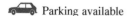 Parking available

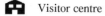 Visitor centre

 Refreshments available

 Toilets

Wheelchair access

FEATURED SITES IN NORFOLK

**Barn Owl is a familiar bird of coastal sites
and on Fenland farms.**

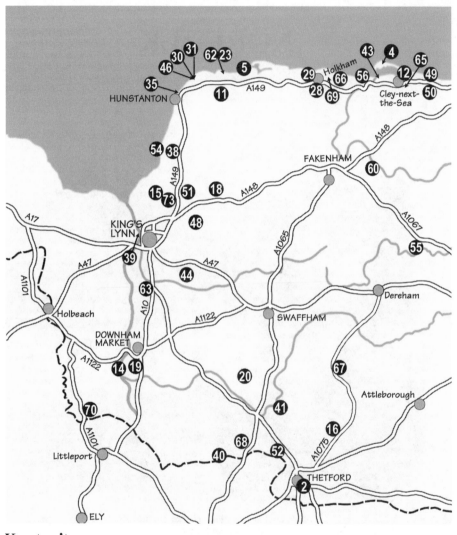

Key to sites

		7	RSPB Buckenham Marshes	14	Denver Sluice
1	NWT Alderfen Broad	8	Burgh Castle	15	Dersingham Bog
2	Barnhamcross Common	9	Buxton Heath	16	NWT East Wretham Heath
3	NWT Barton Broad	10	Cantley Beet Factory	17	Felbrigg Hall
4	Blakeney Point	11	Choseley Barns	18	Flitcham Abbey Farm
5	Brancaster Marsh	12	NWT Cley Marsh	19	Fordham
6	Breydon Water	13	NWT Cockshoot Broad	20	Foulden Common

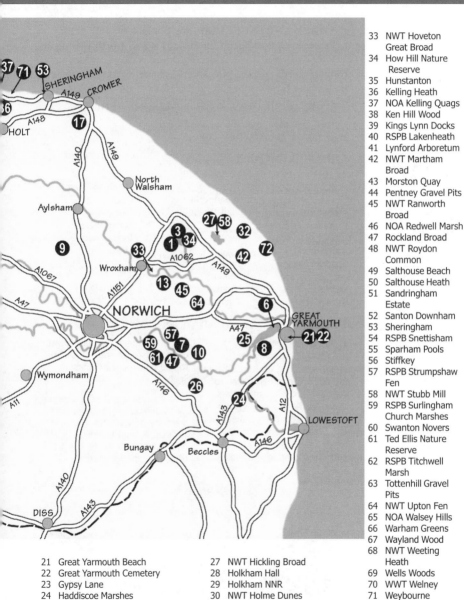

33 NWT Hoveton Great Broad
34 How Hill Nature Reserve
35 Hunstanton
36 Kelling Heath
37 NOA Kelling Quags
38 Ken Hill Wood
39 Kings Lynn Docks
40 RSPB Lakenheath
41 Lynford Arboretum
42 NWT Martham Broad
43 Morston Quay
44 Pentney Gravel Pits
45 NWT Ranworth Broad
46 NOA Redwell Marsh
47 Rockland Broad
48 NWT Roydon Common
49 Salthouse Beach
50 Salthouse Heath
51 Sandringham Estate
52 Santon Downham
53 Sheringham
54 RSPB Snettisham
55 Sparham Pools
56 Stiffkey
57 RSPB Strumpshaw Fen
58 NWT Stubb Mill
59 RSPB Surlingham Church Marshes
60 Swanton Novers
61 Ted Ellis Nature Reserve
62 RSPB Titchwell Marsh
63 Tottenhill Gravel Pits
64 NWT Upton Fen
65 NOA Walsey Hills
66 Warham Greens
67 Wayland Wood
68 NWT Weeting Heath
69 Wells Woods
70 WWT Welney
71 Weybourne
72 Winterton Dunes
73 Wolferton Triangle

21 Great Yarmouth Beach
22 Great Yarmouth Cemetery
23 Gypsy Lane
24 Haddiscoe Marshes
25 Halvergate Marshes
26 Hardley Flood

27 NWT Hickling Broad
28 Holkham Hall
29 Holkham NNR
30 NWT Holme Dunes
31 NOA Holme Observatory
32 Horsey Area

Key points

- Site is a designated SSSI.
- Free access at all times.
- Level terrain along muddy grass paths.
- Observation blind.
- No dogs.

SMALL AND SECLUDED, this Norfolk Wildlife Trust reserve on the edge of the Broads is well worth visiting at any time of year. NWT Alderfen Broad is excellent for many common birds species, plus several scarce insects and plants: truly a site for the all-round naturalist.

Target birds *All year* – Common wildfowl (100%), Cetti's Warbler (hear 50%, see 10%).
Summer – Common Tern (80%).

Other likely bird species

All year		*Summer*
Great Crested Grebe	Green Woodpecker	Common Tern
Cormorant	Great Spotted Woodpecker	Cuckoo
Common wildfowl	Pied Wagtail	Hirundines
Common waterbirds	Common scrub birds	Sedge Warbler
Sparrowhawk	Common woodland birds	Reed Warbler
Common gull species	Siskin	Other warblers
Tawny Owl	Redpoll	*Occasional*
	Other finches	Lesser Spotted Woodpecker

Background information and birding tips

SECLUSION is the chief attribute of NWT Alderfen Broad, which isn't to imply there are no birds or other wildlife to see, just that it lacks the drama of the top Norfolk birding sites. The major plus-point is that I can almost guarantee you will be on your own as you wait patiently for that elusive Cetti's Warbler in the dense undergrowth to show itself, or scan the Broad to find Britain's first Cinnamon Teal!

From the car park, the reserve footpath heads right as you come down the access track. Near the car park, a short boardwalk peels off to the left. At the end of the boardwalk is a 'blind' (the

Alderfen is an established breeding site for Common Terns.

Contacts

Norfolk Wildlife Trust
01603 625540

American word for a fence with a hole in it for observation) giving excellent views over the Broad itself.

Many common duck species will be present whatever time you visit, joined by Great Crested Grebes, Coots, Moorhens and Grey Herons. In Summer, the Broad is home to Common Terns and many Swifts, Swallows and House Martins. In Spring, look out for Black Terns or even a passing Osprey.

The footpath continues along an uneven grass path through dense cover, ideal for skulking Cetti's Warblers. It also runs alongside a small creek, which is home to damselflies and dragonflies in Summer.

The woodland can be alive with many common bird species such as Dunnock, Blackbird, Blue, Great and Coal Tit, Robin, Song Thrush etc. There is also a slim chance of Lesser Spotted Woodpecker.

In Summer, the resident birds are joined by Willow Warbler, Chiffchaff, Blackcap, Whitethroat and Garden Warbler.

Unfortunately, there is no circular route around the reserve, so you will have to retrace your steps when you have seen enough. It is amazing how many things you see on the walk back to the car in a wood seemingly devoid of life on your outward journey!

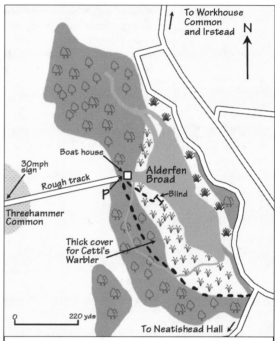

Access details

(Approx. ten miles NE of Norwich)

At Wroxham, turn onto A1062 to Horning. In village turn left to Neatishead. At the crossroads, turn right, go past the Radar Museum and take the next left, signposted 'Threehammer Common'. Go into the village and just before 30mph speed limit sign, turn right

along a track by the side of a house. Follow this very bumpy track to the NWT car park at the end.

Other nearby sites

NWT Barton Broad, Breydon Water, Burgh Castle Marshes, Buxton Heath, NWT Cockshoot Broad, How Hill Trust Reserve, NWT Ranworth Broad, NWT Sparham Pools, RSPB Surlingham Church Marshes, Ted Ellis Reserve.

THIS AREA of common land covered by scrub has established itself as the second best site in the county to see Hawfinches. It can be hard work to cover, but is well worth the effort. Nunnery Lake, a small body of water, is visible from the Common where you may see familiar water birds.

Target birds *Spring* - Wood Lark (late February to mid-June 80%), Nightingale (late April to early June, hear 75%, see 20%). *Winter* - Goosander (80%), Hawfinch (15%).

Other likely bird species

All year	Common scrub birds	Hirundines
Little Grebe	Mistle Thrush	Grasshopper Warbler
Common wildfowl	Long-tailed Tit	Lesser Whitethroat
Sparrowhawk	Blue Tit	Whitethroat
Kestrel	Great Tit	Blackcap
Lapwing	Treecreeper	Chiffchaff
Snipe	Jay	Willow Warbler
Kingfisher	Corvids	
Green Woodpecker	Linnet	*Winter*
Great Spotted Woodpecker	Yellowhammer	Winter thrushes
Sky Lark	*Spring*	*Occasional (Spring)*
Pied Wagtail	Turtle Dove	Hobby
	Cuckoo	Yellow Wagtail

Background information and birding tips

BARNHAMCROSS COMMON is a large expanse of grass heathland that attracts many dogwalkers and joggers. For this reason, I prefer to visit early in the morning when the birding tends to be at its best.

A maze of small paths gives excellent access to all the birds without disturbing them. Access is very difficult for wheelchair users due to boggy tracks, but some areas can be viewed from the road.

During recent Winters the Common has become one of the best places to see Hawfinches in Norfolk, after the decline of the Holkham Park colony. These handsome finches can prove very elusive but if you are familiar with their call (a subtle, but far-carrying 'tick, tick') you should eventually locate the small flock (five or six birds maximum in recent years, with just one recorded regularly in 2000). The area at the back of the playing field is a favoured haunt and they will be most obvious when perched in the tops of the larger trees on the Common.

From late February to mid-June you should hear the mournful song of Wood Lark at Barnhamcross. The best area is across the A134 from the car park, and about 300 yards south (just south of the Nunnery compound). When they are not in song flight, Wood Larks like to perch in the tops of the isolated bushes and trees dotted around the Common.

Nightingales return to the Common in late April and sing from thick cover adjacent to the playing field. They can be extremely difficult to see here – even more so than at other sites, if that is possible! Bear in mind that they stay very close to the ground most of the time and you might stand a chance.

Other birds include Jays and Green Woodpeckers which will usually be heard before you pick them out, normally flying from bush to bush. In Winter, thrushes including Redwings and Fieldfares, are readily seen. Finch flocks will feed noisily in the bushes.

From the east side of the Common you can look into the compound of The Nunnery, headquarters of the British Trust for Ornithology. The small lake in Winter is possibly the most reliable site for Goosander in Norfolk. Common ducks, grebes and geese should also be seen on the lake.

Lapwings are present all year, with maybe a Snipe or two in Winter. Also on the east side of the Common, behind Nunnery Lake, is the Little Ouse River that usually holds a Kingfisher somewhere along its length.

In Summer, the resident birds are joined by several warbler species including Whitethroat, Lesser Whitethroat, Blackcap, Garden Warbler, Willow Warbler, and Chiffchaff. Cuckoos may also show well here in early May.

The telephone wires on the

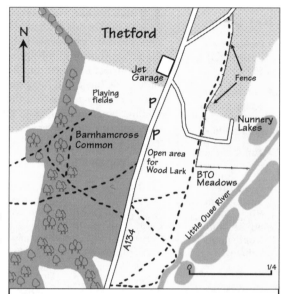

Access details

(Approx. one mile S of Thetford town centre)

Head S from Thetford on A134 (sign-posted Bury St. Edmunds) over new mini-roundabout and through traffic lights until you are out of the housing area. Beyond a petrol station on the right the vista opens out to wide grassy areas either side of the road. Park on the right and walk across the

playing field to the trees and bushes. The Common also continues across the road from the car park where you can view the BTO's Nunnery Lake.

south-west side of this site are a favoured perch of Turtle Doves from the end of April until July, given away by their gentle purring call.

Barnhamcross Common provides an hour or so's gentle birding, especially useful if you have made Thetford your base for a birding break.

Other nearby sites

NWT East Wretham Heath, Fordham, NWT Foulden Common, RSPB Lakenheath, Lynford Arboretum, Santon Downham, Wayland Wood, NWT Weeting Heath.

39

Key points

- Reserve is a designated SSSI.
- Terrain level along gravel footpaths and boardwalks.
- Toilet block at new car park.
- Food, etc available at the public house or in Neatishead village.
- Electric boat runs from near the Barton Angler Country Inn.
- Disabled parking at Heron's Carr.
- Free 24-hour mooring available.

Contacts

Norfolk Wildlife Trust
01603 625540

General Broads Authority
01603 610734

HERE is a site with a very bright future. Extensive work by the Broads Authority and Norfolk Wildlife Trust in 2001 and 2002 has opened this previously difficult-to-visit site to birdwatchers. A boardwalk to a viewpoint over NWT Barton Broad has been constructed, along with a new car park, toilet block and footpath. As improvements to water quality begin to take effect, the variety and quantity of wildlife should also improve. Please reward all this hard work by paying the reserve a visit soon.

Target birds *All year* – Common wildfowl (100%), Cetti's Warbler (hear 60%, see 10%).

Other likely bird species

All year		*Summer*
Great Crested Grebe	Kingfisher	Common Tern
Cormorant	Green Woodpecker	Hirundines
Egyptian Goose	Great Spotted Woodpecker	Migrant warblers
Common wildfowl	Pied Wagtail	*Winter*
Common waterbirds	Common scrub birds	Goldeneye
Sparrowhawk	Common woodland birds	Winter thrushes
Kestrel	Common finches	*Occasional*
Common gull species		Lesser Spotted Woodpecker
		Marsh Harrier

Background information and birding tips

PREVIOUSLY, NWT Barton Broad could only be viewed from a boat but thanks to some incredibly hard work by Norfolk Wildlife Trust and the Broads Authority, all birders should be able to enjoy the delights of this site in 2002.

A car park has been constructed behind the Barton Angler Country Inn, and a new gravel footpath leads from here to a boardwalk through part of the reserve at Heron's Carr. A viewpoint affords excellent views over the Broad but if you like to take your ease, there are regular trips by electric boat around the Broad, complete with a commentary by a warden.

So what can the visiting birder expect to see? Well, nothing very unusual at the moment, but extensive work is being undertaken to improve the water quality to attract more wildlife to the reserve.

Expect to find many common wildfowl species (Tufted Duck, Pochard, Shoveler, etc), with Goldeneye joining them in Winter, and waterbirds (Great Crested Grebe, Coot, Moorhen, etc). Cormorants regularly roost on NWT Barton Broad and Common Terns visit in Summer.

The wet woodland (carr) along the boardwalk should not be ignored as this is home to many common species, including Marsh Tit. Cetti's Warblers should be heard from the thick bushes, though they are devils to see. All three woodpecker species have been recorded, though Great and Green Woodpeckers are the two most commonly seen.

The hard work of NWT and BA ensures that NWT Barton Broad is one to watch in the future. I suggest you reward their hard work by paying Heron's Carr a visit as soon as you can and inject a little cash into the local economy. This may have the effect of damping down some local objections to the development of the reserve.

Other nearby sites

NWT Alderfen Broad, Buxton Heath, NWT Hickling Broad, How Hill Reserve, NWT Hoveton Great Broad, NWT Martham Broad, NWT Ranworth Broad, Sparham Pools, NWT Upton Fen, Winterton Dunes.

Access details

(Approx. 10.5 miles NE of Norwich).

BY CAR: In Wroxham, follow signs to Stalham/Yarmouth/ Cromer/N.Walsham (along A1151). Two miles N of roundabout at junction with A1062, turn right at signs to 'Dried Flower Centre'/ Neatishead. Continue into Neatishead village, and turn right at Ye Olde Saddlery public house and B&B (sign-posted to Irstead).

After 0.7 miles turn right at Barton Angler Country Inn, and the reserve car park is on the left after the pub entrance. Take the obvious new gravel footpath for approx. 500 yards to Heron's Carr. Wheelchair users should not turn right at the Barton Angler Country Inn but instead continue for another 0.8 miles to Heron's Carr (TG 358207) where there is disabled parking only.

BY BOAT: NWT Barton Broad is situated along the River Ant, one day's sail from Wroxham. Mooring for reserve is at Lime Kiln Dyke, following signs for the Barton Angler Country Inn.

Mooring with facilities is available at Neatishead, at the end of Lime Kiln Dyke, or further N at Barton Turf, though this does not give access to Heron's Carr. The whole of Barton Broad can also be seen from your boat.

The electric boat mooring is sign-posted from the new car park by the Barton Angler Country Inn. A warden offers a commentary during each trip.

41

Key points

- A National Trust reserve.

- Control your dog!

- No foot access to western tip (April – end July) to protect terns from disturbance.

- Phone boat company for sailing times.

- Facilities at parking places (Cley, Morston and Blakeney) can be closed off-peak.

- Keep to boardwalks around the visitor centre.

- Avoid roped-off areas.

- Visitor Centre has disabled toilets and sells drinks and snacks. Opening times unpredictable so go prepared! Usually open April – end September.

FAMOUS WITH birders and non-birders alike as a great place to view tern and seal colonies in Summer, Blakeney Point attracts many common, scarce and rare migrants in Spring and Autumn. However, unless you take a boat to The Point to see them you may have to undertake an arduous eight mile round trek along a shingle bank! In Winter thousands of waders roost on The Point.

Target birds

Summer – Nesting terns (100%), Mediterranean Gull (10%). *Spring/Autumn* – Passage seabirds, passage migrants. *Winter* – Waders (100%), Raptors (20%).

Other likely bird species

All year	Common finches	Grasshopper Warbler
Cormorant	Reed Bunting	Goldcrest
Shelduck		Ortolan Bunting
	Spring/Autumn	
Other common wildfowl	Shearwaters	*Winter*
Kestrel	Gannet	Brent Goose
	Whimbrel	Wigeon
Red-legged Partridge	Skuas	Grey Plover
Common waders	Wryneck	Rock Pipit
	Hirundines	Winter thrushes
Common gull species	Richard's Pipit	
Sky Lark	Yellow Wagtail	*Occasional*
Meadow Pipit	Ring Ouzel	Hen Harrier
Pied Wagtail	Bluethroat	Merlin
	Whinchat	Peregrine
Common scrub birds	Wheatear	Short-eared Owl
Corvids	Black Redstart	

Background information and birding tips

A VISIT to Blakeney Point in ideal migrant conditions (fog, drizzle, onshore winds) can seem a very bleak experience. Visit in Spring and Summer sunshine for the tern and seal colonies and it can seem like a naturalist's paradise.

Summer boat trips are popular with tourists interested in seeing Common and Grey Seals on The Point, but the trips are also superb for obtaining close views of Sandwich,

Common, Little and Arctic Terns busily going about the business of raising their chicks. Sharp-eyed birders will manage to pick out a Roseate Tern or Mediterranean Gull if they are lucky.

Along Blakeney Channel you will see many common waders on the mud banks, and see terns as they fish the large inlet. At most times, the trip takes about one hour and you do not land on The Point. However, if the tide is right, the boat does land, extending the

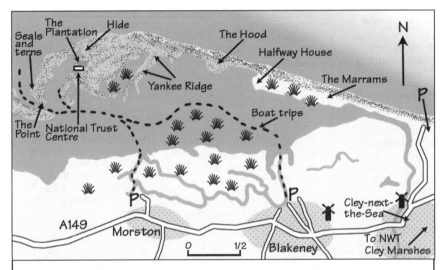

Access details

(Approx. 11 miles W of Cromer.)

You can tackle Blakeney Point the hard way or the easy way. The easy way is to travel by boat from either Morston Quay or Blakeney Harbour. Call contact numbers for sailing times, as these depend on tides. Boats run throughout the year, though tide times dictate whether you are able to land on The Point or not.

Morston is about two miles W of Blakeney village. Obtain boat tickets where the chalk

boards advertise 'Boat Trips' by The Anchor pub on A149. Morston Quay is sign-posted on a brown tourist sign. Follow this rough track to a pay and display car park.

Blakeney Harbour is sign-posted off the A149 down Westgate Street. Follow the road to the quay car park and the moorings for the seal and bird trips are very obvious.

If you want a challenge in Spring and Autumn, the best way to find the birds is by walking from Cley beach car park, out of the village

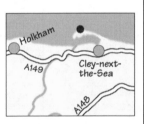

towards Sheringham, then turn left at the sign for 'Beach'. Walk W along the shingle bank for four miles. The going may be easier if the tide is out as you can walk on hard sand.

round trip to two hours. Booking boat trips is essential, especially in school holidays. In 2001, the trip cost £5 for adults and £3.50 for children.

Birdwatchers in Spring and Autumn will be on the look-out for migrants, and should endeavour to walk the whole

length of Blakeney Point from Cley beach car park. This is an arduous walk along a shingle sea wall, and at the end of the eight mile trek (four miles each way) your calf muscles will be complaining bitterly! If you are lucky, the tide will be out enabling you to walk on hard

sand. Please keep clear of Oystercatchers and Ringed Plovers in Spring as they will be trying to nest on the shingle.

For the first mile you will have the sea on your right and a marsh on your left. Scan both at regular intervals for

• **Continued overleaf.**

43

● **Continued from page 43.**

Key points

- **No bikes or wheeled vehicles.**

- **If walking, the terrain is tough.**

- **Difficult wheelchair access. Please phone the warden.**

- **Hearing loop installed for 'sea and bird sounds atmosphere'.**

Contacts

The Warden, 35 The Cornfield, Langham, Holt, Norfolk NR25 7DQ.

01263 740480 (April – Sept)

01328 830401 (Oct – March).

Winter warden: 01263 740241

The National Trust, East Anglia Regional Office 01263 733471 www.nationaltrust.org.uk/ regions/eastanglia/

Blakeney boats:
Graham Bean
01263 740505
Colin Bishop
01263 740753
Roy Moreton
01328 830394

Morston boats:
John Bean
01263 740038
Jim Temple
01263 740791

passing seabirds over the former and geese, ducks and raptors over the latter. The shingle then opens out to an area of stubby vegetation, known as The Marrams. Wait here awhile as the dense plants can hold various species, but they do tend to hide.

I surprised a Peregrine in this area in April 2001, then watched it for an hour as it terrorised waders on the beach. Wheatears are common here on passage, and look out for thrushes, warblers, Goldcrests, finches etc as they make their first landing from the continent.

A mile further on, you reach Halfway House. Don't let the name fool you: this is only Quarter or Three-quarter House depending if you are on your way to The Point or on your way back. Either way, it will feel good to get your feet on solid ground for a few moments after sand and shingle. The bushes around Halfway House are excellent migrant traps.

After a further half a mile, you reach a dune system, known as The Hood, which is good for migrant pipits, chats, thrushes etc. Search the area thoroughly before continuing your journey.

Eventually, you will reach an odd-shaped blue building, which was the old lifeboat station, but now houses the National Trust visitor centre. The area here has three trees, known optimistically as The Plantation, and in this barren landscape they do act as magnets for birds on passage!

The area around the lifeboat station and chalets is excellent

for Wheatears, Whinchats, thrushes, etc in Spring and Autumn. There is also a seat here where you can look over Blakeney Channel and marsh. When the tide permits, Grey Plovers, Curlew, Dunlin, Bar-tailed Godwits, Ringed Plovers, etc can be seen and Brent Geese are present on the marsh until May.

Terns fish the channel from April onwards, but the nesting area is another half a mile from here, at the western tip of The Point. There is no access by foot to the tern colony between April and July.

A boardwalk runs from behind the visitor centre to a hide overlooking a channel. This is good for observing fishing terns in Summer when the tide is in, and geese and waders in Winter, when the mud is exposed. A telescope is useful for this hide.

The boardwalk also leads to the beach. This can be a spectacular place to be when the wind is blowing strongly onshore. Skuas and shearwaters seem to pass closer here than at any other seawatching site in Norfolk (with the possible exception of Sheringham), though there is no shelter.

Blakeney Point also boasts a disabled toilet. The most baffling thing is exactly how the National Trust expects wheelchair users to get to it, as a steep step from the sand onto a boardwalk has to be negotiated. If you have mobility problems, I would phone the warden to clarify things first!

As mentioned before, Blakeney Point is famous for its seal colony. More than 400 can be seen here,

Blakeney's projection into the North Sea makes it a natural stopping-off point for migrants, such as Wryneck which can turn up in Spring or Autumn.

most of them Common Seals. The seals and terns provide a noisy spectacle on the boat trips and I thoroughly recommend it to you even if you are prone to queasiness on boats. Usually I feel ill at the slightest sea-swell, but this trip is a breeze. I am usually more concerned with sorting out the terns ("was that a Roseate which just flew over my head?") and cooing at the baby seals!

In truth, the walk from Cley is usually only undertaken by hardened birdwatchers trying to find rare migrants in Spring and Autumn. Such expeditions in October 2001 produced Lanceolated Warbler, Ortolan Bunting, Barred Warbler, Dotterel and mainland Britain's first twitchable Pallas's Grasshopper Warbler, so you can see that the trudge along the shingle can be well worth the effort.

Other nearby sites

NWT Cley Marshes, Felbrigg Hall, Holkham NNR, Holkham Park, Kelling Heath, Kelling Quags, Salthouse Beach, Salthouse Heath, Swanton Novers, NOA Walsey Hills, Wells Woods.

Key points

- **National Trust site – free access.**

- **Possible charge for main car park.**

- **Road to car park may flood at high tide.**

- **Toilet block near main car park.**

- **Access trail consists of railway sleepers.**

- **Wheelchair users restricted to beach road.**

- **Terrain is level, but at least one stile to negotiate.**

- **Insect repellent advisable in Summer.**

- **Telescope advisable.**

E NJOY this typical North Norfolk marsh, complete with typical marsh birds, without crowds of other birdwatchers. Situated within walking distance of the RSPB Titchwell Marsh reserve along the beach, it can be a productive place, especially in Winter.

Target birds *Resident* - **Bearded Tit (70%), Barn Owl (40%).** *Winter* - **Brent Goose (95%), Seaduck (40%), Raptors (25%).** *Summer* - **Marsh Harrier (70%).** *Spring/ Autumn* - **Passage migrants.**

Other likely bird species

All year	Blackcap	Snow Bunting
Cormorant	Chiffchaff	
Little Egret	Willow Warbler	*Spring/Autumn*
Shelduck		Shearwaters
Kestrel	*Winter*	Gannet
Common waders	Red-throated Diver	Garganey
	Wigeon	Hobby
Common gull species	Teal	Whimbrel
Green Woodpecker	Long-tailed Duck	Skuas
Sky Lark	Common Scoter	Wryneck
Meadow Pipit	Goldeneye	Yellow Wagtail
Pied Wagtail	Red-breasted Merganser	Redstart
Bullfinch		Whinchat
Reed Bunting	Hen Harrier	Wheatear
	Merlin	Ring Ouzel
Summer	Peregrine	Winter thrushes
Terns	Grey Plover	Barred Warbler
Hirundines	Short-eared Owl	Yellow-browed Warbler
Sedge Warbler	Stonechat	
Reed Warbler	Winter thrushes	Firecrest
Whitethroat	Twite	Pied Flycatcher

Background information and birding tips

B RANCASTER MARSH is another coastal site neglected by birders, making it ideal for those wishing to birdwatch on their own. It is an extension of the Gypsy Lane walk to the west.

Close to the small lay-by along the road, listen out for the '*ping-ping*' calls of Bearded Tits in the surrounding reedbed: they can show well here. The start of the track is marked by a National Trust sign about 75 yards back towards the village from the small lay-by. The board says you must obey the by-laws posted on the back of the sign. However, the sign is situated so awkwardly that if you try to read these you will end up in the ditch, which is probably contrary to one of the by-laws.

The path starts off along a rough track through a small reedbed. This is frequented by Reed Warblers in Summer. The

Contacts

The National Trust
01263 733471

trees and bushes around the start of the track are alive with species such as Goldfinch, Greenfinch, Reed Bunting and other common birds.

The path narrows and continues east until it reaches a stile from where you start to get a great overview of the marsh. This is also a good place to watch for Sedge Warblers. Until this point, the vertically-challenged among us will have seen very little of the marsh over the reeds!

All along this section there are bushes to scan for common birds and migrants in Spring and Autumn. There is a distinct possibility of the odd Redstart, Pied Flycatcher, Barred Warbler or Firecrest turning up here in May or, more likely, in September/October.

After the stile, the path consists of two railway sleepers side by side (quite narrow when passing other walkers, especially those clad in winter woollies). The whole path gives excellent views over the marsh. In Winter, expect Hen Harriers and maybe a Merlin with a distinct possibility of a Barn or Short-eared Owl. Flying in and out of the marsh will be small flocks of Brent Geese and Wigeon.

The marsh is quieter in Summer but you should obtain reasonable views of a Marsh Harrier or two. Hirundines should be seen overhead, sometimes being pursued by a Hobby. In August 2001, I discovered a Little Egret here, probably a wanderer from Titchwell.

The path reaches a beautiful cottage with views over the marsh and, if I win the lottery, I

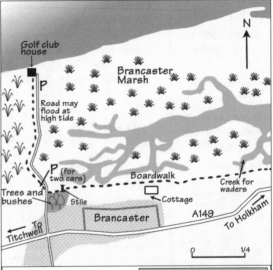

Access details

(Approx. 6.5 miles E of Hunstanton).

Enter Brancaster village on A149 Norfolk coast road and take Broad Lane, signposted 'The Beach'.

There is a small pull-in on the left with room for two cars at the point where the road splits the reedbed. If this is full, follow the road to the car park (you may have to pay the attendant, depending on time of year).

The footpath is 75 yards back towards the village from the small lay-by. Turn left along a track in the reeds and follow for as far as you like (this path is part of The Peddar's Way long distance footpath).

shall be knocking on their door to make them an offer they can't refuse! Just after this cottage, you come across a creek, which is a good place to scan for waders when the tide is out.

From here the path continues with good views over the marsh to your left and bushes to your right. The longer you walk along

towards Holkham, the more you are likely to see, especially in Winter.

If you wish to partake in a spot of seawatching, you should park in the beach car park and view the sea from the beach. In Winter, you should be rewarded with views of divers, grebes and waders, with shearwaters and skuas in Autumn and terns in Summer.

47

Key points

- **Not accessible for wheelchair users.**

- **Free access at all times.**

- **Terrain is level along a narrow, muddy path.**

- **Two hides overlook Breydon Water (accessed up steep steps).**

- **Excellent views available from raised 'sea-wall'.**

- **Telescope essential.**

- **Huge area best viewed an hour before high tide when birds are pushed into NE corner.**

Contacts

General Broads Authority
01603 610734

Boat trips across Breydon Water
01603 715191

BREYDON is a huge expanse of water or, when the tide is out, mud. It is best viewed from the two hides or the footpath along the north-east corner, though you may wish to walk the whole area to maximise your chances of seeing as much as possible. An hour before high tide is best for viewing the waders. A highly recommended way of seeing birds up close, is to have a trip out on an organised boat tour (see Contacts Section below).

Target birds

Winter – Avocet (90%), White-fronted Goose (55%), Rock Pipit (50%), Short-eared Owl (25%). *Spring/Summer* – Avocet (90%), Little Gull (50%), Roseate Tern (10%). *Spring/Autumn* – Passage waders, Little Gull (60%).

Other likely bird species

All year	Pink-footed Goose	Curlew Sandpiper
Cormorant	Wigeon	Black-tailed Godwit
Shelduck	Pintail	Whimbrel
Common wildfowl	Goldeneye	Greenshank
Sparrowhawk	Golden Plover	Spotted Redshank
Kestrel	Grey Plover	Green Sandpiper
Grey Partridge	Knot	Wood Sandpiper
Red-legged Partridge	Bar-tailed Godwit	Common Sandpiper
Common waders	*Spring/Summer*	Black Tern
Gull species	Garganey	Arctic Tern
Barn Owl	Sandwich Tern	*Occasional*
Pied Wagtail	Common Tern	Marsh Harrier
Winter	*Passage*	Hen Harrier
Bewick's Swan	Ruff	Merlin
Whooper Swan	Little Stint	Peregrine
		Little Tern

Background information and birding tips

SUCH A HUGE area can seem a very daunting place to watch birds, but getting there at the right time makes this an accessible place, as the tide will do all your hard work for you. The north-east area is the last to be covered by the tide, so if you reach here about 60 or 90 minutes before high tide, all the waders and roosting terns will have been pushed towards you.

Breydon is the only reliable place to see wintering Avocet in Norfolk. There may be one or two at other sites in the county, but more than 50 stay here from October to March. These are joined by others in Summer, with numbers reaching up to 300 in July and August. Dotted among the Avocets you should see one or two Grey Plovers and Bar-tailed Godwits, along with other species of commoner waders.

If you follow the path from the

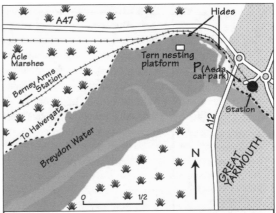

Asda car park along the north shore, passing the two hides, you are able to look out over Acle Marshes on your right. In Winter Hen Harriers are sometimes seen, while Merlins are more infrequent. This area is probably the most reliable site in the county for Short-eared Owls. In Winter up to three birds roost here. A Barn Owl sighting is also possible.

The marshes around Breydon also hold varying numbers of wintering wildfowl. White-fronted Geese numbers seem to be declining here but Wigeon are numerous and you might pick out a few Bewick's or Whooper Swans in the fields. You should also find one or two Rock Pipits as 100 or so over-winter around Breydon.

Common waders will be joined by several more exciting species at passage times in Spring and Autumn. These can include Whimbrel, Spotted Redshank, Little Stint, Ruff and Green, Common, Wood and Curlew Sandpipers. Numbers are usually better in Autumn. Also look out for Black and Arctic Terns at these times.

In Summer, Breydon is frequented by several species of roosting tern. Sandwich and Common Terns are the most numerous, but watch out for Little and Roseate Terns among them. The hides overlook the tern nesting platforms. It is also worth noting that Breydon is a prime site for Caspian Tern, so be alert.

More than half the British records of Broad-billed Sandpiper have been found at Breydon and, in May, Kentish Plovers are almost annual.

Access details

(On outskirts of Great Yarmouth).

BY CAR: **Take A47 into Great Yarmouth, heading straight over the first roundabout (junction with A12) towards the town centre. At the next roundabout go back the way you have just travelled (sign-posted to A47 Norwich). Turn left at the signs to the train station. Go past the station and park in the left hand side of the Asda car park, by the raised 'sea-wall'. Walking adjacent to the wall, continue to the information board. The Weavers Way footpath starts here, going under the road bridge and following the north shore of Breydon**

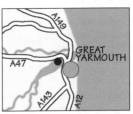

Water to the two hides and beyond to Berney Marshes.

BY BOAT: **There is free 24hr mooring on the River Bure at Great Yarmouth, near the tourist information at TG 521083. Walk south and cross A47 road bridge to the train station and Asda supermarket. Follow directions above. Alternatively be 'green' and catch a train to Great Yarmouth or Berney Arms.**

If you wish, you can continue along the north shore path across the Halvergate Marshes to Halvergate village, a distance of some seven miles. There is an infrequent bus service back to Yarmouth from Halvergate but check times first. See Halvergate site for details.

If you are visiting The Broads area by boat, you can get excellent views of Breydon Water's birds from your vessel. You should only try to get into Yarmouth across Breydon Channel when the tide is coming in; if you try to do it when the tide is going out, you will be carried out to sea on the strong currents!

49

Key points

- **Call in at Strumpshaw Fen for details of whereabouts of Bean Geese.**

- **Free parking.**

- **Access via a rough track that is wet at all times of year. Boots or wellies recommended.**

- **Telescope essential as target species are invariably distant.**

- **Please leave sightings information in hide.**

RENOWNED for its wintering flock of Bean Geese, Buckenham also attracts a large number of Wigeon. In Summer, several nationally declining breeding species raise their young on the marshes, making this a very important bird reserve. This site incorporates RSPB Cantley Marsh.

Target birds
Winter – (Taiga) Bean Goose (85%), White-fronted Goose (85%), Water Pipit (40%). *Summer* – Breeding waders, Marsh Harrier (55%), Hobby (40%).

Other likely bird species

Winter	Barn Owl	Snipe
Wigeon	Short-eared Owl	Curlew
Teal	Winter thrushes	Redshank
Pintail		Black-headed Gull
Other wildfowl	*Summer*	Yellow Wagtail
	Egyptian Goose	
Common waterbirds	Gadwall	*Spring/Autumn*
Winter raptors	Shoveler	Garganey
Golden Plover	Oystercatcher	Passage waders
	Avocet	Little Gull
Common gull species	Lapwing	

Background information and birding tips

ENGLAND'S only regular wintering flock of Bean Geese has made the RSPB's Buckenham Marshes famous. These birds are usually present from November until mid February and in 2001, the flock had dwindled to just 50 birds by February 10. A week later they had all departed (and guess who turned up to see them on the latter date?) A small flock of White-fronted Geese also over-winters on the marsh.

Visiting birdwatchers wanting to see Bean Geese should call in at the RSPB Strumpshaw Fen reception hide (see page 162 for instructions) before continuing to Buckenham Marsh. They can then find out the best place to view the flock on that day, as the geese can roam over a wide area.

There is a hide overlooking Buckenham Marsh. To reach this, cross the manned level crossing at Strumpshaw and follow the road/track to the parking area, next to the river. Walk to the hide by the derelict windmill. Alternatively, park at Buckenham Station (TG 351056) and cross the railway line on foot to the access track.

In Winter, as well as Bean and White-fronted Geese, you will also see thousands of Wigeon. These birds generally take no notice as you walk along the access track as they are too busy feeding.

Raptors and owls regularly patrol the fields in Winter, Peregrine being the most regularly noted. Barn Owls can be encountered at most times of year but I have never been very lucky at this site. One or two

Contacts

RSPB Mid Yare Office
01603 715191

RSPB East Anglia Office
01603 661662

Water Pipits can usually be found around the pools near the hide, though they are elusive at times.

At dusk an enormous corvid roost of up to 15,000 birds provides one of the best bird spectacles in the Broads. They arrive in groups of 100-500, from all over the area, to roost in the carrs to the north of Buckenham and act as a timely reminder to those working in the reedbeds that it is time for home.

In Summer, Buckenham is an important breeding area for several species that are declining rapidly on the national stage. These include Sky Lark, Yellow Wagtail, Redshank, Snipe, Shoveler and Lapwing. Egyptian and Greylag Geese also breed as does Meadow Pipit. Marsh Harrier and Hobby frequently cause panic as they hunt over the marsh. One or two Avocets are seen occasionally.

In Spring and Autumn, the site attracts several species of passage waders. Ruff, Black-tailed Godwit, Green and Wood Sandpipers and Little Stint are the most regular species, but anything can turn up. Recent rarities include Pacific Golden Plover and Pectoral Sandpiper (and a White Pelican, but we can safely ignore that one). Little Gull and Garganey are recorded regularly on passage.

This is an important reserve for birds, but to be honest, not so good for birdwatchers: viewing can be quite poor and most species are usually distant. There is always something to see here but better views can be obtained at sites nearby (except for the Bean Geese of course).

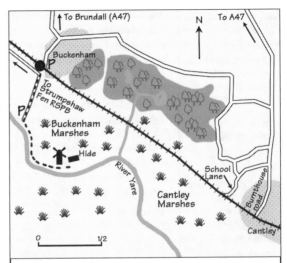

Access details

(General area: approx. seven miles E of Norwich)

From Norwich take A47 to roundabout sign-posted to Brundall. Continue on minor road for 0.4 miles, and bear left at the sharp bend onto The Street (sign-posted Brundall Station). Follow the road around mini-roundabouts and across the traffic-calmed area.

After 1.1 miles you go under a railway bridge, then reach a sign for Strumpshaw Fen RSPB (follow the RSPB signs if you want information on where to see the Bean Geese). Turn right (Stone Road) and follow signs for

the Household Waste Disposal Centre. Go past this centre, then turn right after 0.7 miles, sign-posted to Buckenham Station (Station Road). After half a mile, park in gravel car park by the old railway station. Carefully cross the railway line, and head left for the derelict windmill along the wide, rough track.

One other thing to note, is that there is no boat mooring at Buckenham, even though the River Yare runs adjacent to the reserve. This addition would make it an ideal place for Broadland tourists to visit during their holiday.

Other nearby sites

Breydon Water, Burgh Castle, Cantley Beet Factory, Great Yarmouth Beach, Hardley Flood, Rockland Broad, NWT Sparham Pools, RSPB Strumpshaw Fen, RSPB Surlingham Church Marshes, Ted Ellis Reserve.

51

Key points

- **Terrain is mainly level along tracks and grass paths. Some steep steps though most can be avoided.**

- **Path alongside Breydon Water is level and well maintained, good for wheelchair users.**

- **Telescope essential for good views of raptors.**

- **Free access at all times.**

- **Free 24-hour mooring close by.**

- **Boat trips available from Goodchild's Marina, just to the south of the Roman ruin.**

Contacts

General Broads Authority
01603 610734

Boat trips
01603 715191

THE REMAINS of a Roman fort provide a viewing platform across a fine expanse of extensive marshland that is good for wintering wildfowl and raptors. You will also be able to take a productive walk alongside the southern shore of Breydon Water for close views of waders and wildfowl.

Target birds   *All year* – Avocet (80%). *Winter* – raptors (25%), Short-eared Owl (15%).

Other likely bird species

All year	*Winter*	*Summer*
Little Grebe	Sky Lark	Peregrine
Great Crested Grebe	Meadow Pipit	Winter thrushes
Cormorant	Pied Wagtail	Stonechat
Common wildfowl	Common scrub birds	*Summer*
Common waterbirds	Common woodland birds	Common Tern
Marsh Harrier	Corvids	Cuckoo
Sparrowhawk	Common finches	Hirundines
Kestrel	Reed Bunting	Sedge Warbler
Red-legged Partridge	*Winter*	Reed Warbler
Grey Partridge	Bewick's Swan	Other warblers
Common waders	Whooper Swan	*Spring/Autumn*
Common gull species	White-fronted Goose	Passage waders
Barn Owl	Wigeon	*Occasional*
Great Spotted Woodpecker	Goldeneye	Lesser Spotted Woodpecker
	Hen Harrier	Bearded Tit
	Merlin	Hobby

Background information and birding tips

THE ROMAN fort at Burgh Castle affords superb views over the marshes of Langley, Beighton, Reedham, Halvergate, Chedgrave, Acle, South Walsham and Burgh Castle. In Winter, this is a great place to sit and scan for raptors and wildfowl.

A telescope is probably essential to get the best out of your visit, and it can get very cold up there on the hill, but your reward should include views of Marsh and Hen Harriers, along with Peregrine, Merlin, Short-eared Owl and wild swans and geese.

The bushes and trees around the fort are magnets for common woodland birds, including Lesser Spotted Woodpeckers. Search these trees in Spring and Autumn for migrants such as Redstarts, Pied Flycatchers and Firecrests. Below the fort is a reedbed that sometimes attracts Bearded Tits, but more likely will hold a Reed Bunting or two.

The path below the fort that joins the Angles Way, adjacent to the Church Farm Country Club, can be muddy at all times of year. Avoid it by walking along the top path by the church.

Time your visit correctly and you should get close views of many species of wader from this footpath. The best time to arrive is about an hour before high tide when the waders are pushed up to this western end of Breydon Water.

Avocets can be found here all year round and are joined by species such as Dunlin, Ringed Plover, Bar-tailed Godwit, Greenshank, Green Sandpiper and Little Stint at various times of the year. In the Summer of 2001, a couple of Spoonbills were regular visitors.

The Angles Way, a wide, well-maintained footpath, runs for about three and a half miles to Great Yarmouth. This is ideal if you are travelling by public transport, as you can catch a bus to Burgh Castle and walk back to Yarmouth or vice versa. There is always something to see, though views of most birds may be distant.

Finally, you may wish to take an organised boat trip from Goodchild's Marina, to the south of the Roman fort, to get close views of the thousands of waders on Breydon Water. Phone 01603 715191 for further details.

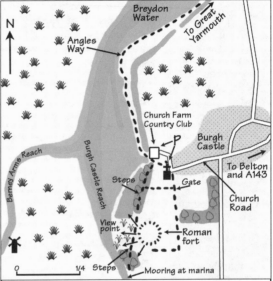

Access details

(Approx. three miles W of Great Yarmouth).

BY CAR: From Great Yarmouth, head S on A12. Follow signs for Burgh Castle and Belton on brown tourist signs (also holiday parks, caravan and camping site and marina) along A143. In Belton, take first right turn, following the brown tourist sign for Burgh Castle. At the T-junction, turn left into Church Road and follow to the church and Church Farm Country Club. Park by the church or in the pub car park. Follow the public footpath, adjacent to the church, to the Roman ruin for a panoramic view over

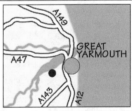

the marshes. Alternatively, walk down the left side of the pub car park to the footpath that runs below the fort and along the southern shore of Breydon Water.

BY BOAT: The nearest mooring is at Burgh Castle Marina, along the River Waveney. This is accessed at the western end of Breydon Water. A (sometimes muddy) public footpath runs north to the Roman fort.

Other nearby sites

Breydon Water, RSPB Buckenham Marsh, Cantley Beet Factory, Great Yarmouth Beach, Great Yarmouth Cemetery, Haddiscoe Marshes, Halvergate Marshes, Hardley Flood, Rockland Broad, NWT Sparham Pools, RSPB Strumpshaw Fen, Ted Ellis Reserve.

Key points

- **Difficult to find – walk the route in daylight to avoid getting lost!**

- **No facilities other than a car park.**

- **A torch is essential.**

- **Insect repellent advised.**

- **Level terrain, but paths can be muddy so wear boots, especially early in the season (May).**

- **Stay on the tracks at all times as there are many delicate plants on site.**

- **Managed by Norfolk Wildlife Trust.**

Contacts

Norfolk Wildlife Trust
01603 625540

SEVERAL PAIRS of Nightjar traditionally occupy this expanse of heath, but it is rarely visited by birdwatchers. A maze of footpaths criss-cross the heath, so only explore if you have a good sense of direction! Woodcock show better here than anywhere else I've visited in Norfolk.

Target birds *Summer* – Woodcock (99%), Nightjar (70%).

Other likely bird species

Summer	Great Spotted Woodpecker	Other warblers
Sparrowhawk		Goldcrest
Kestrel	Sky Lark	Jay
Turtle Dove	Hirundines	Common finches
Cuckoo	Common scrub birds	Yellowhammer
Tawny Owl	Lesser Whitethroat	*Occasional*
Green Woodpecker	Whitethroat	Hobby

Background information and birding tips

BUXTON HEATH is a handy site for Nightjars if you are staying in Norwich or Wroxham, though numbers lag behind other sites (Roydon Common, Salthouse Heath, etc).

The area the Nightjars frequent can be hard to find if you haven't visited the site before but Buxton has the advantage of (usually) being free of other birders or dog-walkers. There seem to be areas quite close to the car park which should support Nightjars but I have never seen or heard any except in the area described.

Once you have found the right area, wait for dusk when the Nightjars become active. You should get excellent flight views of one or two roding Woodcock. They seem to come out much earlier here than at other sites, perhaps to make up for the tardy Nightjars.

You should also hear Tawny Owls hooting, and may see

Green Woodpecker, Jay, Yellowhammer, Turtle Dove, Stock Dove, Sparrowhawk or Kestrel along with common woodland and scrub birds. Overhead, Swallows, Swifts and House Martins help keep the midges away from you but they may fall prey to a dashing Hobby.

Once you've located the correct area it is obvious that the habitat is ideal for these Nightjars. From the wide sandy track (after wiping away the cobwebs acquired from the 'gorse arch walk') look to the flat area of land to your right with a few rusty red plants growing on it. A track leads right which is also a good place to try for Nightjars.

The Nightjars here seem to like a lie-in as they always start *'churring'* later than at other sites. In fact, they sometimes fail to *'churr'* at all and the first you will know of their presence is when something silently flaps, ghost-like, past your ear. You will have just become accustomed to the owl hooting, the Pipistrelle Bats fluttering overhead and the

Access details

(Approx. 7.5 miles N of Norwich).

From Norwich, head N on A140 (to Aylsham/Cromer), then left along B1149 (sign-posted to Horsford). After about five miles, turn right into The Heath (third minor road right after Horsford village).

Look for a track on the left, opposite the first house on the right.

On foot, don't bear right from the car park but continue straight on along the path that runs next to the continuing access track. (If you reach a cattle grid you have gone wrong). Head on the grass path to a metal gate about 50 yards along (not the metal gate nearest the cattle grid).

Past the gate the path splits into two. Take the right-hand path for about 200 yards until it forks again. Head right through an archway of gorse bushes (you may need to duck!) to a junction with a wide sandy track (about 500 yards). You will now see the habitat becoming more Nightjar-friendly so breathe a sigh of relief!

Turn right onto the sandy track and follow for about 500 yards, (when it begins to go up a slight incline, you know you are in the correct area). Where the track levels out, stop because this is the

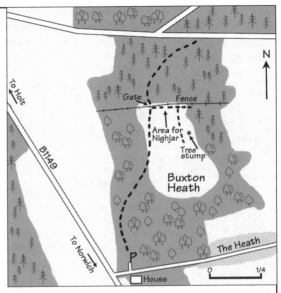

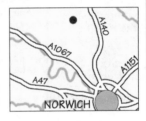

Nightjar area (if the bushes and trees start closing in around this wide track, you have gone too far). You should meet a wide track on the right, which is also a good place to listen for the churrers (there is a beech stump on the left about 300 yards along this track which is a favoured Nightjar perch).

Woodcocks squeaking and honking, when a suggestion of a dark shape startles you. Eerie, but very tranquil!

I can personally guarantee that the midges will love you for your effort, especially if you forget your insect repellent but, with luck, you may also find one or two Glow Worms on your way back.

As a postscript, the habitat looks good for Wood Lark,

Tree Pipit and Nightingale but I have never seen or heard any of them here. Please let me know if you have any success at this site with these three sought-after species.

Other nearby sites

Breydon Water, NWT Cockshoot Broad, Great Yarmouth Beach, NWT Hickling Broad, Horsey, NWT Ranworth Broad, NWT Sparham Pools, Swanton Novers, NWT Martham Broad, Ted Ellis Reserve, NWT Upton Fen.

55

Key points

- **Access at all times.**

- **Keep to walkways and be aware of factory traffic.**

- **Muddy at all times so walking boots advised.**

- **To view the pits you MUST obtain a security pass.**

- **Terrain is very uneven by pits but you can see Cetti's Warbler without leaving the road.**

- **Obey all on-site instructions.**

- **Donation asked for (minimum £1 in 2002).**

- **Sightings book in reception.**

- **Shop and public house at the mooring site.**

Contacts

General Broads Authority
01603 610734

British Sugar, Cantley,
01493 700369

THIS area of lagoons in a working factory environment can be excellent for waders if water levels are favourable and it is a good place to encounter Cetti's Warblers.

Target birds *Spring/Summer* - Avocets breeding on pits (90%), Cetti's Warbler (hear 80%, see 35%), passage waders (80%). *Winter* - Raptors over Limpenhoe Marshes (with patience 20%).

Other likely bird species

All year	*Ringed Plover*	Hirundines
Common wildfowl	Little Stint	Sedge Warbler
Common waterfowl	Curlew Sandpiper	Reed Warbler
Shelduck	Dunlin	Whitethroat
Sparrowhawk	Ruff	Blackcap
Kestrel	Snipe	Chiffchaff
Water Rail	Curlew	Willow Warbler
Lapwing	Redshank	
Green Woodpecker	Greenshank	*Winter*
Sky Lark	Green Sandpiper	Winter thrushes
Pied Wagtail	Wood Sandpiper	
Meadow Pipit	Common Sandpiper	*Occasional*
Long-tailed Tit		Marsh Harrier
Reed Bunting	*Summer*	Hobby
	Black-headed Gull	Hen Harrier
Spring/Autumn	Common Tern	Merlin
Little Ringed	Turtle Dove	Peregrine
Plover	Cuckoo	Barn Owl

Background information and birding tips

CANTLEY Beet Factory can seem a daunting place but may produce some outstanding birdwatching. If water levels are ideal, passage wader numbers can be impressive (for instance, more than 50 Green Sandpipers in one day in August 2001).

You cannot view any pits from public footpaths **so you must obtain a security pass from the reception area.** The pits are not accessible by wheelchair users, but the Cetti's Warbler area is.

You will see Great Crested Grebes on the river, plus summering Sedge Warblers in bankside bushes with Reed Warblers in the, erm, reeds.

You can follow the footpath alongside the river or turn left up the first concrete road to the railway crossing. This area is excellent for Cetti's Warblers all year as they show better than at most other sites I have visited.

If you have a security pass, you may now turn right at the railway crossing (don't cross the line) and follow the rough, muddy track up to a large reed-fringed pool/pit. In Summer, Shelducks, Avocets and Black-headed Gulls all breed here.

The track runs along three sides of this pool, but be careful not to flush the birds as you are on a raised bank, silhouetted against the skyline. Along the back edge, scan the Limpenhoe Marshes for Peregrine, Hen Harrier, Merlin in Winter or Marsh Harrier and Hobby in Summer. Each species is noted regularly.

The track eventually bears right and cuts between the reed-lined pit and a larger one. The large pit on your left is a good place to see Common Terns in Summer.

This site really comes into its own in Spring and Autumn when the waders are on the move. If water levels are low, the muddy edges can be alive with Green, Common, Wood, and Curlew Sandpipers as well as Ruff, Greenshank, Redshank, Little Ringed Plover, Snipe and Little Stint. Recent rarities include Baird's, Pectoral and Marsh Sandpipers on the pools, with an Icterine Warbler in the bushes by the main footpath.

The rough track rejoins a concrete road, leading back to the public footpath. Once back on the main footpath by the river, turn right to get back to the reception area. **Don't forget to sign out and hand in your pass.**

This site is well worth a visit at any time but late July through to October is best to catch the migrating waders.

Other nearby sites

Breydon Water, RSPB Buckenham Marshes, Great Yarmouth Cemetery, Rockland Broad, RSPB Strumpshaw Fen, RSPB Surlingham Church Marshes, Ted Ellis Reserve.

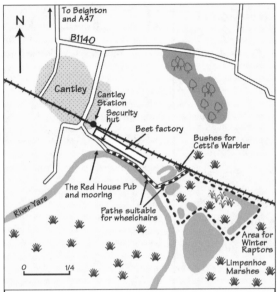

Access details

(Approx. 9.5 miles E of Norwich)

BY CAR: From A47 (Norwich to Great Yarmouth road), turn off at the signs for Cantley and Beighton on B1140. After 200 yards, turn left onto Cox Hill Road (NB: this is still the B1140). Don't go down Acle Road: if you reach Lingwood village you have missed the turn-off. Drive through Beighton to signs for Cantley Station. Follow road over railway line and turn in to the British Sugar site signed 'offices and reception'. Report to reception.

BY BOAT: Moor at The Red House public house on N bank of River Yare about half an hour's 'drive' N of junction with the River Chet. Walk along bank and report to reception.

BY TRAIN: Cantley train station is on the Yarmouth to Norwich line. Walk the short distance (about 100 yards) to the Beet Factory reception area.

GENERAL DIRECTIONS: Reception staff will issue security passes. You will also be asked for a small donation. Follow all on-site instructions and obey the footpath signs. Park where directed.

57

Key points

- **Access at all times.**

- **Best views in early mornings and evenings when birds not disturbed by farm traffic.**

- **Level terrain along uneven, grassy paths.**

- **The farmyard can be viewed from the road.**

JUST A SHORT drive from RSPB Titchwell Marsh reserve, this farmyard attracts Corn Buntings and Yellowhammers throughout the year. It is bordered by a hedge-lined track which attracts migrants in Spring and Autumn.

Target birds
All year – Corn Bunting (60%), Little Owl (40%), Tree Sparrow (20%). *Spring/Autumn* – Passage migrants.

Other likely bird species

All year	Common finches	Winter thrushes
Sparrowhawk	Yellowhammer	Ring Ouzel
Kestrel		Goldcrest
	Summer	Pied Flycatcher
Red-legged Partridge	Hirundines	
Grey Partridge	Whitethroat	*Winter*
Stock Dove	Blackcap	Pink-footed Goose
Sky Lark		Brambling
	Spring/Autumn	
Common scrub birds	Redstart	*Occasional*
Corvids	Whinchat	Barn Owl
	Wheatear	

Background information and birding tips

CHOSELEY BARNS is an unlikely looking site to go birdwatching, but it is the best place in Norfolk to see Corn Buntings. They usually feed around the large drying barn just off the minor road near the RSPB Titchwell Marsh reserve. They are usually joined by many Yellowhammers and an assorted variety of finches and other common birds. Tree Sparrows are

In Winter, the odd Brambling may join the finch flocks.

Contacts
None

also occasionally seen among the mixed flocks.

I suggest you sit quietly in your car by the barn and it won't be long before several of the above species hop in to view. Birds can be present throughout the day, though early mornings and evenings are best because farm traffic is less frequent at these times. In May 2002 a Quail was heard calling in fields around the barn but, as usual, was never seen.

The public footpath running east and west from the barn is bordered by a tall hedge. This hedge attracts migrants in Spring and Autumn, and should be checked thoroughly from late April to late May, and from mid September to early November. Anything can turn up here, due to its ideal position close to the coast.

If you stand on the footpath at the RSPB Titchwell Marsh reserve and look inland, you will see the communications mast and hedge on the hill, demonstrating what an irresistible magnet the area makes for tired migrants. Anything from the humble Goldcrest to the mega-rare Pied Wheatear has been recorded here!

Any tree or fence post in the surrounding fields should be scanned carefully for the resident Little Owls. Take care not to disturb them if you are lucky enough to find one.

Records of Ring Ouzel in April have become regular in recent years, and many other species make this hedge a feeding stop-off in Spring and Autumn. In

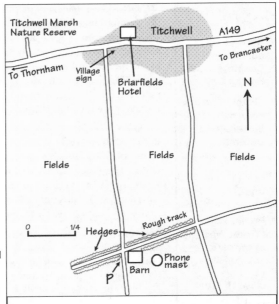

Access details

(Approx. six miles E of Hunstanton).

From the entrance to RSPB Titchwell Marsh on A149, head E to Titchwell village. After 0.4 miles, take the first right turn (where the Titchwell village post is situated on a small green, by the farm. If you reach the Briarfields Hotel you have gone too far).

Keep on this minor road up the hill for one mile. Park

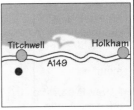

sensibly by the barn and communication tower: DO NOT BLOCK FARM ACCESS. Scan the farmyard for birds, plus walk E or W along the hedge-lined track.

Summer, look out for Blackcap and Whitethroat, which return to breed in May.

Summing up, Choseley Barns makes an ideal quick call-in spot as you travel between more well known places along the Norfolk coast.

Other nearby sites

Brancaster Marsh, Gypsy Lane, NOA Holme Observatory, NWT Holme Dunes, Hunstanton, NOA Redwell Marsh, Sandringham, RSPB Titchwell Marsh, Wolferton Triangle.

Key points

- Reserve open daily except Christmas and Boxing Day.

- Visitor centre is open daily. Easter – mid December (10am – 5pm) Summer (10am - 4pm) Winter

- Permit required (Ticket machine in car park when visitor centre is closed). Free for Norfolk Wildlife Trust members and children under 16, £3.50 for adult non-members.

- Permit is half price for public transport users (bus stop outside visitor centre).

- Free access to East Bank and shingle sea wall.

- Visitor centre stocks an extensive range of bird books, bird food, etc.

FOR MANY generations this site has enjoyed a worldwide reputation as a superb centre for watching birds and is a designated SSSI. Cley is also the quintessential Norfolk reserve: paintings of its windmill with the reserve's reedbed in the foreground are legion! As there is nearly always something to see, with easy access points, this coastal reserve pulls in crowds all year round. If NWT Cley Marshes reserve were a violin, it would definitely be a Stradivarius!

Target birds

All year – Bearded Tit (75%), Barn Owl (50%), Bittern (10%). *Winter* – Water Pipit (50%), Winter raptors (25%). *Spring* – Avocet (99%), Marsh Harrier (95%), Garganey (75%), Red-necked Phalarope (15%), Temminck's Stint (15%). *Summer* – Avocet (99%), Marsh Harrier (95%), Garganey (60%), Roseate Tern (15%). *Autumn* – Passage seabirds, passage waders.

Other likely bird species

All year
Little Grebe
Cormorant
Egyptian Goose
Shelduck
Other common wildfowl
Sparrowhawk
Kestrel
Water Rail
Black-tailed Godwit
Other common waders
Common gull species
Guillemot (at sea)
Razorbill (at sea)
Kingfisher
Sky Lark
Meadow Pipit
Pied Wagtail
Common scrub birds
Corvids
Common finches
Reed Bunting

Winter
Divers

Grebes
Brent Goose
Wigeon
Pintail
Goldeneye
Red-breasted Merganser
Hen Harrier
Merlin
Peregrine
Golden Plover
Bar-tailed Godwit
Rock Pipit
Stonechat
Winter thrushes

Spring
Little Ringed Plover
Whimbrel
Greenshank
Arctic Tern
Yellow Wagtail
Whinchat
Wheatear
Ring Ouzel

Summer
Yellow-legged Gull
Sandwich Tern
Common Tern

Little Tern
Hirundines
Sedge Warbler
Reed Warbler

Autumn
Fulmar
Manx Shearwater
Balearic Shearwater
Gannet
Little Stint
Curlew Sandpiper
Ruff
Spotted Redshank
Greenshank
Green Sandpiper
Wood Sandpiper
Common Sandpiper
Skuas
Kittiwake
Whinchat
Wheatear
Lapland Bunting

Occasional
Jack Snipe
Short-eared Owl
Shore Lark
Twite
Snow Bunting

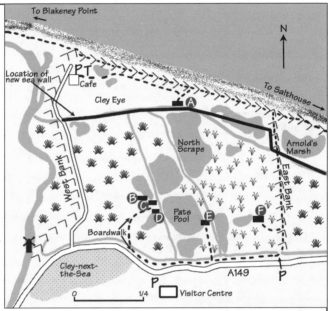

Access details

(Approx. 10.5 miles W of Cromer).

MAIN VISITOR CAR PARK (TG 053441): The main (free) car park is sign-posted off A149 half a mile E of Cley-Next-The-Sea village (car park is landward side of the road). The visitor centre is open from Easter to mid-December. From here, a boardwalk ensures easy access to Dawke's and Teal hides overlooking Dawke's Pool and Pat's Pool respectively.

BEACH ROAD CAR PARK (TG 048452): This is sign-posted 'Beach' off A149 just E of Cley village. £1 fee payable for car parking. There is a toilet block here and a café, which is open from Easter until around the end of August.

EAST BANK CAR PARK (TG 059442): This rough-surface car park is on the seaward side of A149. Heading E from Cley village, go past the visitor centre car park for about 300

KEY

A North Hide   D Teal Hide
B Avocet Hide   E Irene Hide
C Dawkes Hide   F Bittern Hide

yards. If you reach the Walsey Hills 'NOA Watchpoint' sign-post you have gone too far. This car park gives easiest access to the East Bank area of the reserve.

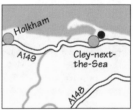

Background information and birding tips

THIS Norfolk Wildlife Trust reserve is a large area to cover, but there are three access points to ease the way. The main entrance is at the visitor centre. Disabled visitors are able to park at the centre itself, whereas able-bodied visitors must park below in the large car park.

Before entering the reserve you must obtain a permit –

either from the visitor centre, or when closed, from the ticket machine in the car park. Norfolk Wildlife Trust members enter free (but must still obtain a permit), while non-members must pay.

Please do not abuse this – the vital work of maintaining the reserve's excellence deserves your support. Access along the

East Bank to the beach is free, and is open at all times.

After obtaining your permit, cross the busy coast road and follow the boardwalk left to the three hides. This is the site's only wheelchair-friendly trail, but it can be very productive. The wide channel running adjacent to the road should be scanned for Kingfisher and Little Grebe,

• **Continues overleaf.**

Key points

- **Toilets (including disabled) at visitor centre.**

- **Toilets (not wheelchair friendly) and café at beach car park.**

- **Wheelchair access to Avocet, Dawke's and Teal Hides along a boardwalk. Take care crossing coast road.**

- **Terrain is level (though access to the visitor centre is up a steep concrete slope). East Bank is narrow and muddy, as are some paths on the reserve itself.**

Contacts

Norfolk Wildlife Trust
01603 625540

Cley Bird Club: Peter Gooden, 45 Charles Road, Holt, Norfolk, NR25 6DA

(Further reading: *The Birds of Cley* by SJM Gantlett) available from 'Books for Birders' 01263 741139

• **Continued from page 61.**

and the fields behind usually hold Wigeon and Teal all year (with larger numbers present in Winter). The flooded fields around here are a favoured haunt of Rock Pipits in Winter.

Along the boardwalk, Bearded Tits can be seen all year with Reed Warblers joining them in Summer. The hides look out to wader scrapes, which are productive at any time of year. Especially look out for Red-necked Phalaropes and Temminck's Stints in May: these two migrant species have become Cley specialities though neither is guaranteed.

The three hides (Avocet, Teal and Dauke's) are also good places to sit to watch the breeding Marsh Harriers drift over the reeds, or a Bittern lazily flap over. Keep your eyes peeled!

You now have to retrace your steps to the road, as there is no circular route from here. Instead of crossing the road to the visitor centre, keep on the path towards the East Bank. This grass path brings you to Irene Hide, which overlooks the same scrape (Pat's Pool) as Teal and Dauke's Hides.

In Spring and Summer, this is *the* place to see Garganey in Norfolk. Cley has a record second to none for attracting rare waders so watch this pool in Spring and Autumn for migrating waders such a Greenshank, Common, Wood and Green Sandpipers, and something rarer that will appeal to twitchers.

After Irene Hide, the path adjacent to the road brings you

to the East Bank. Walk towards the sea wall, scanning for Bearded Tits, which should be seen all year round in the reeds. Water Pipits often feed in the field to the right from December to March.

In Spring, this marshy field is a favourite haunt of Yellow Wagtails. Occasionally, the wagtail flock contains one or two of the scarcer races such as Blue-headed and White. Also look out for the resident Barn Owl over the fields.

Towards the beach, you may wish to divert left to Bittern Hide. Again, this is an excellent area to see Bearded Tits, but not Bitterns! More likely you will spot a Water Rail or, in Winter, a Jack Snipe or two.

Closer to the sea wall, you will see Arnold's Marsh to your right. This is usually home to several species of waders, with Avocet guaranteed in Spring and Summer. This is also a favoured roost site of a Roseate Tern or two, but their appearance is unpredictable.

Once on the shingle sea wall, you can turn back to the visitor centre car park, left to the beach car park, or right to Salthouse. If you choose left or right, scan the sea carefully at all times of year. Cley is renowned as a prime seawatching site and if you turn up in favourable conditions - strong onshore winds - during September and October, you will find many telescopes set up on the shingle near the beach car park, all hoping for something special to pass.

In Winter scan for grebes, divers and ducks, in Summer watch out for terns. In Autumn, anything can go past!

From the shingle bank, you can

divert to the North Hide, which overlooks the North Scrape. Several species of waders can be seen here at all times of year, and it is another good spot to look out for the occasional flying Marsh Harrier and Bittern.

The field by the beach car park is known as The Eye. It is home to a flock of Brent Geese in Winter along with many

Wigeon, passage waders in Spring and Autumn, and very occasionally a Lapland Bunting puts in an appearance (usually in Autumn).

It is perfectly possible to spend the whole day at Cley, gently strolling around, stopping off at the hides, seawatching and generally feeling all is well with the world. Whichever of the car

parks you start from, it is possible to take a long, circular route encompassing the whole of the reserve. And don't forget to pause a while on the shingle sea wall to take in the famous vista of Cley windmill.

Work is due to start on improving the sea defences at Cley which may disturb the birds at certain times. The work is scheduled to start in the Summer of 2002 although it may be delayed until 2003.

Sandwich Terns are among several tern species that visit Cley regularly in the Summer.

Other nearby sites

Blakeney Point, Kelling Heath, NOA Kelling Quags, Salthouse Beach, Salthouse Heath, Sheringham, Swanton Novers, NOA Walsey Hills, Warham Greens, Weybourne.

63

Key points

- **Site is a designated SSSI.**

- **Free access at all times.**

- **Boardwalk trail on level terrain.**

- **Free mooring at the reserve entrance.**

- **Wheelchair-accessible hide.**

- **Free parking, but can get full in Summer.**

- **Use insect repellent in Summer.**

Contacts

Norfolk Wildlife Trust
01603 625540

English Nature
01603 620558

Broadland
Conservation Centre
01603 270479

General Broads
Authority
01603 610734

THIS SMALL Norfolk Wildlife Trust reserve, is ideal for a stop-off during a Broadland boating holiday. Several common species of birds can be seen, but this is a site for the all-round naturalist, as it is home to rare plants, butterflies and dragonflies.

Target bird   Cetti's Warbler (hear 65%, see 20%).

Other likely bird species

Resident	Kingfisher	*Summer*
Great Crested Grebe	Great Spotted Woodpecker	Common Tern
Common wildfowl		Cuckoo
Egyptian Goose	Common scrub birds	Hirundines
Common waterbirds	Marsh Tit	Sedge Warbler
	Common woodland birds	Reed Warbler
Sparrowhawk		*Occasional*
Common gull species	Common finches	Lesser Spotted Woodpecker
	Reed Bunting	

Background information and birding tips

PREVIOUSLY a privately owned shooting site, NWT Cockshoot Broad is now part of the Bure Marshes National Nature Reserve (along with Ranworth Broad and Hoveton Great Broad), managed by Norfolk Wildlife Trust. The water quality is gradually being improved with a resultant increase in wildlife.

The fun starts along the approach road to the car park where you can play the little known game of 'Dodge the Dragonfly', as Black-tailed Skimmers love to rest on the Tarmac, only zipping away at the last minute. The site includes a pleasant, shortish, circular walk along a boardwalk (and is thus fully wheelchair accessible) through reeds and alder carr (wet woodland).

In Summer, the river can be quite noisy with boat traffic and boaters enjoying themselves. Even so, this path is good for Reed Warblers, especially if you stand quietly on the first wooden bridge along the trail. On the river, to your left, you should see Great Crested Grebes, Coots and Greylag Geese. Swallows swoop overhead.

Once on the reserve itself (cross the second wooden bridge at the end of the mooring channel), the path runs adjacent to a channel where you may hear the explosive song of a Cetti's Warbler from thick cover, or catch a glimpse of a Blackcap or Garden Warbler. Marsh Tits are relatively common in the woodland.

Stay on the main path to the hide at the end, or fork left through some reeds (excellent for Swallowtail butterflies in Summer). Both ways can be productive, and if you choose one way up to the hide you can always return via the other route.

The hide overlooks Cockshoot Broad itself, and birds seen here regularly include Kingfisher, (perched in the trees on the island) Common Tern, Shelduck, Egyptian Goose, Grey Heron and other common waterfowl.

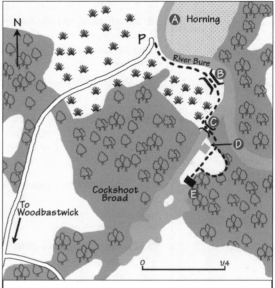

In Winter, the broad holds Pochard, Teal, Shoveler, Cormorant etc. Reed Buntings are resident, as are the commoner woodland species and they are easier to see because of the lack of leaves on the trees. This is a walk for hardy souls at this time of year though. The riverside boardwalk may flood in poor weather years, so I would stick to Spring and Summer.

This reserve is also renowned for its dragonflies and butterflies in Summer. The channel is an excellent place to see Red-eyed Damselflies, and Black-tailed Skimmers are common along the whole length of the boardwalk. I suggest an early morning walk for the best of the bird activity followed by a search for the dragonflies as the heat of the sun brings them out.

As the water quality of Cockshoot Broad improves, the wildlife variety and quality can only improve with it. Hopefully, the nesting platforms will be rebuilt to see the return of Common Terns as a breeding species. A Bittern was reported from here in June 2001, showing the potential of this quiet, picturesque place.

Other nearby sites

Breydon Water, Buxton Heath, Great Yarmouth Beach, NWT Hickling Broad, Horsey, NWT Hoveton Great Broad, How Hill, Ranworth Broad, RSPB Strumpshaw Fen, Ted Ellis Reserve, NWT Upton Fen, Winterton Dunes.

Key
A Ferry Inn
B Bridge - good for Reed Warbler
C 24hr mooring
D Dragonfly viewing platform
E Hide

Access details

(Approx. eight miles NE of Norwich).

BY CAR: From B1140 (Acle to Wroxham road), turn off at the signs for Woodbastwick. In the village, head E past the church, following signs for Ranworth.

Out of the village, the road bends sharply right, but you go straight on down a narrow road sign-posted 'River Only'. It ends in a small car park at the River Bure, opposite the Ferry Inn at Horning. The path to the reserve is on the right of this car park.

BY BOAT: Head E from Wroxham along River Bure to Horning. In Horning, about 100 yards after the Ferry Inn on the left, there is a mooring channel on the right, 24 hours stay maximum. The path into the reserve starts at the end of this channel (TG 346160).

65

Key points

- **Can be very bleak and birdless!**

- **Not suitable for wheelchair users.**

- **Wrap up warm!**

- **Terrain is level on an uneven path. Walking boots recommended.**

HERE IS a site best visited when the weather is particularly harsh, forcing wintering wildfowl on to the unfrozen waters of the Hundred Foot Drain – and that's bad news for fair-weather birders, because on this walk there is nowhere to shelter from the elements.

Target birds *Winter* – Goosander (65%), Peregrine (40%), Smew (10%).

Other likely bird species

Winter	Barn Owl	Common finches
Winter wildfowl	Sky Lark	Yellowhammer
Common waterfowl	Meadow Pipit	Reed Bunting
Lapwing	Pied Wagtail	Corn Bunting
Redshank	Winter thrushes	
Curlew	Corvids	*Occasional*
Common gull species	Starling	Winter raptors

Background information and birding tips

DENVER SLUICE is at its best when all other lakes and pools are frozen, because it keeps the Hundred Foot Drain free of ice even in the most hostile of conditions. In turn, this makes it *the* place to see Goosanders in west Norfolk.

Once you have climbed the bank near the pub, turned left and negotiated the stile, you will see the Hundred Foot Drain stretching in front of you with the sluice just visible in the distance. Walk as far as you like along this raised bank watching the water and fields for anything that moves.

On a particularly good 'Denver Day' the first thing you might see

The local gulls and farmland species are regularly preyed upon by Peregrines.

Contacts

None

is a limping brass monkey. If you are the sort of birdwatcher who moans when your feet and hands go numb in the cold then this is not the walk for you.

Scan towards the sluice to check if there are many birds on the Drain, as this is not always the case. The best birds are usually near the sluice, but as you walk, keep scanning the fields for raptors such as Peregrine and Hen Harrier.

Barn Owls are seen regularly and Short-eared Owls may also be encountered. Also keep an eye on the telephone wires as they make good perches for Corn Buntings, Yellowhammers, Starlings, Linnets, Goldfinches, etc.

If the fancy takes you, you can keep going past the sluice gates to WWT Welney, where a warm soup and a spell in the heated main hide goes down a treat!

A round walk from the Denver car park to Welney is about 9.5 miles and comes with this warning: there is no respite from the cold wind/snow/rain as there isn't a scrap of cover the whole way. On the other hand, on a frosty, bright morning, this can be a superbly bracing day out!

The area is of very little interest at other times of year. You may as well go straight to Welney in your car and save yourself a long, birdless walk.

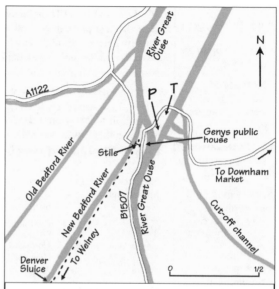

Access details

(Approx. two miles S of Downham Market).

On the A10 bypass, about one mile S of Downham Market. turn on to B1507 (sign-posted Denver/Denver Complex/Denver Mill).

Pass the recently renovated mill, following signs for Denver Sluice. Cross first bridge then park in the obvious large gravel car park on the left. There is a toilet block here but it is sometimes locked in Winter.

From the car park, follow the road to a second bridge and a few yards further on you

will see the Genys public house with a public phone opposite. The footpath to the sluice starts on top of the bank and over a stile. Turn left and walk as far as you want, checking the channel for birds as you go. The sluice is about 1.5 miles from here. WWT Welney is almost five miles away.

Other nearby sites

King's Lynn Docks, Ken Hill Wood, Roydon Common, Sandringham, RSPB Snettisham, Tottenhill, WWT Welney, Wolferton Triangle.

Key points

- **Reserve open at all times.**
- **Majority of reserve is for permit-holders only.**
- **Wide tracks, though some steepish steps.**
- **Boardwalk trail through the bog. Paths can be muddy after rain.**
- **Use insect repellent in Summer.**
- **Dogs should be kept on leads.**
- **Not suitable for wheelchair users, though Nightjars are occasionally viewable by the roadside gate (TF 663284)**
- **Leaflet available by gate.**

Contacts

English Nature
01603 620558

Site Manager
01485 543044

LITTLE VISITED by birdwatchers, Dersingham is the best place in Norfolk to see Nightjars, and one of the few places you might catch a glimpse of a Long-eared Owl. Crossbills and Wood Larks are regular visitors and it is quite likely that you will have them all to yourself!

Target birds *All year* - Wood Lark (40%), Crossbill (10%), Long-eared Owl (5%). *Summer* - Nightjar (90%), Tree Pipit (65%), Marsh Harrier (40%), Grasshopper Warbler (hear 40%, see 5%).

Other likely bird species

All year	Sky Lark	Redpoll
Shelduck	Meadow Pipit	*Summer*
Sparrowhawk	Common scrub birds	Cuckoo
Kestrel		Hirundines
Woodcock	Common woodland birds	Summer warblers
Tawny Owl		Spotted Flycatcher
Green Woodpecker	Goldcrest	
Great Spotted Woodpecker	Corvids	*Occasional*
	Siskin	Lesser Spotted Woodpecker

Background information and birding tips

CLOSE YOUR eyes while wandering around Dersingham Bog NNR and you could easily imagine yourself in the Caledonian Forest: the heady scent of Scots pine could make you believe that you may be attacked by a rogue Capercaillie at any moment.

Dersingham Bog is an area of heavily managed heath and bog that is part of the Sandringham Estate, but managed by English Nature. The warden assures me he does all the work but I reckon management is all down to the grazing cattle! The reserve is not visited by huge numbers of people and is thus one on my favourite places to see Nightjars. It can also be a good place to see Crossbills but they can never be guaranteed.

A visit on a Winter morning may produce a skein or two of Pink-footed Geese overhead while you are spotting common woodland birds along the Woodland Trail (sign-posted from both entrances). All three woodpecker species have been recorded but Great and Green Woodpecker are the two most likely. Siskins and Redpolls feed in the birches. Redwings and Fieldfares may be encountered anywhere on site.

From late February, Wood Larks may be singing on fine days. Also listen out for the moaning call of a Long-eared Owl as it establishes its territory. Keep an ear open too for the sharp *'chip-chip'* of Crossbills in the pines.

Common warblers, including Blackcap, Chiffchaff, Willow and Garden Warblers arrive to breed in Summer. Listen out for the display song of Tree Pipits, which breed on the reserve, and maybe the reeling of a Grasshopper Warbler or two. Marsh Harriers occasionally quarter the heath for prey, sometimes hunting the chicks of Shelduck which breed on the reserve in good numbers.

From mid May onwards, Nightjars 'churrr' from the area around the boardwalk. To reach this area, park in the Wolferton village lay-by and walk towards 'the cliff'. Nightjars can sometimes be seen from near the car park (by the wooden sign-post), but you will probably have to follow the path down some steps to the boggy area.

From the Scissors Crossroads car park, follow the path onto the reserve (do not go up the steps to the Woodland Trail) and the habitat soon opens out to Nightjar country. On a good night (and most are at this site), if you stand on the bog boardwalk you may not know which way to turn next as Nightjars will be displaying, or even perching on the telephone wires, serenading you in the half light. This area is also very good for bats.

Woodcocks should be roding over the woods, Tawny Owls may be hooting and Long-eared Owl chicks might be begging for food from the pines. The perfect dusk chorus!

The cliff viewpoint area is an excellent place to watch migrating birds and also gives a superb overview of the woodland (Crossbills etc may be seen as they fly over the trees).

This superb reserve pays the best dividends during a prolonged visit or frequent visits. You will not see all species present on one trip, unless you are very lucky.

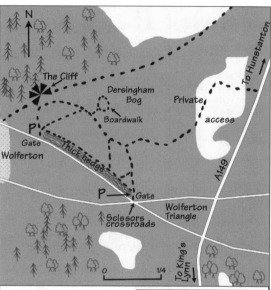

Access details
(Approx. 5.5 miles N of King's Lynn).

Take A149 N towards Hunstanton. After three miles, turn left to Wolferton. After about 300 yards this road reaches a crossroads. Park on the grass near the wooden 'No overnight parking' sign and enter reserve through a kissing gate down a narrow path from this pull-off. This is known as the Scissors Crossroads entrance. Alternatively, at the crossroads bear right and continue for half a mile until you see a large lay-by on

right. The reserve gate is visible from here and there are usually some leaflets at the gate for visitors. If you reach Wolferton village you have gone too far.

When on the reserve, follow the footpaths as sign-posted. The bog and heath habitats here are extremely fragile so stay on the paths at all times.

Other nearby sites
Gypsy Lane, NWT Holme Dunes, NOA Holme Observatory, Hunstanton, Ken Hill Wood, King's Lynn Docks, NOA Redwell Marsh, Roydon Common, Sandringham, RSPB Snettisham, RSPB Titchwell Marsh, Wolferton Triangle.

69

Key points

Key points

- **Norfolk Wildlife Trust Reserve closed in May and June. Open 8am - dusk outside breeding season.**

- **Site is a designated SSSI.**

- **Permit required.**

- **Hides overlook Langmere.**

- **All species can be seen from a public footpath.**

- **Public footpath terrain is flat along a wide sandy track.**

- **Can be wet after rain.**

- **Insect repellent advisable.**

- **Torch needed when walking back to car after seeing the Nightjars.**

Contacts

Norfolk Wildlife Trust
01603 625540

PLAN TO VISIT East Wretham in Spring and Summer when the sought-after species (Nightjar, Tree Pipit, Redstart) are in residence. In Winter, this site holds large numbers of finches and buntings. The public footpath that runs along the southern edge of the reserve is one of the best birdwatching footpaths in Norfolk.

Target birds *Spring/Summer* – Nightjar (90%), Wood Lark (90%), Tree Pipit (80%), Redstart (60%), Crossbill (15%), Long-eared Owl (5%).

Other likely bird species

All year	Nuthatch	Cuckoo
Little Grebe	Treecreeper	Warblers
Ruddy Duck	Jay	Spotted Flycatcher
Sparrowhawk	Siskin	
Kestrel	Redpoll	*Occasional*
Woodcock	Yellowhammer	Goshawk
Stock Dove		Golden Pheasant
Barn Owl	*Spring/Autumn*	Hawfinch
Tawny Owl	Passage waders	
Kingfisher		
Woodpeckers	*Summer*	
	Hobby	

Background information and birding tips

EAST WRETHAM HEATH is a superb reserve that holds many sought-after Breckland species. The best time to visit is on an early Spring morning for Wood Lark, and a late Spring evening (May/June) for Nightjar, but the reserve is closed at these times to protect breeding species. Do not despair – all birds can be seen from a public footpath that runs to the south of the reserve.

My first walk of the year along this footpath is usually on a bright, calm, early March morning, heading west (signed to Brandon). After a short while you will get excellent views of Langmere, a lake on your right. Alternatively, there is a gate on your left, which leads to Ringmere, a smaller lake.

The water levels in these meres varies greatly, but Pochard, Tufted Duck, Mallard, Ruddy Duck (a scarce species in Norfolk), Gadwall and Little Grebe seem to be present at all times of year.

If water levels are low, scan the muddy edges of the meres for passage waders such as Snipe, Greenshank, Green, Wood and Common Sandpipers. I tried to do this in 2001 only to find the water levels so high that I could only just see the roof of the flooded hide overlooking Langmere.

Follow the track past Langmere, listening out all the time for Crossbills, Siskins and Redpolls in the trees along the path and on the reserve. After about a quarter of a mile, there is a clearing on your right, which is an excellent place to listen for

Wood Lark on the reserve. You should have seen Green and Great Spotted Woodpeckers by now, as well as Coal Tit, Long-tailed Tit and Mistle Thrush.

April is a good time to watch out for displaying Sparrowhawk and Goshawk. The former species is virtually guaranteed to show, and Goshawks are certainly in the area. Crossbills will be breeding by now, so listen out for their loud 'chip, chip' calls.

From mid May, this footpath is a great place from which to see and hear Nightjars. Follow the path until you reach a wide, sandy track on your left. The land opens out here to a bracken-covered area with mature pine trees dotted around as far as the eye can see. Between mid May and the end of August, this is a superb place to see Nightjars at dusk, especially the old beech stump by the path.

Long-eared Owl is another Wretham breeding speciality. so listen for the begging squeaks of the young at dusk in May. In Summer, look out for Redstarts and Spotted Flycatchers in the trees and bushes along the whole length of this track, though the former is easier to see on East Wretham reserve itself. A little further on, the path is enclosed by mixed woodland, a good place to see Redpolls.

You can follow this track to where it joins a T-junction of two minor roads. Straight ahead is Fowlmere (on your right, through thick bracken and bushes) which is good for common waterfowl and wildfowl, and in Spring 2001 and 2002 a Ferruginous Duck

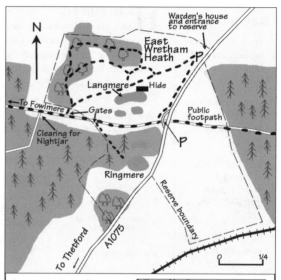

Access details

(Approx. four miles NE of Thetford).

From Thetford head E on A11 to roundabout where you take A1075 (sign-posted to Watton and East Dereham). After the level crossing the reserve car park is sign-posted on a brown tourist sign on left, just over two miles from the roundabout.

The reserve can be viewed from the public footpath, which starts from the lay-by 200 yards S of the car park. Follow directions above to

the level crossing. Cross that, then there is a left-hand bend with a deer warning sign. The lay-by is on the left immediately after the sign (1.2 miles after the level crossing). The public footpath is signed to Brandon 16km and the Peddars Way 2km.

took up temporary residence for a few weeks.

Mixed woodland on the reserve holds breeding Redstarts in Summer and Hawfinches occasionally in Winter, so it is worth venturing onto the heath itself (when open) if you wish to see these species.

I have to say that this track is the best public footpath for birds in Norfolk with the exception of the one that cuts through the RSPB Titchwell Marsh reserve. Starting from the late February Wood Lark/Goshawk/Crossbill extravaganza through to the Summer Nightjar spectacular, this is the perfect place to be.

71

Key points

- **Free access to woodland and lake trails at all times.**

- **Terrain is along rough tracks or across fields.**

- **Part of woodland trail is along a gravel path, quite steeply uphill.**

- **Lake trail is not suitable for wheelchair users.**

- **Map available from Hall ticket office.**

Useful contacts

Felbrigg Hall
01263 837444

The National Trust,
East Anglia Regional
Office
01263 733471

HEAD FOR Felbrigg if you enjoy birdwatching as part of a walk. There is a stretch of ancient woodland surrounded by parkland on this National Trust estate, plus a small lake to wander round. Non-birding members of the family can look around the house, visit the restaurant or café, or spend all your money in the Trust shop.

Target birds *All year* – Common woodland birds
(100%), Lesser Spotted Woodpecker (30%). *Spring/Autumn* – Redstart (50%), Pied Flycatcher (40%), Wood Warbler (30%).

Other likely bird species

All year	Great Spotted Woodpecker	Hirundines
Cormorant	Sky Lark	Reed Warbler
Egyptian Goose	Meadow Pipit	Blackcap
Common wildfowl and waterbirds	Pied Wagtail	Chiffchaff
		Willow Warbler
Sparrowhawk	Common scrub birds	Spotted Flycatcher
Kestrel		
Woodcock	Nuthatch	*Winter*
Common gull species	Treecreeper	Wigeon
	Jay	Goosander
Stock Dove	Common finches	Brambling
Barn Owl	Reed Bunting	Winter thrushes
Little Owl		
Tawny Owl	*Summer*	
Green Woodpecker	Cuckoo	
	Hobby	

Background information and birding tips

FELBRIGG HALL itself is of little interest to birdwatchers, but the grounds of the estate are fantastic for a leisurely stroll. There is a small lake, which holds several species of common wildfowl and waterbirds and an expanse of ancient woodland, home to many common breeding birds – including Redstart and Wood Warbler in the past.

For the lake walk, follow the signs from the car park along purple way-marked paths. Basically, you head for the small church, then diagonally right up the hill. Head for the two tall trees on the hilltop to reach a the

gate. Go through the gate, and turn right, down the hill to the lake. The footpath circles the lake and leads back to the hall. Scan the water for common ducks (Pochard, Mallard, Gadwall and Tufted Ducks) which are sometimes joined by one or two Goosanders in Winter.

The lake has a reed-lined edge, which is frequented by Reed Buntings all year round and Reed Warblers in Summer. Also scan the lake and surrounding fields for the resident Egyptian Geese.

The woodland trail starts from the entrance to the walled garden. Take the gravel path up steepish hill, through a stand of mature trees. Fifty yards up this path, there is a paddock-type area where the trees are less densely spaced. This is the best place to see Redstarts, Wood Warblers and Pied Flycatchers in Spring and Autumn. In Summer, look out for Spotted Flycatchers in the woods.

Further on, the gravel track splits into several muddy, grass paths, all of which you can use to enter the wood. Great Spotted Woodpeckers are usually very much in evidence, but Lesser Spots can be very elusive. I have found the large trees closest to the car park to be best for the latter species, especially in late March when they give themselves away with their harsh calls, drumming and butterfly-like display flight. Occasionally, they even get in the large, lone trees in the fields towards the lake, where they show really well.

All in all, Felbrigg Hall grounds are a superb place for a stroll at any time of year. Visiting birdwatchers can spend as long as they like wandering around the woods or lake (or both) and they are likely to encounter many common species of bird along the way.

In Spring and Summer, they may have the added bonus of being able to see one or two scarce breeding birds, and in Autumn, who knows what may be lurking in the woods as this is a very under-watched site. Firecrest, Red-breasted Flycatcher, Yellow-browed Warbler, etc must be distinct possibilities.

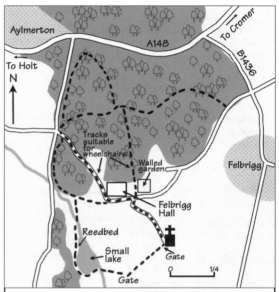

Access details

(Approx. 2.5 miles SW of Cromer).

Felbrigg Hall is extremely well sign-posted off A148 (Cromer to Holt/Fakenham road), on brown National Trust signs.

Follow these signs to the car park by the hall. From the car park, the two trails

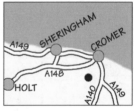

(woodland and lake) are well sign-posted.

Other nearby sites

Blakeney Point, NWT Cley Marshes, Kelling Heath, NOA Kelling Quags, Salthouse Beach, Salthouse Heath, Sheringham, Swanton Novers, NOA Walsey Hills, Weybourne.

Key points

- **Hide is open at all times though Wednesdays can be disturbed by management work on the farm.**
- **Free car park.**
- **Wheelchair accessible hide.**
- **Log book in hide.**
- **Fieldguide in hide.**

PROBABLY THE best place in Norfolk to see Little Owl, Turtle Dove and Kingfisher, with Barn Owl virtually guaranteed, this fantastic little farm reserve should not be missed. Carefully managed for wildlife, this site is good all year round.

Target birds
All year - Little Owl (90%), Barn Owl (70%), Marsh Tit (65%). *Winter* - Pink-footed Goose (30%), Tree Sparrow (20%), Corn Bunting (20%). *Summer* - Marsh Harrier (70%).

Other likely bird species

All year	Tawny Owl	Winter thrushes
Little Grebe	Kingfisher	
Egyptian Goose	Green Woodpecker	*Spring/Autumn*
Teal		Passage waders
Common wildfowl	Great Spotted Woodpecker	Yellow Wagtail
Common waterfowl	Pied Wagtail	*Summer*
Sparrowhawk	Corvids	Turtle Dove
Buzzard	Bullfinch	Hirundines
Kestrel		Migrant warblers
Red-legged Partridge	Other common finches	Spotted Flycatcher
Grey Partridge	Yellowhammer	*Occasional*
Water Rail	Reed Bunting	Garganey
Lapwing	*Winter*	Hobby
Snipe	Grey Wagtail	

Background information and birding tips

THIS WORKING FARM is a hidden treasure! Money donated by the Wildfowl and Wetlands Trust, DEFRA and Countryside Stewardship Scheme goes towards managing the site as a haven for wildlife. This is how all farms could and should be, but it is a sign of the times that I feel the need to praise RS Cross & Son (the owners) for their efforts.

On a Winter's day, the bushes and trees around the car park can be dripping with birds. Yellowhammers and Chaffinches are present in impressive numbers (I counted 75-plus of the former and 100-plus of the

latter in February 2001). A few Tree Sparrows and Corn Buntings are usually present, but not guaranteed. Marsh Tit is a certainty in Winter along with one or two Bullfinches. Pink-footed Geese sometimes feed in the large field opposite the car park in Winter, but be very careful not to flush them. In November 2001, this flock was joined by a Red-breasted Goose.

From the hide, Little Owls are virtually guaranteed. They sit in the large fallen tree directly in front of the hide or on the large logs in the field to the left of this tree. Barn Owls breed on site and are seen throughout the year, but

Contacts

RS Cross & Son,
Abbey Farm, Flitcham,
Norfolk.
01485 600227

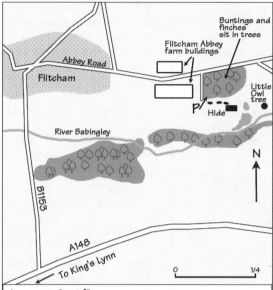

patience may be needed. Tawny Owls also breed but are seldom seen (only heard). In contrast, a pair of Egyptian Geese can be seen (and certainly heard!) displaying from late January and they remain at the farm to breed.

A Buzzard is sometimes seen patrolling the skies throughout the year, while Hobbies occasionally fly over the farm from May to September (most in evidence between July and August). Marsh Harriers are reported daily during the Summer months but their appearances are erratic, so no best time can be recommended.

Other Summer breeders include Whitethroats, Lesser Whitethroats, Spotted Flycatchers, Blackcaps, Willow Warblers and Chiffchaffs. This is one of the best sites in Norfolk to see Turtle Doves, which love to sit on the telephone wires running across the reserve. Kingfishers usually perch on the poles in the water just out from the hide.

There is a field-guide in the hide for use by visitors plus a log book to record all your sightings. There is also the chance to purchase a bag of bird seed.

All in all, this is a cracking little place with plenty to see at all times of year. I sat in the hide one evening in July 2001 and saw a Kingfisher, a female Marsh Harrier, a Barn Owl (constantly on show), a family of Egyptian Geese, a Sparrowhawk sitting by the hide and 14 Turtle Doves on the wires, all within a 50 minute visit. And looking in the log book, this was a common haul for visitors.

This site is a shining example of how farming and wildlife

Access details

(Approx. 7.5 miles E of King's Lynn).

From King's Lynn take A148 (Cromer/Fakenham road), and then turn left onto B1153 at Hillington, sign-posted to Flitcham. In Flitcham, turn right into Abbey Road and drive for half a mile until you have just past the farm buildings on the right. Beyond the farmhouse, there is a small sign on the stone wall 'Abbey Farm Bird Hide' sending you down a short

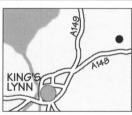

track. Park at the end on the mud: the two hard-standing spaces are reserved for orange badge holders. The hide is along a short concrete path and is wheelchair friendly.

conservation can be comfortable bedfellows. It is frightening to contrast this

farm with the bird-less 'agri-deserts' so often encountered these days.

Other nearby sites

Dersingham Bog, Hunstanton, Ken Hill Wood, Pentney Gravel Pits, NWT Roydon Common, Sandringham, RSPB Snettisham, Tottenhill Gravel Pits, Wolferton Triangle.

Key points

- Free access at all times.

- The bridge is accessed along a wide, rough track up a slight incline.

- Early mornings in late May are best.

FORDHAM presents the only real chance wheelchair-bound birders have of seeing Golden Orioles. Essentially, birders should stand (or sit) on the bridge over the poplar-lined channel and wait for the birds to fly across from one side to the other. This is a very sensitive site so it is essential that the welfare of the birds is your first priority (see page 10 for the Birdwatcher's Code of Conduct).

Target bird Golden Oriole (15%).

Other likely bird species

May/August	Kestrel	Pied Wagtail
Great Crested Grebe	Turtle Dove	Common scrub birds
	Stock Dove	
Cormorant	Hirundines	Common woodland birds
Common wildfowl	Kingfisher	
	Green Woodpecker	Whitethroat
Common waterbirds	Great Spotted Woodpecker	Blackcap
Sparrowhawk		Common finches

Background information and birding tips

THIS IS ANOTHER 'secret' site for Golden Orioles which is visited by hundreds of birdwatchers each year (see also Lakenheath). When Oriole activity died down at Lakenheath a few years ago, I started visiting Fordham instead and obtained flight views of the Orioles every time I went. The birds also called

A flash of yellow may be all you see of Golden Oriole.

Contacts

None

throughout the day from mid-May to mid-June even when they didn't show themselves.

However, in recent years, I have had very few sightings, and Lakenheath is now the better site again! In fact, on my trip to Fordham in June 2001 I didn't even hear the Goldies. The local farmer hadn't heard any either, but there were apparently two pairs present.

More worrying was the assertion by the farmer that in 2000, birders discovered an Oriole nest in the poplars and a constant group formed to look at them, frightening the birds off the nest. If true, it is a disgraceful episode. Birdwatchers who have the welfare of the birds as their highest priority will be content with poorish views as the Orioles fly across the canal and not approach too close. **If you see any bad behaviour at this site please report it and/or put a stop to it.**

While waiting for the Orioles to appear, you will be entertained by a few common species such as Cormorant and Grey Heron flying over, while the channel should produce a Great Crested Grebe and maybe even a Kingfisher. A Hobby may flash through in pursuit of a Swallow, Swift or House Martin.

The bushes lining the Cut-off Channel are good for Whitethroats and Blackcaps and listen out for Turtle Doves 'purring' in the vicinity. Watch out for Mink swimming across the water, usually pursued by an angry Moorhen or two.

One more word of warning: beware of ticking off distant

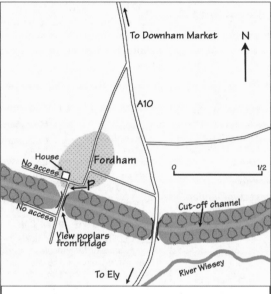

Access details

(Approx. 2.5 miles S of Downham Market).

From Downham Market follow A10 along bypass, sign-posted to Ely (do not go into Downham itself). After about two miles, turn right at the sign to Fordham. Follow this road for half a mile, then go straight on when the 'main' road bends sharply left. After about 200 yards turn left, opposite the house, into a rough car park. Walk onto the bridge to view the poplars either side of the Cut-off Channel.

Green Woodpeckers as they fly across the Channel. Many a time I have witnessed over-anxious birdwatchers count a Yaffle as a Golden Oriole, and for once I am not included on that list of stringers!!

Other nearby sites

NWT East Wretham Heath, Foulden Common, RSPB Lakenheath, Lynford Arboretum, Santon Downham, Wayland Wood, NWT Weeting Heath, WWT Welney.

77

Key points

- Terrain is flat along rough grass tracks.

- Not suitable for wheelchairs though birds can be heard, and sometimes seen, from car park.

- Boots recommended after rain.

- No facilities

- Early mornings from late April to the end of May best, though dusk not bad either.

S PRING MORNINGS are a joy on Foulden Common as the site will be alive with birdsong, a perfect start to a day's birding in Norfolk and, if you are lucky, you may even glimpse a Nightingale in this area of thick bushes and hedges.

Target birds Nightingale (hear 80%, see 25%).

Other likely bird species

Spring	Hirundines	Willow Warbler
Sparrowhawk	Common scrub birds	Long-tailed Tit
Kestrel		Marsh Tit
Turtle Dove	Lesser Whitethroat	Corvids
Cuckoo	Whitethroat	Common finches
Green Woodpecker	Blackcap	
Sky Lark	Chiffchaff	Yellowhammer

Background information and birding tips

F OULDEN COMMON still holds a few pairs of Nightingales. They can be very hard to see but, as soon as you get out of your car, you should hear them singing.

When you hear one, follow the beautiful song to

the thick bush from which it is emanating. The trick now is to wait patiently for the bird to show. Do not disturb the bush to try to get a glimpse, but look towards the ground for the best chance of seeing the skulking songster.

While you are

Great patience is needed before you see a Nightingale but you should hear them at Foulden Common.

Contacts
None.

waiting, you should be entertained by several species of commoner bird. Yellowhammers show well, as do Green Woodpeckers. Cuckoos seem to show here better than at some sites; they favour the twiggy trees just inside the gate. If you get there early in the morning in mid-May you should see one or two displaying from the top of one of these trees.

Turtle Doves also breed on the Common, as do Whitethroats, Lesser Whitethroats and many common species. On a fine Spring morning, this place can have a deafening dawn chorus!

My preferred route, Nightingales permitting, is to go through the gate in the car park then head left along the obvious track. There are thick bushes to your left that are good for Lesser Whitethroats, Nightingales etc. Cross the rough grass field and go through a gap in the hedgerow, checking for common birds all the way. Blackcaps usually show well in the hedge here, as do Whitethroats.

Once through the hedge, turn right and follow the path to the main track. Turn right to get back to the car park. There are one or two isolated bushes along the main track which can hold Nightingales and they can be easier to see here than in the continuous bushes near the car park.

You can explore the Common further if you wish. There are several tracks zigzagging the fields, but I have found that the route above gives ample opportunities to sample the rich birdlife of Foulden.

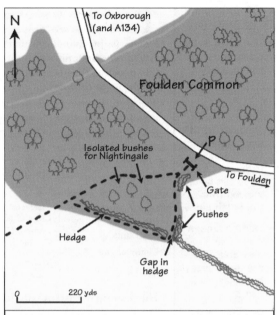

N

To Oxborough (and A134)

Foulden Common

Isolated bushes for Nightingale

P

To Foulden

Gate

Bushes

Hedge

Gap in hedge

0   220 yds

Access details

(Approx. 9.5 miles E of Downham Market).

From A134 (King's Lynn to Thetford road) turn off at Stoke Dry to Oxborough and the Iceni Village. Follow minor road to Oxborough village, turning right at the church and public house (sign-posted Oxborough Hall). Follow this road (do not turn into the hall) to a sharp right hand bend sign-posted Foulden.

The road passes through a wood (start listening for Nightingale now!) and the turn-off to the small car park

A1122   SWAFFHAM   A1065

A134

is on the right 0.6 miles from the sharp bend.

The car park surface is very pitted so watch the suspension of your car. Enter the Common through a farm gate adjoining the car park, and follow paths, homing in on the singing Nightingales.

Other nearby sites

NWT East Wretham Heath, Fordham, Ken Hill Wood, RSPB Lakenheath, Lynford Arboretum, Sandringham, Snettisham RSPB, WWT Welney, NWT Weeting Heath, Wolferton Triangle.

79

Key points

- **The RSPB hut is open from May to August when a warden monitors the Little Terns.**

- **Tern colony not accessible to wheelchair users, but flying birds can be viewed from the north pier.**

- **Mediterranean Gulls also viewable from the north pier for wheelchair users.**

- **Many facilities in town.**

Contacts

RSPB East Anglia Office
01603 661662

The possibility of seeing scarce species (it's the best place in Norfolk to see Mediterranean Gulls and Black Redstarts) just minutes from the glittering attractions of Great Yarmouth town centre, makes this location ideal for a family outing if your relatives don't share your enthusiasm for the great outdoors.

Target birds *All year* – Mediterranean Gull (90%).

Winter – Snow Bunting (20%). *Summer* – Little Tern (100%), Black Redstart (75%), Roseate Tern (10%).

Other likely bird species

All year	*Summer*	
Cormorant	Meadow Pipit	Manx Shearwater
Kestrel	Common finches	Balearic Shearwater
Oystercatcher		Gannet
Ringed Plover	*Summer*	Arctic Skua
Turnstone	Little Gull	Great Skua
	Common Tern	Little Gull
Common gull species	Sandwich Tern	Kittiwake
Sky Lark	*Autumn*	
	Sooty Shearwater	

Background information and birding tips

THROUGHOUT the year, Great Yarmouth beach between the two piers is a reliable site to find several Mediterranean Gulls loafing. I found seven birds in various stages of plumage along the beach in October 2001 and three in January 2002.

In Summer, there is a Little Tern colony nesting in the North Denes area near the caravan park. The dunes are an SSSI, but are heavily disturbed by holiday-makers at this time of year. Nevertheless, in 2001, 261 pairs of Little Terns managed to nest on the beach though in 2002 vandals wrecked the site.

From the road, you can just see the roof of the RSPB shed poking above the dunes. From this hut, you can watch the comings and goings of the tern colony and also watch the consternation on the warden's face as the local Kestrel swoops in to take another hapless chick from the beach.

The panic this causes among the colony has to be seen and heard to be believed. To combat this predation, the RSPB has introduced sewer pipes for the terns to nest under, and very cute they look in their new houses too!

From mid June, the chicks will dash up to the returning parents to collect their cargo of small fish. Running in and out of the area will be a Ringed Plover or two and flying along the shore should be Common and Sandwich Terns plus the usual gull species. Roseate Terns are seen regularly in Summer but usually only first thing in the morning before being disturbed by the ubiquitous dog walkers.

Always keep an eye on the sea as anything can pass by. I picked out a Little Gull here in June 2001, a species the warden hadn't seen before. Also noted on that day were Goldeneyes, Common Scoters and Kittiwakes. The area is not noted for its seabird passage, but in November 2001, there were several Great and Arctic Skuas at sea, as well as Kittiwakes and a Manx Shearwater.

Amazingly, Sky Lark and Meadow Pipit breed in the dunes, despite unbelievable disturbance by all and sundry. Perhaps the 2002 vandalism will lead to greater protection for this SSSI.

In summary, this is a superb spot to sit and watch the activities of a tern colony for an hour or so. The fact that the colony is of the exquisite Little Tern makes it even more compelling viewing for the visitor.

In Winter, the dunes to the north of the town hold a smallish flock of Snow Buntings, but the area is large and disturbed by dog walkers. Park by Jellicoe Way and scan the extensive dune system. The buntings also get onto the beach where the Little Terns nest.

Great Yarmouth is also a noted breeding site of Black Redstart. They can be found around the power station to the south of the town. The whole area from the power station to the industrial estate around the corner is prime Black Redstart territory.

Access details

WINTER: From A47 follow signs to Town Centre/ Seafront onto St. Nicholas Drive. Go over the traffic lights (the road is now called Euston Road) to the pay and display car park at the end, adjacent to the toilet block. Walk on to the beach to search for the Med Gulls, usually between the two piers.

For Snow Buntings, park in the area described in the Summer section below and search the dunes.

SUMMER: Follow directions as above but instead of parking, turn left (N) and follow this road for about a mile. Park on road near turn-off sign-posted to Caistor (Jellicoe Way) by The Iron Duke pub (just at the start of the caravan park).

Walk E towards the sea through the North Denes SSSI to the RSPB hut. Bus number 003 runs from Yarmouth along this road to the caravan site.

For Black Redstarts, follow Winter directions, but do not enter car park. Instead, turn right and follow the road along the seafront for about 2.5 miles. Scan the derelict buildings on the front by the power station (TG 531050) for the Black Redstarts, or continue around the corner to the industrial estate (TG 531043).

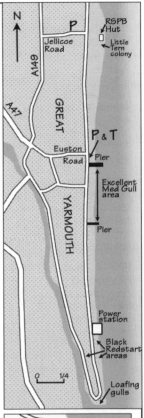

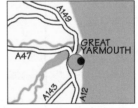

Other nearby sites

Breydon Water, RSPB Buckenham Marshes, Burgh Castle, Cantley Beet Factory Flood, NWT Hickling Broad, How Hill Estate, Rockland Broad, RSPB Strumpshaw Fen, Ted Ellis Reserve, Winterton.

Key points

- **The gates are open from 7.30am – 4.30pm (October 1 to March 31) and between 7.30am and 7pm for rest of year.**

- **Level terrain. Some Tarmac tracks, other paths are uneven or on grass.**

- **Please show due respect for the graves and be careful where you walk.**

- **No dogs.**

MATURE TREES and a peaceful atmosphere ensures that a pleasant stroll here in Spring or Autumn may well produce a rare or scarce migrant. Your walk will almost certainly reveal several species of common migrants such as Song Thrush, Robin, Goldcrest, Redwing, Fieldfare, etc to brighten your day.

Target birds *Spring/Autumn* - Passage migrants

(anything is possible).

Other likely bird species

Spring/Autumn		Yellow-browed Warbler
Wryneck	Whinchat	Other warblers
Hirundines	Wheatear	Pied Flycatcher
Bluethroat	Ring Ouzel	Red-backed Shrike
Black Redstart	Winter thrushes	
Redstart	Barred Warbler	
	Firecrest	

Background information and birding tips

THE BUSHES and trees in the cemetery are a magnet for migrants in Spring and Autumn. The number of migrants is usually dictated by the weather conditions. If you are planning a migrant-hunting trip, watch the BBC weather forecast the night before (much better than ITV). In Spring, you are looking for high pressure over Europe, with a low pressure system over Britain, hopefully combined with easterly winds. Better still is fog or rain on the east coast!

In Autumn, look out for clear skies in Scandinavia, with low pressure over Britain. Onshore winds are a bonus. The high pressure system encourages birds to migrate, before hitting the nasty weather over Britain,

Delicate Yellow-browed Warblers regularly turn up in Autumn.

Contacts

None.

which forces them to land. In Great Yarmouth cemetery, hopefully!

During both seasons, the above conditions should bring several weary travellers for you to find. Both the north and south of sections of the cemetery should be searched thoroughly, but care must be taken to respect non-birding visitors. Though the tradition of birders visiting the site is now well-established, please remember this is a graveyard.

On entering the cemetery, you should know whether there has been an arrival of birds by the number of Goldcrests present. A 'fall' of this species is usually a good indicator of the presence of other goodies lurking in the bushes. Patience may be needed to see the birds as some of the cover is quite thick. The bushes can easily be reached by way of grass paths throughout the cemetery.

In Spring, Ring Ouzels and Wheatears are among the earliest arrivals. Warblers making landfall should include the first Willow Warblers of the year along with Blackcaps and Chiffchaffs, which may have over-wintered in the cemetery grounds. Later, Spotted Flycatchers may drop in, with Redstarts and Pied Flycatchers. In April 2002 a Wryneck spent several days in the southern section.

Autumn is probably a better time to visit as virtually anything can turn up. Yellow-browed and Pallas's Warblers may be among the more regular Pied Flycatchers and Firecrests. The cemetery hosted a Red-flanked Bluetail in 1994, emphasising this site's

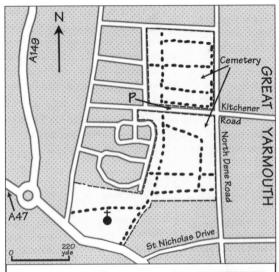

Access details

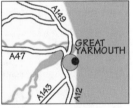

From A47, follow signs to 'Town Centre/Sea Front' to St. Nicholas Drive. Turn left at traffic lights into North Dene Road (sign-posted to coach/lorry car park). Turn left on to Kitchener Road (which is just after the coach park) and follow down to the cemetery gates, about 150 yards along. The cemetery is split into two sections, North and South, and both can be accessed on foot from the road.

ability to attract anything in the right conditions!

Great Yarmouth cemetery is best ignored for the rest of the year, though having said that, I found two Waxwings here in February 2001, so nothing is that certain.

In summary, this site cannot be guaranteed to produce any exciting finds but in Spring and Autumn the opportunity exists for an inquisitive birder to find anything – from a 'fall' of humble Robins or Goldcrests to a 'first' for Britain!

Other nearby sites

Breydon Water, Cantley Beet Factory, Great Yarmouth Beach, Hardley Flood, NWT Hickling Broad, NWT Sparham Pools, RSPB Strumpshaw Fen, Ted Ellis Reserve, Winterton Dunes.

83

Key points

- Terrain is level.

- Access along a narrow, uneven grass path.

- Can be wet and muddy at all times of year.

- No facilities (toilets at RSPB Titchwell Marsh reserve and Brancaster beach car park).

S ANDWICHED between Brancaster Marsh and Titchwell, this is a quiet area for birdwatchers to enjoy a variety of habitats, including marsh, reedbed, beach and sea. This site doesn't have the extensive wader scrapes of its more illustrious RSPB neighbour, but close views of several sought-after species can be had here in solitude.

Target birds *All year* – Marsh Harrier (Winter = 15%, rest = 90%), Bearded Tit (65%), Barn Owl (40%). *Winter* – Sea duck (40%), raptors (35%). *Spring* – Garganey (30%).

Other likely bird species

All year		Grey Plover
Little Grebe	Reed Bunting	
Cormorant	*Summer*	*Spring/Autumn*
Shelduck	Terns	Shearwaters
Sparrowhawk	Cuckoo	Gannet
Kestrel	Hirundines	Passage waders
Red-legged Partridge	Sedge Warbler	Skuas
Grey Partridge	Reed Warbler	Passage migrants
Common waders	Lesser Whitethroat	Yellow Wagtail
Sky Lark	Whitethroat	*Occasional*
Willow Tit	Blackcap	Little Egret
Stonechat	Chiffchaff	Hobby
Linnet	Willow Warbler	Avocet
Bullfinch	*Winter*	Water Pipit
	Brent Goose	Twite
		Snow Bunting

Background information and birding tips

T HIS WALK will suit people who like to do their birdwatching away from the crowds. The range of birds is similar to that encountered on RSPB Titchwell Marsh reserve, though numbers are lower because there are no wader scrapes. It is worth remembering this footpath when the sun is shining in your eyes at Titchwell (in the mornings), as you can look across to the same reedbed from Gypsy Lane.

The footpath passes through trees and bushes which are excellent for commoner species (along with Willow Tit all year and warblers in Summer including,

Lesser Whitethroat, etc) and the odd migrant in Autumn and Spring.

After about 400 yards, the path opens out onto an extensive reedbed where you should see Marsh Harrier and Bearded Tit. Because this walk is quiet, you may get harriers flying overhead as they cross from one reedbed to the other. They are present all year, though can be elusive in Winter. I discovered this walk when 1993's Purple Heron dropped in, so the potential exists for you to find something really special.

Once past the reeds, the raised

Contacts
None.

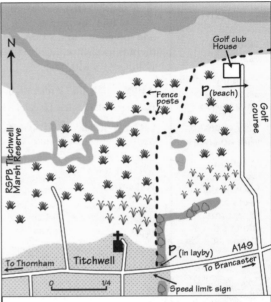

path crosses a marsh. This is an excellent place for raptors, geese and ducks in Winter and the commoner wader species all year round. Garganey are regular visitors in Spring, and the Summer months bring Sedge and Reed Warblers to the area.

As the path bears right, look for raptors perched on old fence posts. Merlin, Peregrine, Hen Harrier, Short-eared and Barn Owls all hunt the area in Winter, with the latter species present all year. Follow the path east to the coast and onto the beach. In Winter, all the species encountered at Titchwell on the beach and on the sea can be seen here, though there will be less pairs of eyes to spot things.

Waders on the beach should include Ringed Plover, Knot, Oystercatcher, Turnstone, Sanderling, Bar-tailed Godwit, Grey Plover, etc, and the sea should produce Red-breasted Merganser, Goldeneye, Slavonian Grebe, Eider, Common Scoter, Long-tailed Duck, Red-throated Diver, etc. Summer will see a similar range of waders with Little, Sandwich and Common Terns passing constantly.

Autumn seawatching should produce Manx Shearwater. Keep an eye open for any of the four species of skua harassing the terns, though Arctic Skua will be the most numerous.

This walk will almost certainly not produce as many birds as the adjoining RSPB reserve, but with patience, should reward the visitor with an impressive array of species. For instance, on a 30 minute power-walk in August 2001 (just to see what was

Access details

(Approx. 5.5 miles E of Hunstanton).

On entering Titchwell village on A149 from Thornham (travelling E), park in small lay-by on left, opposite the national speed limit sign. If travelling W, the lay-by will be on the right just before the 40mph signs. There is room for about four cars.

Follow the public footpath N.

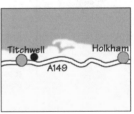

Alternatively, park in Brancaster Beach car park (TF 772451) and walk W along the beach to this footpath where it meets it on the shore.

around), I saw five Little Egrets, several family parties of Bearded Tits, and a female and juvenile Marsh Harrier being mobbed by a pair of Sparrowhawks over my head. All of this without another person in sight. Bliss!

Other nearby sites

Brancaster Marsh, Choseley Barns, Holkham NNR, Holkham Park, NWT Holme Dunes, NOA Holme Observatory, Hunstanton, NOA Redwell Marsh, RSPB Snettisham, RSPB Titchwell Marsh, Wells Woods.

85

Key points

- **Telescope essential.**

- **Terrain is uphill on a Tarmac pavement.**

- **Very exposed, with no shelter.**

- **Excellent vantage point for wheelchair users to scan for raptors, though the bridge slope is steep.**

HARDY SOULS will find this bleak marsh is excellent in Winter for raptors such as Marsh and Hen Harriers and sometimes wild swans and geese. However, because there is no shelter, fair-weather birders need to choose their visiting days with care.

Target birds

Winter – Bewick's Swan (70%), Marsh Harrier (60%), Hen Harrier (35%), Short-eared Owl (15%).

Other likely bird species

Winter

Cormorant	Rough-legged Buzzard (2000/01 & 2001/02)	Sky Lark
Whooper Swan		Meadow Pipit
White-fronted Goose	Kestrel	Pied Wagtail
Shelduck	Merlin	Common scrub birds
Wigeon	Peregrine	Winter thrushes
Teal	Lapwing	Corvids
	Curlew	Common finches
Common waterbirds	Common gull species	Reed Bunting
Sparrowhawk	Barn Owl	

Background information and birding tips

THE VANTAGE point for Haddiscoe Marshes offers no shelter from the elements, so I suggest you only visit in fine weather with good visibility. In these conditions, the view of the marsh from the bridge is superb.

A wide range of raptors grace the marsh, though none can be guaranteed on any given visit.

Overall, there is always something to see, though you may have to wait two or three hours to produce a decent list of desired species. By this time, your toes will no longer feel a part of your body.

Marsh Harriers, Kestrels and Sparrowhawks are the most likely raptors, though Short-eared Owls

Hen Harriers are a possibility, but by no means guaranteed at Haddiscoe.

Contacts

None

are recorded regularly. Barn Owls are frequent visitors to the marsh, but Peregrine, Merlin and Hen Harrier are seen less regularly.

While you are scanning for raptors and owls, you should find one or two Bewick's Swans. Whooper Swans and White-fronted Geese are less regular, but not impossible. If you are very lucky, you might catch up with the wintering Rough-legged Buzzard that has graced Haddiscoe Marsh for the past two Winters (she likes to sit on the low power cables running across the marsh).

The marsh also holds many common species ranging from Goldfinch, Greenfinch and Meadow Pipit, to grazing Wigeon, Teal and Mute Swan and nervous Lapwing and Curlew.

The hardy birdwatcher may wish to walk across the marsh, and they can indeed do so. A public footpath runs along the north-east side of the canal, accessed across the A143.

In fact, you might like to walk the eight mile or so circular route, following the River Yare to Breydon Water at Berney Arms, and back to Haddiscoe alongside the River Waveney, but you will have to achieve it in Wellingtons! You may also walk along the road to get a different viewpoint of the marsh, but be very careful of the fast-moving traffic.

If you ask me, it is much more sensible (if standing on a high bridge in a wind-chill of −10°C can be called sensible) to scan the area from Haddiscoe bridge, from where you can dash occasionally to the car for a respite from the elements.

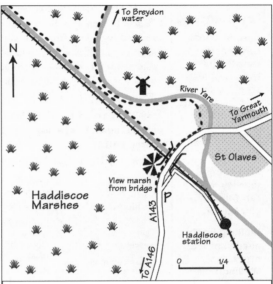

Access details

(Approx. 6.5 miles SW of Great Yarmouth).

FROM GREAT YARMOUTH: **Head S on A12 to junction with A143 (sign-posted Belton, Burgh Castle and Beccles). Continue for 5.5 miles to the village of St. Olaves. Pass through the village and after half a mile cross the steep bridge (over the canal and railway). At the bottom of the bridge, turn immediately left and park on the wide, Tarmac verge (sign-posted Haddiscoe Station – if you reach Haddiscoe village, you have gone too far). Walk back to the road bridge to view the marsh on your left.**

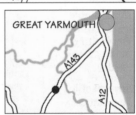

FROM NORWICH: **Leave A47 Norwich bypass on A146. Head SE for approximately 13.5 miles. Take first exit at roundabout with the junction of A143 (sign-posted Great Yarmouth). After approximately five miles, pass through the village of Haddiscoe and continue for another 1.5 miles. Park on the right, just before the steep bridge over the canal and railway (park by signs for Haddiscoe station).**

Other nearby sites

Breydon Water, Burgh Castle Marshes, Great Yarmouth Beach, Halvergate Marshes, Hardley Flood, NWT Hickling Broad, Horsey, Stubb Mill, RSPB Surlingham Church Marshes, Ted Ellis Reserve.

Key points

- **Berney Arms can only be reached by train (request-stop), or by foot from Great Yarmouth.**

- **Free access at all times.**

- **Plan your journey carefully before you set off.**

- **Walking boots needed at least, probably Wellingtons.**

- **£1.10 single train fare from Yarmouth to Berney Arms (2001).**

- **Several stiles to negotiate.**

- **Well-marked footpath across very muddy, wet fields.**

Useful contacts

General Broads Authority
01603 610734

RSPB Mid-Yare Office
01603 715191

CLOSE VIEWS of several species of raptor, normally only seen at a distance at other sites, will be a possible reward for your efforts to reach this area of marshland adjacent to Breydon Water. Berney Arms Marsh can only be reached by train from Yarmouth, followed by an exposed walk across Halvergate Marsh or alongside Breydon Water.

Target birds

Winter – Marsh Harrier (75%), Peregine (40%), Barn Owl (60%), Hen Harrier (50%), Rock Pipit (40%), other Winter raptors (25%), Merlin (15%), Short-eared Owl (15%).

Other likely bird species

Winter	Kestrel	*Occasional*
Cormorant	Golden Plover	Bewick's Swan
Shelduck	Lapwing	Whooper Swan
Wigeon	Common gull species	White-fronted Goose
Teal		
Avocet	Sky Lark	Pink-footed Goose
Other common wildfowl	Meadow Pipit	Twite
	Ruff	Snow Bunting
	Winter thrushes	Lapland Bunting

Background information and birding tips

HALVERGATE and Berney Arms Marshes are probably only worth visiting between late October and early March. The walk described is much more fun if you start your journey by train. Getting off at Berney Arms Station really gives you a sense of being dropped off in the middle of nowhere!

You can walk along the north shore of Breydon Water from Great Yarmouth, but then you have to get back again, leaving you with a bleak eight mile round trek. So, get the train from Yarmouth, walk across Halvergate Marsh, then catch the bus back to Yarmouth train station.

When you inform the train driver you wish to get off at Berney Arms Station, his reaction will be one of surprise or pity, but tell him anyway. Once on the 'platform' at Berney, you have two choices: cross the railway line and head SE towards the windmill, continuing along the north shore of Breydon Water back to Great Yarmouth, or head NW across the marsh following the Weavers' Way footpath.

Choose the former and you will shortly reach the RSPB birdwatching screen which overlooks a pool. This is a good place to encounter common wildfowl species in Winter, possibly Avocet in Summer, and passage waders in Spring and Autumn. Garganey is regularly recorded on passage. The Berney Arms public house is nearby, though opening times are a bit hit and miss.

If, like me, you want to get away from it all, choose the walk across the marsh. From the train platform, head right (away from the rail line) through a gate, and follow the Weavers' Way signs across the muddy fields.

Basically, head for the large church in the distance (Halvergate), carefully noting the direction of each footpath sign nailed to every gate. Eventually, you reach a windmill where you bear left to Halvergate village.

Frequently scan the fields as raptors will appear as if out of nowhere. If you see anything in the air, stay still and you may be rewarded with a Hen or Marsh Harrier lazily flapping overhead, or a Merlin or Peregrine zapping past. Short-eared Owls are regularly seen here, though Barn Owls are more common.

Small flocks of birds in the fields may contain such goodies as Twite, Snow Bunting, Rock Pipit or Lapland Bunting, though Halvergate Marshes is a huge area, so the chance of seeing all these species is remote. You will sometimes see scarcer wildfowl species such as White-fronted Goose, Bewick's Swan and Whooper Swan.

For those who get nervous at the thought of crossing three miles of marsh in Winter, fear not, as I can confirm that mobile phones work the whole way across. Seriously though, Halvergate is a flat area, but the trip shouldn't be taken lightly. There isn't a scrap of cover on the walk, and it can get very cold.

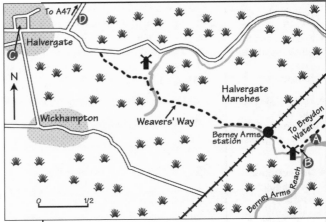

Key
A Berney Arms public house
B RSPB screen
C Bus stop and shelter
D Scan marsh from the road

Access details
(On eastern outskirts of Great Yarmouth).

For station or the start of the walk from Great Yarmouth, follow instructions given for Breydon Water.

Catch the train to Berney Arms Station: *This is a request-only stop so remember to tell the driver you want to get out here before you set off!*

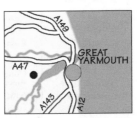

BOAT MOORING: There is free 24hr mooring on the River Bure at Great Yarmouth, near the tourist information at TG 521083. Walk S and cross A47 road bridge to the train station and Asda supermarket.

The walk ends in Halvergate village. If you have timed your walk correctly, and you have done your homework, you will be in time to catch a bus back to Great Yarmouth station (tell the driver where you want to get off). From the marsh, bear left onto the road and walk all the way up the hill to the brick bus shelter (TG 422069).

The wimp's option is to park your car at approximately TG 434066 (do not block access) and walk out onto the marsh, or scan the marsh and pools from the road running north from Halvergate to the A47 Yarmouth road. This road is about 1.3 miles in length and can be very productive.

Other nearby sites
Breydon Water, RSPB Buckenham Marshes, Burgh Castle Marsh, Great Yarmouth Beach, Haddiscoe Marshes, Hardley Flood, NWT Hickling Broad, RSPB Strumpshaw Fen, NWT Stubb Mill.

Key points

- **Free access at all times along public footpaths.**

- **Terrain is level along an uneven, narrow, grass path.**

- **Not suitable for wheelchair users.**

- **Free 24-hour mooring at Chedgrave.**

- **Telescope useful.**

- **Three narrow gateways to negotiate. If you are heavily built (like me!) you may need to climb over them.**

Contacts

General Broads Authority
01603 610734

VIEWS OF THIS privately-owned, extensive flooded area can easily be obtained from a public footpath alongside the River Chet. The site is excellent for common wildfowl all year round, though they can be distant. Regular shooting disrupts the area in Winter, so be prepared for occasional birdless visits.

Target birds *All year* – Common wildfowl (100%).

Other likely bird species

All year	Great Spotted Woodpecker	Common Tern
Little Grebe	Sky Lark	Cuckoo
Great Crested Grebe	Meadow Pipit	Hirundines
Cormorant	Pied Wagtail	Sedge Warbler
Egyptian Goose	Common scrub birds	Reed Warbler
Common wildfowl	Cetti's Warbler	Whitethroat
Common waterbirds	Common woodland birds	Other warblers
Sparrowhawk	Corvids	*Spring/Autumn*
Kestrel	Common finches	Passage waders
Water Rail	Reed Bunting	Yellow Wagtail
Common gull species	*Summer*	*Winter*
Kingfisher	Marsh Harrier	Goldeneye
Green Woodpecker	Hobby	Goosander
		Winter thrushes

Background information and birding tips

HARDLEY FLOOD is a privately-owned stretch of water that holds many species of common waterfowl. In Winter, the large lake can be covered in Tufted Duck, Goldeneye, Wigeon, Pochard, Teal, Mallard, Gadwall, Shoveler, Shelduck and feral geese. A large number of Coots congregate on the lake, presumably attracted by the enormous amount of bread thrown to them by Broadland tourists in the Summer. Many Great Crested Grebes also gather here in Winter.

One major drawback is the fact that this stretch of water is regularly hunted by the shooting fraternity in Winter, so you may

be confronted with a distressing scene. Listen out for gunfire when you get out of your car/boat to avoid a disappointing visit.

My suggested route starts at the bottom of a lane (described in the Access section) and cuts through a marshy field along a public footpath. After a quarter of a mile, there are some dead trees, which regularly attract Great Spotted Woodpeckers and Sparrowhawks.

The footpath runs alongside the River Chet, which also holds common waterbirds throughout the year.

In Summer, look for Reed and and Sedge Warblers. Also keep an

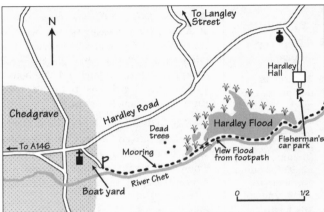

eye open for a flash of blue bulleting over the river's surface: that'll be one of the regular Kingfishers!

The footpath then passes Chedgrave mooring point, though there are no facilities here. Continue another half a mile to view Hardley Flood itself. After heavy rain, you can stand on the wooden bridge listening to the surge of water as it flows into Hardley from the river, thus demonstrating how this place got its name. Having said that, water levels may drop sufficiently to expose a few areas of mud that attract waders, especially at passage times.

At any time of year, this is a duck-watcher's paradise. This site is under-watched so I am certain many a rare duck has gone unnoticed over the years (Blue-winged Teal has been recorded). In fact, it is so under-watched that I wouldn't be surprised if a Bittern hasn't remained undiscovered in the extensive reedbed on the western edge of The Flood. This reedbed also looks good for Bearded Tit, though I have never seen or heard them here.

In Summer, many common ducks remain on site, joined by Common Terns. Hundreds of Swallows, Swifts and House Martins swoop over the water's surface, sometimes hunted by a Hobby. Black Terns regularly visit in Spring and Autumn, and watch out for that Osprey dropping in!

Access details

(Approx. ten miles SE of Norwich)

Leave A47 Norwich bypass at A146 (sign-posted to Lowestoft & Norwich). Head SE for seven miles, turning left to Chedgrave and Langley. In Chedgrave village, take the first left, sign-posted Langley. At crossroads, go straight across (Hardley Road), past the church on the right. Take next right (dead end, sign-posted 'Boatyards and Playground'). Continue for under half a mile and park by the wooden gate just before the road bears right into the boatyard. DO NOT BLOCK ACCESS. If there is no room here, park in the village.

Follow public footpath signs alongside the channel, then alongside the River Chet for about half a mile to view Hardley Flood on the left.

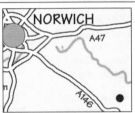

OR: **Continue along Hardley Road for 1.5 miles, turning right at the old, round church. Follow down to Hardley Hall (it says Hall traffic only, but you may go through to the fisherman's car park). Beyond the Hall yard park in grass car park by the bailiff's hut. Hardley Flood can be 'scoped from here. Be warned that the fishermen can be unwelcoming so it may be best to park as directed above.**

BY BOAT: **Mooring situated along the River Chet, approximately a 30 minute sail from the junction with the River Yare. Moor at Chedgrave Common, not at the boatyards.**

Other nearby sites

Breydon Water, Burgh Castle Marshes, Cantley Beet Factory, Great Yarmouth Beach, Haddiscoe Marshes, Halvergate Marshes, Rockland Broad, RSPB Strumpshaw Fen, RSPB Surlingham Church Marshes, Ted Ellis Reserve.

Key points

- Reserve open all year.
- Reserve is a designated SSSI.
- Access by permit (members free, £2.50 for non-members in 2002, under-16s free).
- Visitor centre open daily from April to September (10am-5pm)
- Refreshments available from shop (plus books etc).
- Toilets, including wheelchair access.
- Most of trail is boardwalked other paths can get muddy after rain.

HICKLING is a five star reserve, where, at any time of year, you can easily spend a whole day getting good views of several sought-after species. It has recently established itself as the best place to see Bittern in Norfolk, usually in flight, but fairly reliable nonetheless. In Summer, a trip on the electric boat to the tree tower, Swim Coots and Rush Hills Scrape is a must.

Target birds
All year - Marsh Harrier (80%), Bearded Tit (65%), Bittern (30%), Cetti's Warbler (hear 50%, see 20%), Crane (5% on reserve, 50% in general area). *Winter* - Smew (35%), raptors (25%). *Summer* - Hobby (65%), Avocet (60%), Garganey (50%), Grasshopper Warbler (hear 45%, see 20%).

Other likely bird species

All year

Great Crested Grebe
Little Grebe
Cormorant
Common wildfowl
Sparrowhawk
Kestrel
Woodcock
Common gull species
Barn Owl
Tawny Owl
Kingfisher
Green Woodpecker
Great Spotted Woodpecker
Sky Lark
Meadow Pipit
Pied Wagtail
Marsh Tit
Jay

Other Corvids
Redpoll
Common finches
Reed Bunting

Summer
Little Gull
Yellow-legged Gull
Common Tern
Turtle Dove
Cuckoo
Hirundines
Sedge Warbler
Reed Warbler
Lesser Whitethroat
Whitethroat
Garden Warbler
Blackcap
Chiffchaff
Willow Warbler

Spring/Autumn
Slavonian Grebe

Black-necked Grebe
Little Ringed Plover
Ringed Plover
Little Stint
Curlew Sandpiper
Dunlin
Ruff
Greenshank
Green Sandpiper
Wood Sandpiper
Common Sandpiper
Little Gull
Black Tern
Yellow Wagtail

Winter
Goldeneye
Winter thrushes

Occasional
Savi's Warbler

Background information and birding tips

HICKLING is my favourite Broadlands reserve because it never fails to deliver a great day of nature watchng.

All trails start at the visitor centre. From there you have a

choice of several paths, and all can produce the goods. In Summer, it is worth booking a boat trip in a traditional 'reed lighter' from the visitor centre upon your arrival. This warden-aided trip explores areas not normally open to visitors and is well worth the cost. There is nothing more pleasant on a hot day than cruising along the channels with the wind rustling the reeds and your hair (unless you are bald like me).

My normal Summer route starts along the Bittern trail, accessed from the road immediately behind the visitor centre. It wends its way along a wide, sandy track to the Bittern hide (don't mistake the small boathouse for the hide as you will get your feet wet and see nothing)! Along the way you should already have ticked off Reed, Sedge, and Willow Warblers as well as Chiffchaff, Whitethroat and Reed Bunting, and most probably Bearded Tit in the trackside reeds.

The Bittern hide (fully wheelchair accessible) overlooks reeds, which are good for Marsh Harriers, as well as Bitterns. The harriers are usually near the trees at the back of the marsh. Be patient if you definitely want to see a Bittern: they usually show every couple of hours or so! While you are waiting, look out for dragonflies on the pond or maybe a Hobby or two. Check the logbook in the hide for recent sightings.

The track continues to Whiteslea Lodge which is strictly private and is the Summer home of the Cadbury family. Bear right onto a rough grass path, which runs through bushes to the Observation Hut. This path is not yet wheelchair accessible – surely it can only be a matter of time before NWT join it with the boardwalk to make a circular route for wheelchair users.

In July 2001, the hut was

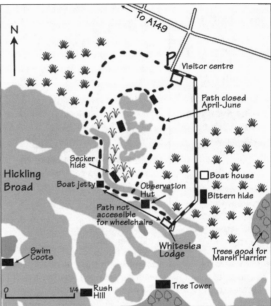

Access details
(Approx. 13 miles NE of Norwich)

From Great Yarmouth head N towards North Walsham on A149. About one mile N of Potter Heigham turn right at the sign-post to Hickling. Follow to Hickling Green, then turn right at Greyhound pub (following brown tourist signs with a duck logo). Turn left about 300 yards past the pub, still following the brown

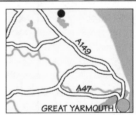

duck signs. This leads down to the Norfolk Wildlife Trust's car park, about 1.5 miles from the pub.

closed due to it sinking into the swamp. I was assured the wardens would get around to mending it. And so they should - they were in it when it started sinking! When the hut re-opens, you will get a good overview of the reeds and marsh, excellent for Marsh Harrier and Bearded Tit.

Where the rough grass path joins the boardwalk of the Swallowtail Trail, there is a short boardwalk leading to a viewing platform which offers a chance to scan Hickling Broad for waterfowl such as Tufted Duck, Great Crested Grebe, Mute Swan, Grey Heron, etc. This is also a superb place to

● **Continues overleaf.**

93

Key points

- **Most hides are wheelchair-friendly.**

- **Summer boat trips available May 18th to September 15th but booking essential (only way of reaching Swim Coots and Rush Hill Scrape).**

- **Free use of binoculars on board the boat.**

- **No dogs**

Contacts

The Warden, Hickling Broad National Nature 01692 598276

Norfolk Wildlife Trust 01603 625540

- **Continued from page 93.**

linger awhile to see what pops up. In July 2001 I had a pair of Marsh Harriers food-passing, an adult Bearded Tit feeding a juvenile, and a Swallowtail butterfly all in the same field of view.

Also in this area is the old Secker Hide which overlooks the marsh and the Broad, but it can only be entered after climbing up steep steps, so it remains inaccessible to wheelchair users. Cetti's Warblers can be heard from the thick bushes around Secker Hide, but you will do well to catch a glimpse.

If you wish to go on a boat trip, they leave from the visitor centre. This costs about £6, but is well worth the money. On your trip, you will visit the Tree Tower, which is a metal structure giving superb views of the whole reserve. You should see Marsh Harrier from here but sufferers of vertigo should stay on solid ground.

On the boat trip, you will next visit either Swim Coots or Rush Hill Scrape. These parts of Hickling are similar in that you reach them via a narrow, reed-fringed channel, good for Reed Warblers, Swallowtail butterflies, Norfolk Hawker dragonflies, etc. They each have a single, thatched hide overlooking a scrape. Both are good places to see Marsh Harrier, Garganey, Teal, Avocet, Yellow-legged Gull, Little Gull, breeding Black-headed Gull, Reed Warbler, Sedge Warbler, Reed Bunting, etc.

The scrapes are also excellent places to encounter passage waders such as Little Stint, Green, Wood Common and Curlew Sandpipers in both Spring and Autumn. In 2002 the boats run from May 18 to September 15 at 10am and 2pm, Sunday to Thursday. The fares are £6 adults, £3 children and £5 NWT members.

Once back on the main reserve, the boardwalk continues to the visitor centre, thus completing a circular route. Along the way, you may wish to visit one or both of the hides overlooking the pools for the chance of more waders, usually the same range of species encountered on the boat trip.

Alternatively, from the jetty, you could retrace your steps towards the hut, then cut across a narrow grass path off to your left (closed April-June). This cuts through the marsh back to the hides and visitor centre.

In Winter, the Hickling area is renowned for its raptors. These are best seen from the Stubb Mill roost (see Stubb Mill site page 164), but may be encountered anywhere on the reserve. By day, Hen Harriers, Merlins, Marsh Harriers and Peregrines patrol the extensive marshes and dunes in the area, spreading from Sea Palling in the north to Haddiscoe Marshes to the south. This means that they can be very elusive during daylight hours, but come in to roost about an hour before dark every evening.

The Summer walk described above can seem quiet in Winter, but Bearded Tits should still show well during windless days. Cetti's Warblers sing occasionally when it is sunny, and Bitterns sometimes fly over the reeds to

You will need to go on the boat trip to Swim Coots or Rush Hill Scrape to stand a chance of recording Garganey in Spring and Summer.

new feeding areas. If the pools are frozen, Bitterns may be seen feeding out in open areas and the Bittern hide is a very good place to watch from in these conditions.

Cranes are resident in the Hickling area but they are best seen at dusk from Stubb Mill or in fields around the Horsey Mere area. You may see one or two flying over Hickling reserve, usually betraying their presence by their evocative 'cronk, cronk' calls.

In recent Winters, NWT Hickling Broad has hosted one or two Smew among the common wildfowl. The Broad should be scanned for Tufted Duck, Goldeneye, Teal, Gadwall, Mallard, Pochard, Shoveler and the occasional Ruddy Duck.

If you are unlucky, this place can seem very deserted, especially in Winter, but patience is usually rewarded with some very good birds at all times of year. For me this is a fantastic reserve, not only for

birds, but also for people and other wildlife. The whole place abounds with animals, plants and insects, making it a must visit place for the all-round naturalist.

A visit to Hickling will not produce all the target species (unless you are very lucky), but there is always something to see. Also see Stubb Mill information (page 164) for details of the raptor roost at Hickling.

Other nearby sites

NWT Barton Broad, Breydon Water, RSPB Buckenham Marshes, NWT Buxton Heath, NWT Cockshoot Broad, Great Yarmouth Beach, Great Yarmouth Cemetery, Horsey area, How Hill Trust, Rockland Broad, Stubb Mill, NWT Upton Fen, Winterton Dunes.

Key points

- **Terrain is mostly level, mainly on muddy tracks. Some Tarmac roads on the estate.**

- **Deer Park is open daily 7am - 7pm in Summer, (6pm in Winter).**

- **Only limited access to other parts of the grounds - remain on designated routes.**

- **Facilities on site include toilets, a pottery, a café (open from Easter), and a public house.**

- **Wheelchair access along the estate roads. Woodland paths may be too muddy, especially in Winter.**

Contacts

Holkham Hall
01328 710227
www.holkham.co.uk

IN THIS large country estate – just like those seen in Merchant/Ivory films – a beautiful wood surrounds a lake, which is good for waterfowl, especially in Winter. There are plenty of common birds to see all year round, and Holkham is the best place in the county to see Lesser Spotted Woodpecker, Tawny Owl and Nuthatch.

Target birds *All year* - Tawny Owl (Winter best – 80%), Lesser Spotted Woodpecker (25%), Hawfinch (Winter best – 10%).

Other likely bird species

All year	Stock Dove	Goldeneye
Great Crested Grebe	Barn Owl	Grey Wagtail
	Green Woodpecker	Winter thrushes
Little Grebe	Great Spotted Woodpecker	
Cormorant		*Summer*
Egyptian Goose	Sky Lark	Hobby
	Meadow Pipit	Cuckoo
Other common wildfowl		Summer warblers
	Common scrub birds	Spotted Flycatcher
Common waterbirds	Goldcrest	
Sparrowhawk	Marsh Tit	*Passage*
Kestrel	Nuthatch	Honey Buzzard
Woodcock	Treecreeper	Goshawk
		Redstart
Red-legged Partridge	Common woodland birds	Wood Warbler
Grey Partridge	Jay	Pied Flycatcher
Lapwing	Other corvids	
		Occasional
Common gull species	*Winter*	Brambling
	Pink-footed Goose	

Background information and birding tips

IT'S SAD to start on a sour note: this used to be a good site to see Hawfinches but reports of this declining species are now few and far between. By all accounts, this is due to disturbance from birdwatchers! Having said that, Holkham is still an excellent place to see woodland species difficult to locate in other parts of the county.

At the north gate, before you even enter the estate grounds, you will see Blue and Great Tits

Robins, Dunnocks and Blackbirds. Stand for a few moments at the Gatekeeper's Cottage where you will almost certainly get outstanding views of a Nuthatch or two on the bird table or on the walls around the gates.

Once through the gates, walk west (right) along a muddy track, checking the gardens to your right for Marsh Tit and other more common woodland species. It shouldn't be long before a Great Spotted Woodpecker makes its presence known with its *'chick'* alarm call.

Follow this track down to the Earl Of Leicester monument (TF 884436), checking the trees and leaf litter for birds as you go. In Winter, a small number of Bramblings can sometimes be found among the Chaffinches, Goldfinches and Greenfinches rummaging about in the dead leaves below the mature trees in this wood. Careful attention to the tree trunks should produce a Treecreeper or two and Long-tailed Tits and Goldcrests will be active in the bushes and trees.

In Winter, Holkham Hall has become renowned for its roosting Tawny Owls. In seven consecutive years of visiting I have only dipped on these beauties once. At the monument, the muddy track becomes a grass path. Look along this track to a large, flat-topped cedar tree a few yards down on the right. This is the roost site for the owls. They can be extremely difficult to locate, but in the Februarys of 2000, 2001 and 2002 they were in exactly the same place; near the top just to the right of the thick branch curving off to the right. The Tawny Owls breed in the park, but are difficult to locate during the breeding season.

After finding the owls, keep on the grass track to the lake. You are guaranteed to see Egyptian and Greylag Geese here, plus other common wildfowl (Tufted Duck, Pochard, Mallard etc). In Winter, these are joined by Goldeneye, one or two Pink-footed Geese and maybe a Black-necked Grebe if you are lucky. You can follow the path through

- **Continues overleaf.**

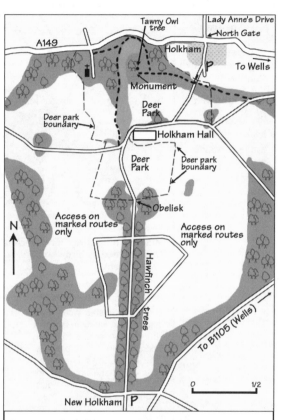

Access details

(Approx. 12 miles E of Hunstanton).

Holkham Hall's northern entrance is sign-posted off A149 between Burnham Overy Staithe and Wells-Next-The-Sea. Turn off main road to the signed car park. This is free, but can be muddy in Winter. Walk S (right) along access road through the estate's main gates. My most productive walk is on the muddy track W to the lake through an area of mature woodland.

To enter the estate from the

south, turn onto B1105 (sign-posted Fakenham) from A149 at western end of Wells. Take the first turn-off right (after 1.1 miles) and follow for 1.7 miles to the entrance gate at New Holkham. Park carefully and walk on estate roads only.

● **Continued from page 97.**

Key points

- Can get busy with tourists in Summer.
- Early morning is best.
- Also visit the ancient house and garden centre.

Hawfinch sightings have declined following too much disturbance by birdwatchers, so please show due respect if you see one.

the wood to the north or to Holkham Hall to the south.

Lesser Spotted Woodpeckers are seen regularly in the park, but they are easiest to find in March when they display among the leafless trees. Listen for their drumming, and watch out for their amazing, fluttering display flight. The area around the monument is particularly good. Green Woodpeckers also frequent the woods.

Woodcock are present in the park grounds in excellent numbers but seeing one involves looking over the woods at dusk. You may come across one skulking in the leaf litter but this is unlikely!

In Spring and Summer, the woods are alive with bird activity. Summer warblers join the resident species, and if you are lucky you might find a Pied Flycatcher, Redstart or Wood Warbler during Spring migration times. Blackcap, Willow Warbler, Chiffchaff and Whitethroat all breed on site. Another delightful Summer visitor to the estate is Spotted Flycatcher; listen out for their 'squeaky wheelbarrow wheel' call.

On the lake, Great Crested Grebe, Mallard, Coot, Moorhen, Greylag Goose, Tufted Duck and Egyptian Goose should all be encountered at this time of year.

The south side of the park is usually the least disturbed by people, and is now the favoured area for Hawfinches. Most of the species mentioned above should also be in evidence. Be aware though that public access is strictly limited to connected roads in this area of the park.

Other nearby sites

Blakeney Point, NWT Cley Marshes, Holkham NNR, NOA Kelling Quags, Kelling Heath, Salthouse Beach, Salthouse Heath, Swanton Novers, NOA Walsey Hills, Wells Woods.

THOUGH it is huge, comprising several habitats, each with its own special birds, Holkham is easy to cover. The marsh is a goose hotspot in Winter, affording close encounters with White-fronted and Pink-footed Geese. The saltings are a regular site for wintering Twite, Shore Larks and Snow Buntings and several raptor species pass through on a regular basis. The pines and dunes are a migrant magnet in Spring and Autumn, with many scarce breeding birds present on the marsh in Summer.

Target birds

All year - Barn Owl (40%), Bearded Tit (25%). *Winter* - Pink-footed Goose (90%), White-fronted Goose (90%), Twite (90%), Shore Lark (50%), seaduck (40%), raptors (Hen Harrier, Merlin, Peregrine – 30%), Snow Bunting (30%), divers (25%), *Summer* - Marsh Harrier (60%). *Spring/Autumn* - Passage migrants.

Other likely bird species

All year	Siskin	Black Redstart
Little Grebe	Redpoll	Redstart
Egyptian Goose	Reed Bunting	Whinchat
Shelduck		Wheatear
Sparrowhawk	*Winter*	Barred Warbler
Kestrel	Wigeon	Firecrest
Lapwing	Teal	
Snipe	Common waders	Red-breasted Flycatcher
Woodcock	Stonechat	Pied Flycatcher
Redshank	Winter thrushes	
Grey Partridge		*Occasional*
Red-legged Partridge	*Summer*	Hobby
	Spoonbill	Jack Snipe
Tawny Owl	Terns	Bean Goose
Green Woodpecker	Avocet	Barnacle Goose
Great Spotted Woodpecker	Cuckoo	Grasshopper Warbler
	Hirundines	Crossbill
Sky Lark	Spotted Flycatcher	
Treecreeper	*Spring/Autumn*	
Jay	Wryneck	
	Bluethroat	

Background information and birding tips

THOUGH Holkham National Nature Reserve (managed by English Nature) is an excellent site for all kinds of nature, it is also popular with humans too. Once on the reserve in Summer it is easy to get away from the crowds as they are more interested in the beach than the marsh, which is overlooked by a hide.

In Winter, Holkham is a superb place to encounter wild

• **Continues overleaf.**

Key points

- **English Nature reserve, open at all times (gates close at 9pm on Fridays and Saturdays in Summer).**

- **Two hides, wheelchair access to one, plus two viewing platforms on sea side of dunes.**

- **Parking fee may be charged (£2 in Jan 2002).**

- **Tracks and boardwalks are flat. Saltings only reached across a beach, wet mud and vegetation. Paths in woods can be narrow and steepish.**

- **Leaflet available from dispenser in car park (£1).**

- **Continued from page 99.**

geese at close range. Slowly cruise down Lady Anne's Drive, scanning the fields either side for geese. Pink-feet seem to prefer the first few fields, while the White-fronts seem to favour the fields at the far end. Either way, watch the birds from your car as they can easily be spooked. Scan the goose flocks carefully, as regular interminglers include Barnacle, Bean, Greylag and Egyptian, while Lesser White-fronted, small race Canada and Red-breasted are also possibilities for the alert birder. Among the geese will be large numbers of Wigeon.

For those birdwatchers who like hides, wander left at the gate at the bottom of Lady Anne's Drive. The sandy track will take you to the Washington hide, where you can 'scope the geese and Wigeon flocks on the marsh. The pools here will also hold common ducks such as Mallard, Gadwall, Pochard, Shoveler, Teal, and Tufted Duck. Also look out for common waders such as Curlew, Golden Plover, Lapwing, Snipe, Redshank etc.

There is always the possibility of a raptor flying over the marsh too. Regular species include Peregrine, Merlin, Hen Harrier, Kestrel and Sparrowhawk, with Barn Owl and Short-eared Owl also possible. The reeds near the hide are the haunt of Bearded Tits but they can be elusive.

From the Washington hide, walk either along a boardwalk to the beach, then turn right back to Holkham Gap for the winter finches, larks and buntings (see below) or continue on past Meols House to the Joe Jordan hide. I don't know the origins of the

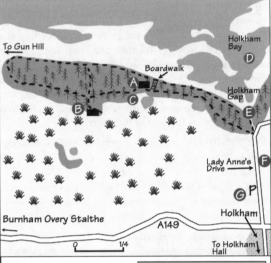

Key
A - George Washington Hide
B - Joe Jordan Hide
C - Meols House
D - Twite and Snow Bunting area at low tide.
E - Viewing platform
F & G - Fields for geese

Access details

(Approx. 13.5 miles E of Hunstanton).

From A149 between Burnham Overy Staithe and Wells-Next-The-Sea, turn down Lady Anne's Drive towards the sea (opposite the brown tourist sign to the Pottery and Holkham Hall).

Parking is permitted all along this road, on the verges. Park at the bottom and follow the boardwalk to the Gap or turn left along a sandy track to the hides For this guide, I have classed the sandy track to the right as Wells Woods.

name but I can safely guess that it has nothing to do with the Manchester United 'hardman' striker of the same name!

This hide also looks out over Holkham Marsh, but at a slightly different angle. The hide can be difficult to find, but is situated where

the main track splits into four. At the point where the main track turns into a grass path, turn left down a very narrow path through the bracken, to the Jordan hide. Access is up steep steps, so it is not suitable for wheelchair users.

In Winter, Holkham Gap is famous for its wintering Twite

100

flock. These are sometimes joined by varying numbers (up to 100 in early 2002) of Snow Buntings and, rarer still, Shore Larks. Their feeding area is reached from the car park by walking along the boardwalk straight ahead to the beach (about 300 yards). There is a viewing platform here, but the birds tend to be further out in the short vegetation uncovered when the tide goes out.

Head right from the boardwalk along the beach/mud (you can walk as far as Wells Harbour if you wish) and scan the area. Wheelchair users may scan the saltings from this viewing platform, though the birds will almost certainly be too far away to identify! Also note that sand may have blown over the boardwalk making wheelchair

access to the platform difficult.

Walking boots or Wellingtons are recommended as you may need to walk across the saltings to find the birds. I am not advocating flushing these flocks, but if you wander a few yards then scan, wander and scan, then you should get good views without disturbing the birds. The Twite, Snow Buntings and Shore Larks will be so busy feeding that if you stay still they will probably edge closer to you.

Other common birds here can include Greenfinch, Goldfinch, Meadow Pipit, Sky Lark and Pied Wagtail and you may be lucky enough to locate a Jack Snipe while you are scanning for the finch flocks. Raptors such as Peregrine and Merlin regularly

Spring migrants such as Firecrest are a real possibility at Holkham Pines

• **Continues overleaf.**

Key points

- **Bike parking rails behind Washington Hide and at Holkham Gap viewing platform.**

- **Telescope very useful.**

- **Use insect repellent in Summer.**

- **Do not touch any strange objects on the beach — unexploded missiles turn up occasionally.**

Contacts

English Nature
01603 620558

Site Manager
01328 711183

- **Continued from page 101.**

sweep across the saltings in pusuit of the feeding birds.

If you walk to the raised grassy dune at the back of the saltings you can obtain reasonable views of Winter sea-birds such as Red-breasted Merganser, Eider, Goldeneye, Great Crested Grebe, Slavonian Grebe, etc. In January 2002, more than 10,000 Common Scoters were seen here and a King Eider has also overwintered. Waders such as Dunlin, Sanderling, Turnstone, etc. should also be encountered in the saltings and on the beach.

In Summer, Holkham Gap is of very little interest as the area is badly disturbed by holiday makers. I suggest you walk left along the sandy track from the car park to the hides. Along the track, you will get good views of Wren, Long-tailed Tit, Blackbird, Blackcap, Whitethroat, Willow Warbler, Chiffchaff, etc.

Always check the first pond on your left as a Little Grebe or two are usually present. In the reeds and scrub by the hide you should see Reed and Sedge Warblers and maybe even a Bearded Tit. The pools hold breeding ducks such as Gadwall, Tufted Duck, Shoveler and Pochard as well as Coot and Moorhen.

Marsh Harriers regularly hunt over the marsh, but these can give closer views from the Jordan hide. Avocets, Lapwings, Redshanks, Snipe, Shelduck, Oystercatchers, Sky Larks, Yellow Wagtails etc can all be seen on the marsh but can be distant. Large numbers of Swifts, Swallows and House Martins hunt over the pools, sometimes swooping over you along the path. Hobbies sometimes hunt.

From the Joe Jordan hide there is a large dead tree straight out from the front window which holds a large number of Cormorants. Holkham marsh has become a regular haunt of Spoonbills in Summer though of course they cannot be guaranteed.

While non-birders are building sand castles on the pristine beach, you can watch Sandwich, Common, and Little Terns fishing in the sea. The latter species sometimes nest on the beach, so watch out for any fenced-off areas. However, most seem to have moved to Gun Hill to the west, a long walk along the beach for humans but a mere minute's flight for a tern!

In Spring and Autumn, the woods and dunes hold the greatest attraction. These areas attract migrants freshly arrived from the continent. Regular Spring arrivals include Whinchats, Wheatears, Ring Ouzels, Goldcrests and various warblers.

Autumn seems to be the better time to find Pied Flycatchers, Wood Warblers and Redstarts in the woods, along with some scarcer visitors such as Firecrest, Red-breasted Flycatcher and Yellow-browed Warbler.

This is a (if not *the)* prime site for Pallas's Warbler. These Siberian jewels usually join up with roving tit flocks. These flocks follow circuits through the woods so, rather than following the birds, stay in one place and wait for them to come to you. Meols House is a good spot.

Wrynecks are relatively frequent visitors to the dunes. Rarities include Dusky and Radde's Warblers and Britain's one and only Red-breasted Nuthatch! There is often an influx of continental Jays in Autumn as well as Woodcock.

There are many paths criss-crossing the woods and dunes, which offer the visiting birdwatcher ample opportunity to find their own special birds at migration time. Please stick to these paths though, as the dunes and woods are home to other rare and scarce wildlife such as the Natterjack Toad.

Other nearby sites

All year - Blakeney Point, NWT Cley Marshes, Holkham Hall, NWT Holme Dunes, NOA Holme Observatory, RSPB Titchwell Marsh, NOA Walsey Hills.

Summer - Kelling Heath, Salthouse Heath , Swanton Novers.

Spring/Autumn - Wells Woods, Weybourne.

NORFOLK WILDLIFE TRUST'S Holme Dunes reserve is one of the best places in Norfolk to find your own rare, scarce and common migrants in Spring and Autumn. It is also the best place in the county to see Barn Owl throughout the year, Long-tailed Duck in Winter and Lesser Whitethroat in Summer. It could take you a whole day to cover this site properly, especially at migration times.

Target birds *All year* – Barn Owl (85%). *Summer* –
Black-tailed Godwit (90%), Avocet (80%), Little Tern (75%), Lesser Whitethroat (60%). *Spring/Autumn* – Passage migrants, passage waders. *Winter* – Long-tailed Duck (60%), Snow Bunting (25%).

Other likely bird species

All year
Little Grebe

Great Crested Grebe
Fulmar
Cormorant
Sparrowhawk
Kestrel
Oystercatcher
Lapwing
Ringed Plover
Turnstone
Tawny Owl

Great Spotted Woodpecker
Sky Lark
Meadow Pipit
Pied Wagtail
Goldcrest
Nuthatch
Treecreeper
Corvids
Bullfinch
Reed Bunting

Summer
Terns
Cuckoo
Hirundines
Sedge Warbler
Reed Warbler
Whitethroat

Blackcap
Other warblers
Spotted Flycatcher

Spring/Autumn
Shearwaters
Gannet
Little Ringed Plover
Little Stint
Ruff
Whimbrel
Greenshank
Green Sandpiper
Wood Sandpiper
Common Sandpiper
Skuas
Kittiwake
Terns
Auks
Long-eared Owl
Wryneck
Richard's Pipit
Tawny Pipit
Yellow Wagtail
Redstart
Whinchat
Wheatear
Ring Ouzel
Winter thrushes
Barred Warbler

Yellow-browed Warbler

Firecrest

Red-breasted Flycatcher
Pied Flycatcher
Red-backed Shrike

Winter
Divers
Grebes
Brent Goose
Wigeon
Teal
Common Scoter
Goldeneye

Red-breasted Merganser
Hen Harrier
Golden Plover
Grey Plover
Knot
Stonechat
Winter thrushes
Siskin

Occasional
Velvet Scoter
Merlin
Peregrine
Hobby
Short-eared Owl

Grasshopper Warbler

Key points

- **Open 10am – 5pm every day except Christmas Day.**

- **Permit needed (NWT members free, non-members £2).**

- **Reserve is a designated SSSI.**

- **Public footpath along dunes open at all times.**

- **Toilets at the start of rough access track.**

- **The visitor centre sells books, snacks and drinks (no toilet here).**

- **Two hides on Holme Marsh.**

- **Four hides at eastern end of main reserve.**

● **Continues overleaf.**

• **Continued from page 103.**

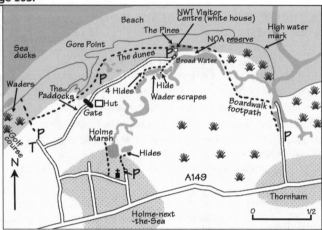

Access details

(Approx. two miles NE of Hunstanton).

From Hunstanton take the next left turn off A149, (sign-posted NOA Watchpoint/NNT Reserve). After about half a mile turn right onto a rough track just before you reach the toilet block (if you need the facilities, go now as there are none on site). Go slowly down this track or you will do irreparable damage to your trusty motor. Park on left by the visitor centre (the white house) at the end of the track. The hides are accessed by walking back past the NOA grass car park, the beach is along the footpath through the pines.

HOLME MARSH: Heading E into Holme on A149 take last turn left before you leave the village (Eastgate Road). Continue along

this road then bear right (signed to 'Sunnymead Holiday Park'). Park carefully by the concrete bollards after about 100 yards. Take the kissing gate to your right and follow the obvious path to the two hides overlooking a pool and bushes.

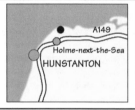

Background information and birding tips

WHERE do you start with a site as good as this? There are numerous access points to view the reserve, all of which produce good birds at most times of year. I will describe several areas including Holme Marsh, Gore Point, The Pines, The Dunes, The Paddocks and the wader scrapes.

Gore Point: This is an excellent place to see seaduck in Winter, particularly at high tide. The best way to get there is to park at the toilet block in Holme, near the golf course. Walk across the golf course (watch out for stray golf balls and obey all course officials' instructions), through the

dunes and onto the beach. Gore Point is to your right. Long-tailed Duck is a speciality here, but there may be thousands of Common Scoter on the sea as well.

Directly to the left of the junction of the beach and golf course, a receding tide reveals a small marsh, which is a haven for waders. If you approach quietly and slowly, you will obtain stunningly close views of Knot, Dunlin, Sanderling, Bar-tailed Godwit, etc. Good fieldcraft is needed to avoid disturbing these waders as they busily feed on the saltings.

If you are lucky, you may

find the small flock of Snow Buntings on the beach in Winter, though these birds roam far and wide. In Summer, several species of wader nest on the raised shingle bank by the beach, so take care not to disturb them. Little Terns occasionally nest here too. If they don't, you will still see them out to sea, along with Common and Sandwich terns. Please be aware that the tides and currents along this coast have claimed many a life.

The paddocks: In Spring and Autumn, head for The Paddocks. Drive along the rough access track, and park just past the warden's hut.

Walk up the bank onto the dune footpath boardwalk, and turn left. After about 100 yards there is a field on your left with many thick bushes scattered around.

Do not enter the paddocks, but view from the perimeter fence. Wait patiently for birds to appear out of the thick cover: possibilities include Barred Warbler, Red-backed Shrike, Redstart, Pied Flycatcher, Turtle Dove, etc. The paddocks also attract Wheatear in Spring and Autumn. If you keep walking left, you reach the golf course and dunes, which may hold pipits and larks. **Do not trespass onto the golf course**, as the budding Nick Faldos become very grumpy.

The dunes: You may follow the boardwalk east all the way to the NWT visitor centre and the area of pines. If you choose to walk, scan the dunes and bushes regularly for anything that moves! Do not stray from the paths as you might trample a Natterjack Toad or a scarce plant or two. Alternatively, once you have scanned the paddocks, drive down the track and park by the white house at the end which is the NWT visitor centre. The roped-off grass car park on the right is for visitors to the adjoining NOA Holme Observatory site only.

The pines: These are at the back of the NWT visitor centre and attract migrants during Spring and Autumn. Regular drop-ins include Redstart, Pied, Red-breasted and

Other nearby sites

Brancaster Marsh, Dersingham Bog, Gypsy Lane, NOA Holme Observatory, Hunstanton, Ken Hill Wood, NOA Redwell Marsh, Sandringham, RSPB Snettisham, Wolferton Triangle.

Spotted Flycatcher, Firecrest and Crossbill. Again, check the surrounding dunes for pipits, larks and Wryneck.

The wader scrapes: These are reached by walking from the NWT visitor centre, past the NOA car park then bearing immediately left down a wheelchair accessible track. The bushes along here hold Sedge Warblers in Summer, along with common scrub birds. The first hide is wheelchair friendly but the path beyond becomes rough grass. The hides overlook a couple of scrapes made famous as the site of the first Norfolk breeding record of Black-winged Stilt.

Spring and Autumn should produce a number of species including Greenshank, Whimbrel, Green Sandpiper and Ruff. In Summer, you may get very close views of Avocet and Black-tailed Godwit.

Holme Marsh: This is an excellent place to see Barn Owl and Lesser Whitethroat. The two hides (with cushions!) overlook a pool surrounded by bushes, home to Whitethroat, Blackcap, Sedge Warbler and Lesser Whitethroat. The latter species tend to show well from these hides. The large tree to the left of the first hide is a favoured perch of the local Barn Owl.

If you don't see an owl here walk back to the road and follow the public footpath (a rough, wide track) to the right. The path ends at a gate (do not go over the gate) and overlooks several fields, which, with patience, are almost certain to produce a Barn Owl sighting.

Key points

- **Keep dogs on leads.**

- **Boots recommended for Holme Marsh.**

- **Terrain is mainly level along rough tracks, grass paths and boardwalks.**

- **Limited wheelchair access.**

Contacts

NWT Holme Dunes
The Firs,
Broadwater Road,
Holme-Next-The-Sea,
Norfolk PE36 6LQ
01485 525240

Norfolk Wildlife Trust
01603 625540

Key points

- **Owned by the Norfolk Ornithologists' Association.**

- **Permit required from Observatory office. Free to NOA members, £2 for non-members.**

- **If you are visiting both NOA and NWT reserves, you need two permits.**

- **Open from dawn to dusk to members, who are allowed past gate which closes at 5pm but is never locked.**

- **Drinks and snacks available at Observatory office.**

- **Friendly warden to tell you what is around.**

- **Not wheelchair friendly.**

Contacts

Norfolk Ornithologists' Association
01485 525406

SMALL BUT SUPERB – that's the best way to sum up a seven acre reserve that is particularly good for common, scarce and rare migrants in Spring and Autumn. A comfortable hide provides a perfect place from which to seawatch throughout the year. This is a good place to find your own migrants as the reserve is small and easy to cover.

Target birds *All year* – Barn Owl (85%), Marsh Harrier (60%). *Summer* – Black-tailed Godwit (90%), Avocet (80%). *Spring/Autumn* – Passage migrants. *Winter* – Raptors (25%).

Other likely bird species

All year	Reed Warbler	Red-backed Shrike
Little Grebe	Whitethroat	
Great Crested Grebe	Blackcap	*Winter*
	Other warblers	Divers
Fulmar	Spotted Flycatcher	Grebes
Cormorant		Brent Goose
Sparrowhawk	*Spring/Autumn*	Wigeon
Kestrel	Shearwaters	Teal
Red-legged Partridge	Gannet	Goldeneye
Grey Partridge	Skuas	Red-breasted Merganser
Oystercatcher	Kittiwake	Hen Harrier
Lapwing	Terns	Golden Plover
Tawny Owl	Auks	Grey Plover
	Long-eared Owl	Winter thrushes
Great Spotted Woodpecker	Wryneck	Siskin
Goldcrest	Yellow Wagtail	
Nuthatch	Redstart	*Occasional*
Treecreeper	Whinchat	Hobby
Reed Bunting	Wheatear	
	Barred Warbler	Grasshopper Warbler
Summer	Yellow-browed Warbler	Merlin
Terns	Firecrest	Peregrine
Cuckoo		Short-eared Owl
Hirundines	Red-breasted Flycatcher	
Sedge Warbler	Pied Flycatcher	

Background information and birding tips

THIS SMALL reserve, the site of Norfolk's only accredited observatory, attracts migrants by the mist net full in Spring and Autumn. Ringing takes place all year round.

You should be observant all the way along the access track to the grass car park, as the fields to your right are one of the best places in Norfolk to see Barn Owl at all times of year.

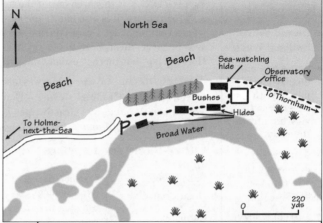

Park in the roped-off grass car park to the right of the track, and not by the white house on the left. Follow the Shrike signs to the entrance of the NOA reserve, to the right of the white house. Before doing any more birding, obtain your permit from the Observatory office situated along the only rough path on the reserve.

In Spring and Autumn, a spell in the seawatching hide could prove a profitable starting point, provided you are able to negotiate the steep flight of steps. Obtain a key for this hide from the Observatory office. The best time for seawatching is at high tide when the birds will be much closer. Some of the small pine trees partially block the view in places. At peak seawatching times, the hide can become quite full, so don't fall out (literally!) over the best viewing spot. And don't ignore this hide in Winter, as this stretch of coast is excellent for divers and seaduck.

There are also two hides along the footpath to the Observatory office, both overlooking a sheltered 'valley' populated by thick bushes. In Spring and Autumn, sit quietly in one of these hides and you will be amazed at what pops out of the thick cover. The sun seems to catch this spot in the afternoons, and due to the shelter of the surrounding pines, the area is highly

Access details

(Approx. two miles NE of Hunstanton).

From Hunstanton head E on A149 to left turn (sign-posted NOA Watchpoint/NNT Reserve). Continue on this road for about half a mile, then turn right onto a rough track just before you reach the toilet block (note there are no facilities on site). Drive slowly as track is very bumpy.

Pass through the entrance gate to the NWT and NOA reserve, telling the person in the hut you are only visiting the NOA part of Holme. If you intend visiting the NWT part of the reserve,

you MUST purchase a separate permit.

Follow the gravel track down to the end and park on the right in the roped-off grass car park. Do not park by the white house unless you have purchased a permit for the NWT reserve.

attractive to tired migrants. Spend as long here as you can.

The only other hide on the NOA reserve overlooks Broadwater and the marsh beyond. This is a good place to watch breeding waders in Spring and Summer. Avocet and Black-tailed Godwits are virtually guaranteed at this time of year. In Winter, watch out for raptors and wildfowl.

Broadwater itself holds common wildfowl species and Reed and Sedge Warblers can be seen in the surrounding vegetation in Summer. Marsh Harriers quarter the marsh at most times of year.

Key points

- Owned by the National Trust.

- Large pay and display car parks, with other areas viewable from the road.

- Some areas accessible for wheelchair users.

- Terrain is level but mostly along muddy paths, especially in Winter.

- Mooring for boats small enough to get under Potter Heigham bridge.

NOT ONLY is this area one of the best places in Norfolk for raptors, it is also one of the best places in Britain where you might see Cranes during the year. This is a large area to cover, incorporating Horsey Mill, Horsey Mere and Horsey Gap, but there is usually much to see.

Target birds *All year* – Marsh Harrier (75%), Crane (40%), Bearded Tit (30%). *Winter* – Hen Harrier (50%), Merlin (25%). *Summer* – Grasshopper Warbler (hear 60%; see 15%). *Spring/Autumn* – Passage migrants.

Other likely bird species

All year	Jay	Other warblers
Little Grebe	Common finches	
Great Crested Grebe	Reed Bunting	*Spring/Autumn*
		Shearwaters
Cormorant	*Winter*	Gannet
Common wildfowl	Divers	Skuas
	Grebes	Wryneck
Common waterbirds	Seaduck	Yellow Wagtail
Sparrowhawk	Bewick's Swan	Ring Ouzel
Kestrel	Whooper Swan	Redstart
Lapwing	Pink-footed Goose	Whinchat
Common waders	Winter thrushes	Wheatear
		Firecrest
Common gull species	*Summer*	Pied Flycatcher
Barn Owl	Hobby	Red-backed Shrike
Green Woodpecker	Sandwich Tern	
Sky Lark	Common Tern	*Occasional*
Meadow Pipit	Little Tern	Short-eared Owl
Pied Wagtail	Hirundines	
Stonechat	Sedge Warbler	
	Reed Warbler	

Background information and birding tips

HORSEY is a large area to cover but can be well worth the effort at any time of year, but as Winter is the most exciting from a birdwatching point of view, that's where I will start.

The main targets in Winter are raptors and Cranes. The small, resident Crane population roams widely during the day, but they have several favourite areas. These include the fields around Brograve Farm (TG 444242),

Walnut Farm (TG 452246) and Horsey Mill itself.

I have found the best place for Cranes (and raptors) is the pull-in on the right 0.6 miles to the south of Horsey Mill on the B1159. If you wait in your car for a while (the longer the better) you should see Crane, Hen Harrier, Barn Owl and Marsh Harrier, and possibly Short-eared Owl and Merlin.

Scan the surrounding fields

regularly, as raptors and Cranes appear as if out of thin air, and usually vanish just as quickly! If you miss any of the above species during the day, visit Stubb Mill in the evening for almost guaranteed views of them.

Also along this road from Horsey Mill to West Somerton, you may find small numbers of Bewick's or Whooper Swans but I haven't seen any during numerous visits in recent Winters. The wintering Pink-footed Goose flock seems to be becoming more elusive too, but again, scan the fields thoroughly along the B1159. They are usually seen in flight, either side of the road in the morning and at dusk.

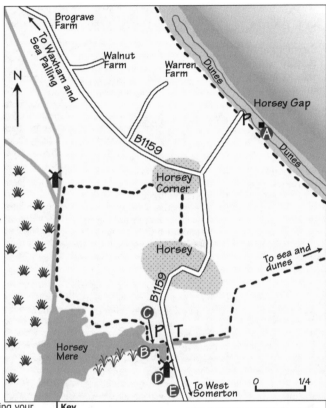

If you fancy stretching your legs, you have a couple of choices. Park in Horsey Mill car park, then cross the main road along the permissive footpath directly to the dunes (a permissive footpath is one that is permitted for use by the owner).

Scan the fields on the way for Cranes and raptors plus Winter thrushes, Meadow Pipits, Sky Larks, waders, etc. Once you have reached the dunes, you can walk left or right along the footpath, or down to the sea. Left is to Horsey Gap, right is to Winterton Dunes.

• **Continues overleaf.**

Key
A - Pill box good for Stonechat
B - Viewpoint for wheelchair users
C - Mooring
D - Horsey Mill
E - Lay-by for raptor watching

Access details

(Approx. ten miles N of Great Yarmouth).

HORSEY MILL: The car park is between Stalham and Martham on B1159, a loop road to the coast off A149 between Great Yarmouth and North Walsham/Stalham. The main Horsey Mill car park is well sign-posted on brown tourist signs about two miles

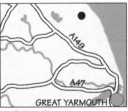

N of West Somerton.

HORSEY GAP: exactly one mile N of Horsey Mill car park. Heading N on B1159, there is a sharp left bend with a rough track to the right. This track leads to a large beach car park with access to coast and dunes.

Key points

- **Small shop at Horsey Mill for snacks and drinks.**

- **Boats for hire in Summer from shop at mill.**

- **Telescope recommended.**

Contacts

Warden
01493 394961

The National Trust, East Anglia Regional Office
01263 733471

General Broads Authority
01603 610734

Rowing boat hire
01493 393511 (£10 for half a day in 2001).

• **Continued from page 109.**

Horsey Gap is good for seaduck such as Long-tailed Ducks, Red-breasted Mergansers, Common and Velvet Scoters, or scarcer grebes such as Slavonian and Red-necked. You should also get reasonable views here of Red-throated Divers.

Along the dune footpath, you will almost certainly encounter one or two handsome Stonechats: the derelict pill box seems to be a favoured perch. A few Snow Buntings may be present on the beach during some Winters. Of course, you can also gain access to the coast by parking in the Horsey Gap car park (see Access section) and this may be a wise alternative in bitterly cold weather!

Alternatively, from the mill car park, you can walk past the mill to a viewpoint over the mere and reeds. This is an excellent place for wheelchair users to sit to scan for raptors, Cranes, wildfowl and Bearded Tits. The viewpoint is part of the new 'Easy Access' network of trails. The longer you sit here, the more you will see, with Marsh Harrier being virtually guaranteed.

Across the dyke from the viewpoint is a narrow, muddy footpath running along the northern edge of Horsey Mere, accessed from the mill car park.

Along this path, you cross a rough field, before going up a couple of steps to a raised bank. This does not give views over the mere but is a suitable place to wait for raptors and Cranes coming in to roost, though not as good as Stubb Mill.

This footpath continues to Horsey Corner, from where you can get back to the car park by taking either the road, or the dune footpath via Horsey Gap. The choice is yours.

The centre of attention at times of Spring and Autumn passage will be the dunes (as far south as Winterton and as far north as Sea Palling). I suggest you park in the Horsey Gap car park and explore the dunes and bushes as far as you wish.

Wheatears are seen regularly, as early as mid to late March, with Ring Ouzels not far behind. Bushes should be scanned for Redstarts, Wrynecks, Pied Flycatchers, Goldcrests, warblers, Whinchats, Tree Pipits, Red-backed Shrikes, etc. Anything is possible, so keep your eyes peeled.

Whimbrel may be passing overhead or stopping off in the fields around the dunes. Marsh Harriers will almost certainly be seen, but Hen Harrier sightings drop off during these periods. Barn Owl is another resident that can still be seen in the fields and dunes at these times.

Other nearby sites

Breydon Water, Burgh Castle, Buxton Heath, NWT Cockshoot Broad, Great Yarmouth Beach, Great Yarmouth Cemetery, NWT Hickling Broad, Haddiscoe Marshes, Halvergate Marshes, NWT Stubb Mill (Winter), NWT Ranworth Broad, Winterton Dunes.

At sea, the wintering ducks will be departing, being replaced by Little, Sandwich and Common Terns. In Autumn, the ducks return and the terns may well be harassed by passing skuas. All four species are recorded annually, although Arctic Skua is the most common. Other possible passage birds at sea include Razorbill, Guillemot, Manx and Balearic Shearwaters, Kittiwake and Little Gull.

Summer is probably the quietest time to pay a visit. Marsh Harriers usually show well in the fields across the road from Horsey Mill, but the Cranes will be very elusive.

On the mere, Common Terns are very active and noisy, and close views can be obtained from a boat (either your Broadland hire boat or from a hired rowing boat – see phone number in contacts section). You may also be lucky enough to see Bearded Tits in the reeds from the viewpoint accessed along the short footpath from Horsey Mill.

Reed and Sedge Warblers are common around the Mere, and *hirundines* sweep across the car park, dodging visitors as they go. Swallows even nest in the thatched toilet block in the car park. At this time of year they are sometimes pursued by a Hobby or two.

In the dunes, Stonechats are raising their families. Grasshopper Warblers can be heard reeling from nearby bushes but are hard to locate. Whitethroats and Reed Buntings are busily feeding their young and usually show well in the bushes along the dune footpath and around the Horsey Gap car park. At sea, terns are constantly coming and going while Ringed Plovers trot along the beach. Also look out for Grey Seals offshore.

The dunes in Summer attract a wide range of scarce species of wildlife including Grass Snake, Natterjack Toad, Emperor Dragonfly, Essex Skipper and Dark Green Fritillary and also many different varieties of plants. The all-round naturalist could spend the whole day in the dunes area of Horsey alone!

The sheer variety of species to be seen is worth the effort of covering this extensive area. In Winter, I tend to drive around, scanning for birds, or pull off and wait for an hour or two at a good vantage point. In times of passage, it can be an exciting place to explore to find your own birds – concentrate on hedgerows and bushes and you may strike lucky.

Views of perchng Merlin may be few and far between, but this small falcon is a regular sighting in Winter.

Key points

- **Part of Bure Marshes National Nature Reserve.**

- **Can only be reached by boat.**

- **Open between April and mid-September, (Sunday to Thursday, 10am - 5pm).**

- **Free temporary mooring for reserve visitors, free 24-hour mooring opposite at Salhouse.**

- **Admission £1 (includes guide booklet). Children free.**

- **Fully boardwalked.**

- **Two hides, both up sets of stairs.**

- **No dogs.**

- **Free binoculars in hides.**

- **Insect repellent advisable.**

Contacts

English Nature, Norfolk Office.
01603 620558

HOVETON IS a small scenic reserve which can only be reached by boat. A variety of common bird species can be seen on a stop-off during your Broadland boating holiday and there are many other attractions to make this a place to recommend for the all-round naturalist.

Target birds *Summer* - Common Tern (May to the end of July, 95%). *All year* - Marsh Tit (50%), Marsh Harrier (20%), Lesser Spotted Woodpecker (very secretive here, 1%).

Other likely bird species

All year		*Summer*
	Green Woodpecker	Cuckoo
Great Crested Grebe	Great Spotted Woodpecker	Hirundines
Cormorant	Pied Wagtail	Sedge Warbler
Common waterfowl	Goldcrest	Reed Warbler
Gadwall	Long-tailed Tit	Blackcap
Teal		Chiffchaff
Other common wildfowl	Other common woodland birds	Willow Warbler
Kingfisher	Treecreeper	*Occasional*
	Jay	Hobby

Background information and birding tips

HOVETON GREAT BROAD is a Site of Special Scientific Interest within the Bure Marshes National Nature Reserve complex. It is managed by English Nature, and is a very scenic place to visit when on a Broads boating holiday. While I would not pay £30-plus to hire a boat for the morning to visit specifically, as part of a holiday itinerary it is well worth spending an hour here.

I found it difficult to obtain accurate information about opening times, it being different in at least three places I have checked! You'll be pleased to hear the times given in Key points comes straight from the warden, so should be totally reliable.

Teal are among the common wildfowl species at Hoveton.

From the temporary mooring, you enter the reserve through a wooden gate (on the left as you stand with your back to the river). There is usually a warden present to hand out information leaflets and collect your entrance fee. It is then simply a matter of following the boardwalk around the reserve. This passes through a wet wood (alder carr), past a reed-fringed broad, and back to the river mooring.

One of the two hides overlooks the broad. Common Terns nest on wooden platforms on the lake and Reed and Sedge Warblers should be seen in the reeds and bushes around the edges of the broad. Common waterfowl and ducks such as Great Crested Grebe, Tufted Duck and Grey Heron. Cormorants are likely to be on show and and loafing gull species will include Black-headed and Lesser Black-backed Gulls.

The other hide is a good place to see common woodland birds and wildfowl such as Teal and Gadwall.

Numerous common bird species can be found in the woods as well as slightly more scarce species such as Great Spotted Woodpecker, Marsh Tit and Treecreeper. Lesser Spotted Woodpeckers are present at Hoveton, but during the period the reserve is open to the public, they are very secretive indeed.

All along the trail are information boards telling you about the creation and management of Hoveton Broad and, better still, there are lots of marked plants for ignoramuses like me.

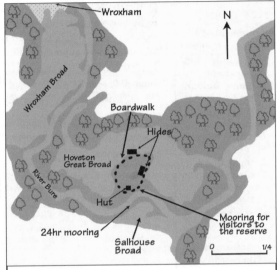

Access details

(Approx 6.5 miles NE of Norwich)

This site can only be reached by boat!

Follow the River Bure E from Wroxham for about 40 minutes. You will pass two entrances to Wroxham Broad on your right, and then an obvious mooring site for Salhouse Broad will come into view, also on the right.

Immediately opposite the Salhouse mooring is temporary mooring for visitors to Hoveton reserve on the left.

The reserve is packed with many scarce plants and dragonflies and makes for a very pleasant stroll for an hour or so. If nothing else, it makes a great place to practise your first mooring after collecting your boat from Wroxham, and to stretch your legs in beautiful surroundings.

Other nearby sites

Breydon Water, NWT Cockshoot Broad, Great Yarmouth Beach, Hardley Flood, NWT Hickling Broad, Horsey, How Hill Trust Reserve, NWT Martham Broad, NWT Ranworth Broad, RSPB Surlingham Church Marshes, Ted Ellis Reserve.

113

Key points

- **Complicated opening hours! Open daily from June – Sept (10am – 6pm. Car park closes at 6.30pm). April/May/October: Mon – Fri (11am – 1pm, then 1.30pm – 5pm); Sat & Sun (11am – 5pm). Check before you visit.**

- **Permit needed (50p in 2001).**

- **Terrain is level along muddy paths. Some gravelled.**

- **Walking boots recommended.**

- **No dogs allowed.**

- **Toilets available.**

- **Insect repellent advisable.**

Contacts

How Hill Trust
01692 678555

HIDDEN away in the Norfolk Broads, this superb reserve is easy to visit by boat or car for a very pleasant stroll through mixed habitats. Another Broadland site for the all-round naturalist.

Target birds *Spring/Summer/Autumn* - Cetti's Warbler (hear 55%, see 20%), Bearded Tit (45%), Marsh Harrier (30%), Little Ringed Plover (25%).

Other likely bird species

Summer		
Great Crested Grebe	Common Tern	Reed Warbler
Shelduck	Turtle Dove	Other warblers
	Cuckoo	Marsh Tit
Other common wildfowl	Kingfisher	Long-tailed Tit
	Green Woodpecker	Jay
Common waterbirds	Great Spotted Woodpecker	Siskin
Sparrowhawk	Sky Lark	Redpoll
Kestrel	Meadow Pipit	Reed Bunting
Oystercatcher	Pied Wagtail	*Occasional*
Lapwing	Hirundines	Hobby
Snipe	Common scrub birds	Lesser Spotted Woodpecker
Redshank	Sedge Warbler	

Background information and birding tips

THIS EXCELLENT, but often ignored, reserve is run by the How Hill Trust. The well-marked circular trail (about one and a half miles long) takes the visitor through many different habitats, each with its own particular bird species.

The car park affords a good over-view of Reedham Marshes, and it is worth pausing awhile for a glimpse of Marsh Harrier. The large grassy area here is an excellent place for a picnic and for active childrens' games.

Once you have purchased a ticket to enter the reserve from Toad Hole Cottage, the path cuts through a meadow, which is one of the best places in Norfolk to see Swallowtail butterflies.

Sedge and Reed Warblers sing from the bushes and reeds in this area.

A hide overlooks the Wolfson scrape where Little Ringed Plovers sometimes breed and Common Terns occasionally visit. Shelducks breed here, along with common waterfowl such as Mute Swan, Moorhen, Coot etc.

Reed and Sedge Warblers sing from the vegetation on the edges of this scrape from May to August. The bushes are home to the resident, skulking Cetti's Warbler. The latter species is rarely glimpsed but its explosive song can be heard throughout the year. Watch out for Bearded Tits in any stretch of reeds around the reserve.

The trail also passes through a

wet woodland (Gale Wood) where you should see Marsh Tit, Willow Warbler, Blackcap, Chiffchaff and many species of common birds. Further on, you will pass through an area of larger trees – a good place to see Great Spotted Woodpeckers and Jays. Crome's Broad is a favoured site for Common Terns and Kingfishers, and, if you are lucky, Black Terns and Ospreys on passage.

If you time your walk perfectly, you may see a Woodcock roding over the woods towards the windmills at dusk: a perfect backdrop for your evening picnic on the grass by the car park on a warm Spring evening.

Expect a pleasant hour or two's walk around a very nice reserve with many species of bird. Most are common but there is always a chance of something scarcer such as Marsh Harrier or Cetti's Warbler to liven up the visit.

The paths can get muddy, but there are some boardwalks and more substantial gravel paths for wheelchair users. In June 2001, some areas were inaccessible by wheelchair. Visitors should phone the reserve well in advance of their visit to ensure access is possible.

Other nearby sites

Breydon Water, Buxton Heath, Cantley Beet Factory, NWT Cockshoot Broad, Great Yarmouth Beach, Hardley Floods, NWT Hickling Broad, NWT Hoveton Great Broad, NWT Ranworth Broad, NWT Sparham Pools, RSPB Strumpshaw Fen, Ted Ellis Reserve, Winterton.

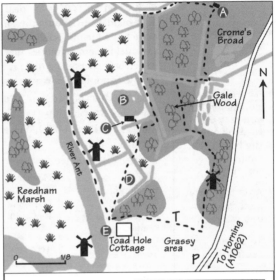

KEY
A - Hide
B - Wolfson Scrape
C - Hide
D - Meadow for Swallowtail
    butterflies
E - Mooring

Access details

(Approx. 11 miles NE of Norwich)

BY CAR: From Wroxham, take A1062 (sign-posted to Potter Heigham) through Horning towards Ludham. After crossing Ludham bridge (if you reach Ludham village you have gone too far) take left turn (sign-posted Turf Fen).

Effectively, this involves going straight on down a narrow lane where the A1062 turns sharply right.

Take second turn left, (just after red phone box), sign-posted How Hill. Follow lane to a sign for How Hill Nature Reserve and park in the car park for Toad Hole Cottage.

Walk across the grassed area towards the blue sign (similar to the one at the edge of the grass), then to the cottage to purchase an entry ticket.

BY BOAT: Head E from Wroxham on River Bure, then N up River Ant.

The reserve's mooring is sign-posted on right, just after third windmill (not counting the one at the junction of the Bure and Ant). It is a short walk to Toad Hole Cottage.

115

Key points

- **Food, toilets and other facilities in town centre.**

- **No walking necessary, but you may wish to stroll along the beach (i.e. sandy, flat terrain).**

- **Area regularly disturbed by dog walkers.**

- **Telescope useful.**

HUNSTANTON is an ideal place to base a birdwatching holiday. In addition to all the facilities you would expect in a bustling resort town, it offers excellent seawatching opportunities that are also accessible for wheelchair users. The town is the best place in Norfolk to see Purple Sandpiper in Winter and Fulmar all year round.

Target birds
All year - Fulmar (80%). *Winter* - Purple Sandpiper (75%), Eider (60%), Common Scoter (40%), Long-tailed Duck (30%), Velvet Scoter (20%). *Autumn* - Passage seabirds.

Other likely bird species

All Year	Gannet	Goldeneye
Cormorant	Skuas	Red-breasted Merganser
Oystercatcher	Guillemot	
Ringed Plover	Razorbill	Grey Plover
Sanderling		Skuas
Dunlin	*Summer*	Bar-tailed Godwit
Turnstone	Tern species	
Kittiwake		*Occasional*
Gull species	*Winter*	Scaup
	Divers	Snow Bunting
Spring/Autumn	Grebes	
Shearwaters	Brent Goose	

Background information and birding tips

AS A BUSTLING seaside town Hunstanton can be busy at all times of year. Though Fulmars are virtually resident, it is probably only worth visiting in Winter when it is relatively quiet - though even at this time of year dog walkers can disturb the waders on the beach.

My favourite birdwatching position is on the prom at the bottom of the cliff. From this vantage point, it is possible to sit in your car and scope the sea while Fulmars fly overhead, except for a short period from mid September to late October. From the sea wall here you also get a good overview of the beach and rocks.

If you wish, you can walk north along the beach for the chance of Snow Buntings, or south where the groynes have become renowned for roosting Purple Sandpipers at high tide (the ski ramp is a favoured spot). However, the sandpipers may get as far south as Heacham beach and Snow Buntings are irregular visitors, usually on the beach to the north of the prom. When the tide is out, Brent Geese feed among the rocks on the beach under the cliffs.

Alternatively, you may view the sea from the top of the cliffs by parking on the road near the lighthouse. This has the advantage of giving the viewer height to see birds at longer range, and the shelters can afford less hardy

Contacts

Hunstanton Tourist Information
01485 532610

seawatchers a degree of, well, shelter.

The number and variety of sea-duck varies from year to year but there is usually something out there. Red-breasted Mergansers, Great Crested Grebes, Goldeneye and Eider are the commonest species and up to 3,000 Common Scoter can range from here to Titchwell. Look out for the white wing-flashes of the scarce Velvet Scoters in among their cousins. Long-tailed Duck used to be very regular here but I haven't been as successful in recent years. The grass area by the shelters can be good for close views of Oystercatcher and Turnstone. Snow Buntings sometimes frequent the large grass car park by the lighthouse.

Hunstanton is always worth visiting on the way to other more illustrious sites to see if there is anything around. In Autumn, especially in strong onshore winds, you may be rewarded with sightings of one or more species of skua (Great and Arctic being the most common) or Manx, Balearic and Sooty Shearwaters. If nothing else, you will usually get fantastic views of Fulmars.

Hunstanton provides a good base for a birding trip. Members of the Hawaiian tourist board were so impressed during a visit to the town that they now recommend all Hawaiians pay a visit to "this beautiful place"! And who am I to argue?

Other nearby sites

Brancaster Marsh, Dersingham Bog, Gypsy Lane, NWT Holme Dunes, NOA Holme Observatory, Ken Hill Wood, King's Lynn Docks, NOA Redwell Marsh, Sandringham, RSPB Snettisham, RSPB Titchwell Marsh, Wolferton Triangle.

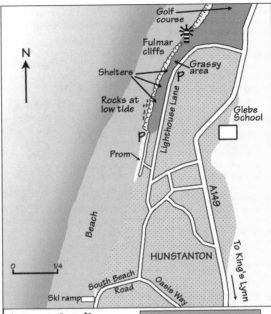

Access details

To the best birdwatching area, follow signs from A149 to 'Cliff Car Park' down Lighthouse Lane (B1161). Park along this road by the large grassed area, near one of the shelters and look out to sea from the cliff-top.

You may also continue towards the town centre, turning right down a small private road after the grassy area (signed 'private road, chalets only' opposite The Golden Lion Inn) – if you reach the main road you have gone too far. Parking here does not present a problem at off-peak times. Turn right at the bottom and park at the end for close views of the cliffs, beach and sea. This is excellent when the weather is foul or for wheelchair users. Walk N or S along the beach if you

wish to stretch your legs.

The jet-ski ramp (approx. TF 668398) for Purple Sandpipers can be reached along the beach by walking about a mile S (towards Heacham), or by car by following signs for 'South Beach and Car Parks' from roundabout on A149. Go down this road (Oasis Way), then straight over the roundabout onto South Beach Road. At the bottom of the short hill, turn left and park about 50 yards along next to a café. Walk up onto the seawall – this is the jet-ski ramp where the Purple Sandpipers roost at high tide.

Key points

- **Many small car parks.**

- **Level terrain on narrow peat tracks.**

- **Several possible Nightjar areas can be viewed from the car.**

- **Torch advisable.**

- **Insect repellent advisable.**

- **Many paths to explore – don't get lost!**

FOR A PERFECT site to end a Summer's day on the North Norfolk coast, head for this area of heath which is an excellent place to see Nightjars.

Target birds   Nightjar (75%), Tree Pipit (75%).

Other likely bird species

Summer	Sky Lark	Yellowhammer
Sparrowhawk	Meadow Pipit	
Kestrel	Hirundines	*Occasional*
Woodcock		Hobby
Tawny Owl	Common scrub birds	Long-eared Owl
Green Woodpecker	Common finches	

Background information and birding tips

KELLING is a large area of heathland famous for its Nightjar population. In my experience, these birds don't show as well as at other sites (Roydon Common, Salthouse Heath, Dersingham Bog, Sandringham) but it is a pleasant area to stroll around and find your own '*churrers*'.

This site certainly doesn't seem to attract many birdwatchers so you may find yourself enjoying the displays of these amazing birds on your own. The Nightjars start

'*churring*' just before dark but don't usually show until dusk.

Once you have found yourself a car park not occupied with a courting couple, you will find yourself with a choice of paths to explore. Any may be good for Nightjars, so listen for the first '*churrings*' and follow the nearest track, **but stay on the path at all times.**

From mid-May until late August, the heath is frequented by Tree Pipits. They are best located by their display song flight, which is Meadow Pipit-like but with a

Woodcock are hard to see on the ground, but begin displaying in twilight.

Contacts
None

diagnostic *'see-er, see-er, see-er'* ending. You should also see common species such as Yellowhammer, Green Woodpecker and Sky Lark. Summer's Swallows, Swifts and House Martins are sometimes hunted by a Hobby, with Kestrel and Sparrowhawk more commonly seen.

There is a slight chance of Long-eared Owl at Kelling, and some of the habitat looks good for Nightingale but I have never heard one here. Woodcocks are regularly seen roding at dusk.

At the southern end of the heath is a wide public footpath (signed on a wooden post). Wheelchair users can access the heath down this track in their car (with care). There is a small lay-by half way down where you can park and listen out for Nightjars. At the end of the track is a wide area in which to turn the car around.

You may get a bit of noise disturbance from the camp sites nearby. As an example, my last visit coincided with a brass band concert. If you are camping yourself, you might just be able to hear Nightjars from your tent/ caravan.

Nearby, Kelling Triangle (TG 090410) used to turn up the occasional Wood Warbler in Spring but they seem to have deserted the area. It may still be worth exploring in Spring for migrants though.

Other nearby sites

Blakeney Point, NWT Cley Marshes, Holkham NNR, Holkham Park, NOA Kelling Quags, Swanton Novers.

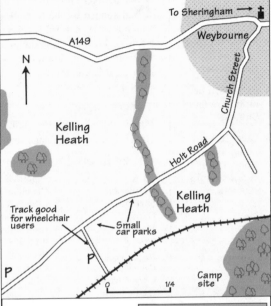

Access details

(Approx. seven miles W of Sheringham).

Follow A149 to Weybourne (about two miles W of Sheringham). Turn off immediately opposite Weybourne church, sign-posted Kelling Heath and NN Railway (Church Street).

Follow this road as it bends to the right and becomes Holt Road. In 0.7 miles, the road passes through a small wood, then opens out to gorse-lined hedgerows.

When you see the hedgerows, look for small, hidden turn-offs onto the heath. The second turn on the left takes you to a grass car park overlooking the

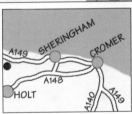

heath (good for wheelchair users to scan the heath).

Also on the left, there is a track marked 'public footpath' that you can drive down to park in the small lay-by along its length (approx. TG 101416). The track leads to the NN railway crossing where you can turn around.

On the right of the road is a large car park, also good for access to the heath.

Key points

- Public footpath, open at all times.

- Paths can be muddy even in Summer.

- Level terrain along a rough track, then steep shingle sea wall.

KELLING QUAGS is an often overlooked reserve managed by the Norfolk Ornithologists' Association which attracts several species of common breeding birds and a few rarities. Because the pool is small, the visiting birdwatcher can obtain close views of many birds, and because it is under-watched, you might just find something special for yourself.

Target birds *All year* – Barn Owl (50%). *Spring* – Sand Martin (95%), Garganey (20%). *Summer* – Little Gull (40%). *Autumn* – Passage seabirds, waders and migrants.

Other likely bird species

All year		
Cormorant	Sandwich Tern	Black Tern
Shelduck	Common Tern	Yellow Wagtail
Gadwall	Little Tern	Whinchat
Shoveler	Sedge Warbler	Wheatear
Kestrel	Reed Warbler	
Red-legged Partridge	Whitethroat	*Winter*
	Blackcap	Divers
Grey Partridge	Chiffchaff	Grebes
Oystercatcher	Willow Warbler	Brent Goose
Ringed Plover		Wigeon
Lapwing	*Spring/Autumn*	Sea ducks
Redshank	Shearwaters	Stonechat
	Gannet	Winter thrushes
Common gull species	Ruff	
Sky Lark	Whimbrel	*Occasional*
Pied Wagtail	Greenshank	Hobby
Meadow Pipit	Green Sandpiper	Winter raptors
	Wood Sandpiper	Short-eared Owl
Summer	Common Sandpiper	
Black-headed Gull	Skuas	
	Little Gull	

Background information and birding tips

KELLING QUAGS, or Kelling Water Meadows as it is also known, is a Norfolk Ornithologists' Association reserve. A hedge-lined track from the parking area leads down to a smallish pool. The hedges and surrounding fields are good in Winter for common finches and thrushes, and Whitethroat, Blackcap etc in Spring and Summer. The hedges should be checked for migrants in Autumn and Spring with Redstart and Pied Flycatcher possible.

In Winter, the pool and surrounding meadow hold small numbers of Gadwall, Tufted Duck, Wigeon, Shoveler etc along with Shelduck and loafing gulls.

This area is a good place to watch out for early arriving migrants such as Black Tern,

Contacts

Norfolk Ornithologists Association,
01485 525406

Garganey, Yellow Wagtail, Sand Martin, etc. Passage waders can include Greenshank, Whimbrel, and Common, Green and Wood Sandpipers.

During Summer, Black-headed Gulls raise their chicks on the island in the middle of the lake and Little Gulls can also be seen on the reserve from May to September. Sand Martins, House Martins, Swallows and Swifts should all be skimming for insects.

After the pool, the footpath splits into two. The right hand side cuts across a 'causeway' through a small reedbed and continues on to a shingle beach. The path straight on wends its way through fields towards Salthouse and Cley.

When walking across the 'causeway', listen for Reed and Sedge Warblers in Spring and Summer. From the beach, you can spend time seawatching. In Summer, Sandwich, Common, and Little Terns will be busy fishing offshore. From July to October watch out for Manx Shearwaters and all four skua species, especially in drizzly or foggy conditions with onshore winds. In Winter, look out for divers, grebes and sea ducks including Red-breasted Merganser, Common Scoter and Long-tailed Duck.

Infrequent visitors can get the impression that there isn't much to see at Kelling, but if you wait for a while something interesting usually turns up. The Quags have a track record of producing some good birds, the most recent being a Dusky Warbler in September 2001. In the Summer of that year, a Quail and White-winged Black

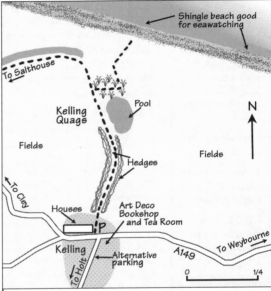

Access details

(Approx. 4 miles W of Sheringham).

On the Cromer side of Kelling village, turn right from A149 (immediately before the left turn to Holt, with the tea room/bookshop on the corner) onto a very small car parking area. Alternatively, park on road sign-posted to Holt, to the left of A149.

Wherever you park, take care not to block resident's

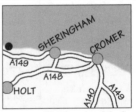

access and be very careful when manoeuvring as the parking is on a blind, double bend.

Follow the track down to the meadows and onwards to the shingle beach.

Tern stayed for a few days. The Marbled Duck that dropped into the reserve during May 2000 is still being discussed to this day as to whether it was a wild bird or a 'fence hopper'.

This is a pleasant one mile walk from the car to the beach and back with plenty of common bird species to be seen along the way. You may even find something special.

Other nearby sites

Blakeney Point, NWT Cley Marshes, Felbrigg Hall, Kelling Heath, Salthouse Beach, Salthouse Heath, Swanton Novers, NOA Walsey Hills, Weybourne.

121

Key points

- **Extensive woodland, with occasional views to Snettisham Marsh and The Wash.**

- **Free access at all times.**

- **Terrain is fairly level with some slight inclines.**

- **A 1.25 mile circular route, or explore as you fancy.**

- **Allow at least two hours to explore.**

- **Obey all 'Private' signs along the route.**

- **Paths can be muddy in Winter, or after rain.**

- **Dogs on leads.**

Contacts

None.

MIXED WOODLAND is a scarce habitat in Norfolk's coastal area, so this large patch situated between RSPB Snettisham reserve and Hunstanton, is well worth a visit. Ken Hill Wood is excellent for many common woodland bird species as well as one or two scarce ones. An added bonus is that you will meet very few other humans during your visit.

Target birds *All year* – Willow Tit (40%),

Lesser Spotted Woodpecker (March = 50%, rest = 20%), Crossbill (20%). *Spring/Summer* – Wood Lark (50%).

Other likely bird species

All year	Goldcrest	Hirundines
Sparrowhawk	Marsh Tit	Warblers
Kestrel	Nuthatch	
Woodcock	Treecreeper	*Winter*
Stock Dove		Pink-footed Goose
Barn Owl	Other common woodland birds	Winter thrushes
Little Owl	Jay	
Tawny Owl	Siskin	*Spring/Autumn*
Green Woodpecker		Redstart
	Summer	Wood Warbler
Great Spotted Woodpecker	Marsh Harrier	Firecrest
Sky Lark	Cuckoo	Pied Flycatcher

Background information and birding tips

CONSIDERING how many birders visit Snettisham, it is surprising how few are tempted to explore this wood. A walk at any time of year will produce encounters with common woodland birds, but you'll also get a nice view over to The Wash in some places, and there may be a few migrants to be found during times of passage.

Ken Hill Wood is a good place to see Crossbills, but as with any site, they can be extremely elusive. In some years hardly any are seen, in others they seem to be in every pine tree. Wood Larks have recently colonised one or two clearings and all three species of woodpeckers are

present. Lesser Spotted Woodpeckers are best seen in March and April when they perform their fluttering display-flight.

The route described below gives the visiting birdwatcher the best chance of connecting with the target species, though feel free to explore further as long as you observe the numerous 'Private Land' signs dotted throughout the wood.

From the car park, take the wide track at the back of the house, which soon narrows and bends into the wood. Not far along this path, there is a sign nailed to a tree stating 'Ken Hill Estates, dogs on leads'. Go through the gate here and you will see a field to your left. Stand at the edge of the field for an overview of The Wash. In Winter, this is a good place to watch Pink-footed Geese leaving their roost at Snettisham. From late February you should see a Wood Lark displaying over this field and, in Summer, watch the area for Marsh Harriers.

Once through the gate, follow the path keeping the field to your left and the wood on your right. After about 500 yards you reach a gate and an obvious barn in the field. Scan for Barn Owls, raptors, etc.

Bear right here into the wood (left takes you down to the coast). The path is fenced on both sides so you cannot go wrong. This area is probably the best for migrants in Spring and Autumn. Pied Flycatchers and Redstarts are regular visitors though neither are numerous. Yellow-browed Warbler, Firecrest, Red-breasted Flycatcher and Pallas's Warbler must all be distinct possibilities in September and October.

The path bears right, then eventually goes down a steepish hill. There are numerous side paths to explore in this area off to the right **(paths to the left are all marked private)**. As you continue down the hill, pine trees become more numerous, so listen for the loud *'chip, chip'* calls of Crossbills.

At the bottom of the hill is a narrow concrete bridge over a small creek. Do not go over this bridge (you will reach the A149), but turn right. About 150 yards after the bridge, the path reaches

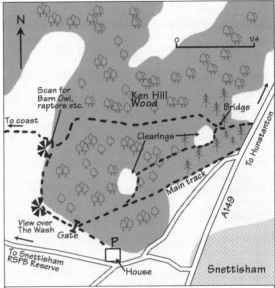

Access details

(Approx. five miles S of Hunstanton).

Turn off A149 between King's Lynn and Hunstanton at brown tourist signs for Snettisham Beach/ Snettisham RSPB. After 0.2 miles, on a left bend, is a house. The car park is behind this house, accessed through a red and white height barrier pole.

Take the wide track behind the house, which then narrows and enters the wood. Follow the paths as described below.

a T-junction with a wider track at a clearing. This is a good area for Treecreeper, Siskin, Coal Tit, Nuthatch and Great Spotted Woodpecker. Turn right to skirt the clearing, then into more pine trees. Not long after this is another clearing, which is a good place to see Green Woodpecker and maybe a Wood Lark.

Turn left at this clearing, then immediately right to bring you back to the gate with the Ken Hill Estates sign. Turn left back to the car park.

Adding the birds seen out towards The Wash and Snettisham, plus all the common woodland birds, you may well have seen 40 species on your walk, depending on the time of year.

Key points

- Free access at all times.

- All dock areas viewable from the road.

- Do not enter any fenced areas.

- Terrain is flat. Hedgerows viewed along a wide, rough track.

- Park sensibly! Do not block access for lorries.

- Low tide is best for gulls at the shellfish outfall.

WHILE this is not the most scenic site in Norfolk, it is *the* place to be seen among gull aficionados, as it has a reputation for attracting rarer species at any time of year.

Target birds *All year* - Glaucous Gull (15%). *Summer* - Yellow-legged Gull (50%).

Other likely bird species

All year		*Summer*
Cormorant	Common gull species	Common Tern
Common wildfowl	Sky Lark	Whitethroat
Oystercatcher	Meadow Pipit	Blackcap
Ringed Plover	Pied Wagtail	
Curlew		*Winter*
Redshank	Common scrub birds	Redwing
Turnstone	Common finches	Fieldfare

Background information and birding tips

KING'S LYNN docks may lack glamour but it is the area most often frequented by gulls and gull freaks! It has a good track record of producing a Glaucous Gull or two in Winter and one lingered here on and off all year in 2001.

Gulls sometimes loaf on the water in the dock near the weighbridge (20 yards into the site on the right). If not, they may be around the Fisher Fleet shellfish factory outfall, about 200 yards down the dock road.

The outfall, situated at the end of the dock road, is on the opposite bank to where you park, immediately before you reach the River Great Ouse. Look for a mud bank with a few large rocks scattered around. Low tide is best, when the gulls pick tasty morsels off the rocks.

In Winter, it is worth checking the River Ouse for common wildfowl such as Tufted Duck and Goldeneye, or maybe Smew or Goosander in harsh weather. In Summer, Common Terns fish the river, competing with the less dainty Cormorants.

The common gull species can still be found here in the Summer months, but this is the time of year when gull enthusiasts eye the flocks to

One or two Glaucous Gulls may be found at King's Lynn Docks in Winter.

Contacts

Associated British Ports: King's Lynn. 01553 691555

pick out a Yellow-legged Gull from its Herring Gull cousins.

If you enjoy impressing your friends by being able to tell an immature Herring Gull from an immature Lesser Black-backed Gull then this is the place for you (or the place to practise ageing gulls if you aspire to this feat). At low tide scan the river banks for waders such as Redshank, Curlew, Turnstone and Oystercatcher.

Though the Fisher Fleet area is relatively quiet, remember that this is a working dock and you should expect heavy lorries to be passing regularly.

After checking the docks, you may wish to scan the extensive hedgerows for common scrub birds (Dunnock, Wren, Robin, etc). Drive to the river, then bear right along a pitted, rough track. This runs for more than 1.5 miles alongside the river, bordered by hedges all the way. This area is especially worth checking in Spring and Autumn for migrants.

In November 2001, a Barred Warbler and a Serin were both present, showing the potential of the site (and demonstrating my potential for peering into dense foliage for hours on end without seeing these special birds)!

The track eventually leads to Lynn Point, which is a good area to find Brent Geese and wintering raptors but you are very exposed to the elements!

In summary, King's Lynn docks are worth a detour from the A149 at any time of year to see what is around. You never know, you might just find Britain's first Audouin's Gull for your efforts!

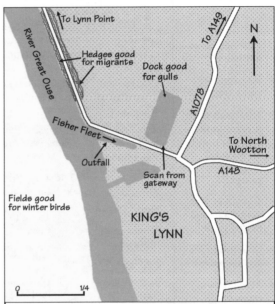

Access details

Follow signs for 'docks' leaving the King's Lynn bypass (A149) at northernmost roundabout onto A148 (sign-posted King's Lynn/South Wootton). At South Wootton, go straight through traffic lights, then the road becomes the A1078 (still signed to the docks). Follow this road for 3.8 miles then turn right into the docks, immediately before the sharpish left bend.

The dock on the right after 20 yards is good for loafing gulls. The Fisher Fleet is straight on from here, with

trawlers docked on the left, (if you reach the river, you have gone too far).

At the River Ouse end of the fleet, there is a small shellfish factory outfall, which is the best place for gulls. PLEASE DO NOT BLOCK THE ROADS. HEAVY LORRIES USE THIS ROAD FREQUENTLY.

Other nearby sites

Brancaster Marsh, Dersingham Bog, NWT Holme Dunes, NOA Holme Observatory, Hunstanton, Ken Hill Wood, NOA Redwell Marsh, Roydon Common, Sandringham, RSPB Snettisham, RSPB Titchwell Marsh, Tottenhill gravel pits, Wolferton triangle.

125

Key points

- **Free access at all times.**

- **Managed by the RSPB**

- **The Flash is on private land and can only be viewed from the footpath.**

- **Terrain is level along narrow, rutted path.**

- **Unsuitable for wheelchairs.**

- **At least two stiles to negotiate**

- **This will eventually become the largest wetland area in the country.**

Contacts

RSPB East Anglia Office
01603 661662

This site has become famous as a dependable place for Golden Orioles. There are likely to be many more species to view here in the future however, as the RSPB is creating an enormous wetland site, Lakenheath Fen, on the edge of the existing reserve, to encourage the return of Bitterns and Bearded Tits. Outside the reserve, the area known as The Flash, regularly attracts Black Terns and Garganey.

Target birds *Spring/Summer* – Golden Oriole (hear 80%, see 30%), Black Tern (50%), Garganey (30%), Wood Sandpiper (10%).

Other likely bird species

Spring/Summer		
Great Crested Grebe	Common Sandpiper	Sedge Warbler
Common wildfowl	Common Tern	Reed Warbler
Shelduck	Turtle Dove	Whitethroat
Common waterbirds	Cuckoo	Other warblers
Sparrowhawk	Great Spotted Woodpecker	Common woodland birds
Kestrel	Sky Lark	*Occasional*
Lapwing	Hirundines	Marsh Harrier
Redshank	Pied Wagtail	Hobby
	Common scrub birds	Lesser Spotted Woodpecker

Background information and birding tips

WHILE Lakenheath is already one of the country's best sites for Golden Orioles, ongoing development promises to turn the wetland areas into a site of national importance, too.

The RSPB intends to make this the largest wetland site in the country. It will consist of vast areas of reedbeds and wet meadows, with a view to attracting Bitterns and Bearded Tits, with poplar plantations for the orioles. Work on the site is progressing and already numbers of Reed and Sedge Warblers have increased along with Reed Buntings. The RSPB intends to open visitor facilities, including a car park and toilets, in two years time. When completed this reserve should be a superb place for birds and birdwatchers alike.

The Golden Orioles have nested here in the black poplars for many years, their numbers being monitored by the Golden Oriole Group.

From mid-May you will almost certainly hear the flutey calls of the males drifting from the poplars, but seeing one takes much patience. Their stunning colours blend in perfectly with their surroundings and you may have to wait quietly for an hour or two for good views of one. The most likely sighting will be a fleeting glimpse as an individual flies.

I suggest a very early morning

visit from mid-May onwards for best results. As the day wears on, the Golden Orioles become quieter, although one can occasionally be seen. It is best to position yourself opposite one of the rides in the wood where you can see the birds flying from one block of woodland to the next.

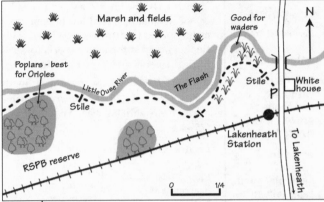

Once the orioles are feeding young, controlled viewing facilities at the nest site may be possible. This is a good way of encouraging birdwatchers to use this site, rather than drawing attention to the others.

Do not enter the woods under any circumstances. The orioles are very sensitive to disturbance, so please stay on the bank at all times. If you see anyone behaving suspiciously, report them to RSPB staff.

Walking to the poplars you will pass small patches of reeds where singing Reed Warblers will entertain you. Sedge Warblers will be singing from many of the nearby bushes and Whitethroats are also extremely numerous.

The abundant marshy pools, viewable only from the public footpath, are good for passage waders. After about half a mile there is a large flooded area across the other side of the Little Ouse River,

Access details

(Approx. 13 miles SE of Downham Market and 9.5 miles W of Thetford).

Situated off B1112 (Feltwell to Lakenheath road). From Feltwell, head S through Hockwold cum Wilton. Cross over a channel, then just after the next bridge (over the Little Ouse River) turn right into the car park. This car park is not very obvious, but is situated opposite a white house. If you reach Lakenheath station you have gone too far.

Walk back towards the Ouse

along a very short footpath, then bear left onto the raised grass bank (following the footpath sign, keeping the river on your right. If you reach the bridge you have gone too far). Follow this raised bank for about a mile and a half to the poplar trees.**

know as The Flash. Black Terns should be encountered here in May, and Garganey and Wood Sandpiper are recorded almost annually.

A Hobby may flash through, pursuing the many hirundines over the water, and Marsh Harriers are occasionally seen. Scan the far bank of The Flash for passage waders.

The poplars may also hold Lesser Spotted Woodpecker and Hawfinch but don't hold

your breath for a sighting. You should hear the gentle purring of Turtle Dove and Cuckoo.

For those interested in county boundaries, you will have to keep an eye on which birds you tick off for Suffolk and which you count for Norfolk. The Little Ouse is the county border, so the poplars are technically in Suffolk while The Flash is in Norfolk. For those people less 'sad' than me this does not matter one single jot!

127

Key points

- **Managed by Forest Enterprise.**

- **Terrain is flat, with hard paths and rough gravel/ grass trails.**

- **Wheelchair access is generally good, especially in arboretum.**

- **Keep dogs under control as several each year are bitten by adders.**

- **Toilets, with disabled access, are situated nearby at Lynford Stag (TL 814919).**

- **Excellent FC footpath map available (see Contacts section).**

Contacts

Forest Enterprise
01842 810271

High Lodge Forest Centre
01842 815434

PART OF the huge Thetford Forest in The Brecklands of Norfolk, Lynford has become the best place in the county to see Hawfinches in Winter, with a good chance of finding many of the area's speciality species (Nightjar, Wood Lark, Crossbill and Tree Pipit) in Spring and Summer.

Target birds
All year – Lesser Spotted Woodpecker (30%), Crossbill (20%). *Winter* – Hawfinch (40%). *Spring/ Summer* – Nightjar (90%), Tree Pipit (85%), Wood Lark (75%).

Other likely bird species

All year	Common woodland birds	Hirundines
Little Grebe	Nuthatch	Garden Warbler
Sparrowhawk	Treecreeper	Spotted Flycatcher
Kestrel		
Woodcock	Jay	*Occasional*
Tawny Owl	Siskin	Goshawk
Kingfisher	Redpoll	Long-eared Owl
Woodpeckers		Grey Wagtail
Marsh Tit	*Spring/Summer*	
	Cuckoo	

Background information and birding tips

THE ARBORETUM, set within the huge Thetford Forest area of Norfolk, is run by Forest Enterprise which maintains several tracks through the woods. Some of these are suitable for wheelchair users, others not, but most of the key species can be seen by those with mobility difficulties. Similar birds can be found nearby at the Lynford Stag picnic site, which also has toilet facilities, including ones for wheelchair users.

Between December and March Lynford has become *the* place to see Hawfinch in the county but they can be hard to find. To locate them, it will be easier if you are familiar with their *'tick, tick'* call. They can be seen in the tops of the hornbeam trees in the arboretum itself but patience is needed.

Early mornings seem best as the birds are easily disturbed when people arrive with dogs and children later in the day. Individual birders have their own favourite place to see Hawfinch: some tell you to head for the large trees in the field at the back of the lake, others to hang around the entrance to the arboretum. In truth they roam over a large area. This is also one of the best places to see Crossbills in Norfolk but numbers vary from year to year, and they can be very elusive.

At the back of the arboretum is Lynford Lake, which is good for common wildfowl and waterfowl. Many common woodland species also frequent the arboretum, and you should obtain good views of Green and Great Spotted Woodpeckers, Marsh Tit, Treecreeper and Nuthatch.

In Spring and Summer, I prefer

to park in the car park to the south of the arboretum. This car park gives you access to the colour-marked trails. Both the blue (1.5 miles) and the green (1 mile) trail lead you to the scenic west end of Lynford Lake, which is excellent for Summer visitors, including Garden Warbler.

The longer trail leads you up Sequoia Avenue, which is where I have had most success with Crossbills at Lynford. Watch out for them flying overhead, almost always alerting you to their presence by their loud *'chip, chip'* contact calls. Both trails lead to a bridge over the narrow part of the lake where you may be lucky enough to see a Kingfisher.

This southern car park is a highly recommended spot for Nightjar, Wood Lark and Tree Pipit. From the car park, turn right along the top of a meadow (good for butterflies) until you reach a wooden barrier. Go over the barrier (don't worry, it is to keep out cars, not people), and scan the clearing on your right for Nightjars in the evening and Wood Larks in the morning. Tree Pipits are most easily seen when they display during May and early June. Listen for their song which ends with a descending *'seeer, seeer, seeer'.*

Long-eared Owls breed in Thetford Forest but you will be extremely lucky to see one. The best chance is in May when the hungry young squeak to attract the attention of the adults. Goshawk is the other scarce species of the area.

The whole area is ever changing, as some parts of the wood are felled and previously cleared areas regenerate. Any

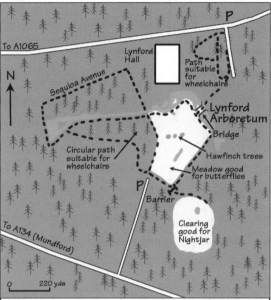

Access details

(Approx. 7 miles NW of Thetford).

Lynford is served by two car parks: On A134 (Downham Market to Thetford road) at the Mundford roundabout take the exit N to Swaffham. Then take first right turn, signed to Lynford Hall. Follow road past the hall to the car park sign-posted on the left (disabled drivers may park in the arboretum itself, signed on the right).

Alternatively, at the roundabout at Mundford

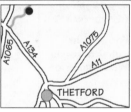

head S towards Thetford, but immediately take the minor road on left sign-posted to Lynford Lakes. Follow the road to the left turn, sign-posted to the lakes. Park in the designated car park at the end of this rough track.

clearing in the area should hold its own Nightjars or Wood Larks; they are there for you to discover your own special place! One such clearing is accessed opposite the minor road to West Toffs at TL 838879, an excellent spot for both Nightjar and Wood Lark.

There are also many areas to the south of Lynford which are worth exploring, though not covered here because they are in Suffolk (e.g. Mayday Farm, TL794834).

Key points

- Free access at all times.

- Managed by Norfolk Wildlife Trust.

- Site is a designated SSSI.

- Terrain is level along grass and mud paths. Can be wet at all times of year.

- Not wheelchair friendly.

- Mooring available at West Somerton (£2 per night).

- Facilities in public house in West Somerton.

Contacts

Norfolk Wildlife Trust
01603 625540

General Broads Authority
01603 610734

MARTHAM is a lesser-known Broadland site, close to Hickling and Horsey, which attracts many of the species associated with its larger neighbours. The two public footpaths that border Martham are excellent places to see wintering raptors, Bearded Tits and common wildfowl.

Target birds *All year* – Marsh Harrier (80%), Bearded Tit (55%), Cetti's Warbler (hear 50%, see 15%), Crane (25%). *Winter* – Common wildfowl, Hen Harrier (40%).

Other likely bird species

All year	Great Spotted Woodpecker	Other warblers
Great Crested Grebe	Sky Lark	*Winter*
Cormorant	Meadow Pipit	Pink-footed Goose (in flight)
Common wildfowl	Common woodland birds	Winter thrushes
Common waterbirds	Corvids	*Occasional*
Sparrowhawk	Common finches	Bewick's Swan
Kestrel	Reed Bunting	Whooper Swan
Common gull species	*Summer*	Smew
Barn Owl	Common Tern	Merlin
Kingfisher	Sedge Warbler	Peregrine
	Reed Warbler	Hobby

Background information and birding tips

I FEEL it is a great shame that Martham Broad is often overlooked, as it is a Norfolk Wildlife Trust site that offers some close encounters with many sought-after species.

A walk along the eastern footpath towards Horsey Mill should reward the visiting birdwatcher with good views of Marsh Harrier at any time of year, and the chance of Hen Harrier, Merlin and Peregrine overhead in Winter. Cranes regularly fly over at all times of year. If you catch the light right – early morning – you will get stunning views of some or all of the above species!

If you wish to see Martham Broad itself, take the footpath from West Somerton village. This footpath affords views over the water for close encounters with many species of common wildfowl at all times of year. You should expect Tufted Duck, Pochard, Mallard, Gadwall, Teal, Shoveler and Shelduck, though numbers decrease during the Summer months.

Bearded Tits show best at the southern end of the Broad, though usually only in flight. If you want closer views, go to Hickling Broad nearby. In the wood itself, you should hear a Cetti's Warbler or two if the sun is shining. They are more vocal in Spring, but I heard one here in November 2001. They can often be more obliging here than at other sites.

Scarcer visitors such as Smew, Scaup and grebes sometimes supplement the common birds at Martham in Winter, and Black Terns occasionally drop in on passage.

In Summer, Reed and Sedge Warblers take up residence, and Common Terns frequently visit the Broad. Having said that, Summer is probably the quietest time to visit, though you are guaranteed to see Marsh Harrier, especially from the north-eastern footpath.

This path runs north from the pull-in by West Somerton channel to the road, halfway between the village and Horsey Mill. Turn right (as the path reaches the road) to complete a circular route back to West Somerton, though watch out for traffic. It is very easy to forget about cars when a Hen Harrier is hovering next to you or a flock of Cranes is flying overhead!

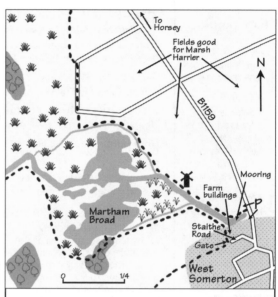

Other nearby sites

Alderfen Broad, NWT Barton Broad, Great Yarmouth Beach, Great Yarmouth Cemetery, Hardley Flood, NWT Hickling Broad, Horsey, How Hill Trust, NWT Stubb Mill, NWT Upton Fen, Winterton Dunes.

Access details

(Approx. nine miles N of Great Yarmouth).

BY CAR: **From A149 (Cromer to Great Yarmouth road) take B1152 NE to Martham (two miles S of Potter Heigham). Continue through Martham to West Somerton, then head N on B1159 towards Horsey. Park in one of the two large pull-ins by the channel, 200 yards after the tricky junction with the B1159 to Winterton.**

Take the waterside footpath to view the fields along the eastern side of Martham Broad (good for raptors), or walk back into West Somerton for about 75 yards and turn right into Staithe Road (best views of the Broad and reeds). After 100 yards, bear left past the farm to where the Tarmac joins a rough path. Where the grass path starts, turn right through a kissing gate to follow the southern side of the channel. This path reaches a wood in a quarter of a mile. Pass through another kissing gate and, after a further 100 yards, a narrow path runs through the trees to the water's edge.

BY BOAT: **For small craft only, as you will have to negotiate Potter Heigham bridge. West Somerton moorings are situated N of Potter Heigham bridge. You have to sail across Martham Broad to get to the moorings. Approximately a 40 minute trip from Potter Heigham.**

Key points

- Difficult to view the marsh from a wheelchair.

- National Trust Tower is accessed up steep stairs, but marsh can be seen from car park.

- Tower and toilets usually locked in Winter (*always* locked when I have visited).

- Pay-and-display car park.

- Arrive about an hour before dark for best results.

F AMED as the place from which to catch boats to Blakeney Point, Morston is not so well known as a fantastic place to stand and watch raptors and Brent Geese flying in to roost in Winter. Until now, that is!

Target birds *Winter* - Brent Goose (90%), Hen Harrier (75%), Barn Owl (60%), Merlin (20%).

Other likely bird species

Winter	Grey Plover	Rock Pipit
Great Northern Diver (in 2000 and 2001)	Other common waders	Meadow Pipit
		Pied Wagtail
	Common gull species	Corvids
Common waterfowl		Common finches
Kestrel	Sky Lark	

Background information and birding tips

T HOUGH rarely visited by birders in Winter, Morston can pay dividends for the patient viewer. The observation tower provides an excellent vantage point to view raptors on the marsh as they pass through to roost at Warham Greens. Hen Harriers tend to come into roost quite late on in the day, and Merlin is by no means guaranteed but there should be plenty to keep you occupied until they do appear.

For instance, in February 2001, I found a Little Egret here and was entertained by two Barn Owls hunting along the sea wall, one of which flew right over the car and landed on a post in the car park. Shortly after, several skeins of Brent Geese flew across the magnificent orange sky (or Norfolk Sunset as it is known to those privileged to witness it) to roost on the main channel. Sometimes birdwatching can be

Lapwings can be found in the muddy channels at Morston Quay and also in the nearby farmland.

Contacts

The National Trust
01263 733471

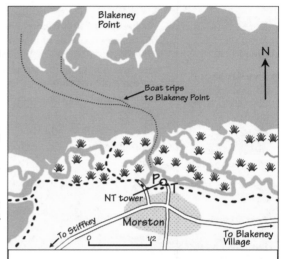

hard work, but experiences like that make the effort well worthwhile.

In recent Winters, Morston has gained a reputation as a reliable site to see Great Northern Diver. One occasionally winters in the main Blakeney Channel. Views can be distant from the car park, but you can walk out onto the marsh along a muddy footpath to get closer.

The muddy channels close to the observation tower provide good views of Redshank, Curlew, Ringed Plover, Grey Plover, Dunlin and Lapwing when the tide is out. I had a pleasant surprise in January 2001 when I found a Greenshank feeding in one such creek. Was it an early arrival or hardy wintering individual?

If you do walk along the paths, watch out for feeding flocks of finches and larks. There is a chance that you may encounter Twite or Rock Pipits mixed in with the Sky Larks and finch flocks. You can walk out onto the marsh, east towards Blakeney harbour or west towards Stiffkey. If you take the latter route, after about a mile, you reach what is called Stiffkey Fen. This is a privately owned area of flooded fields, which attract passage waders, (such as, Wood, Common, Curlew and Green Sandpipers, Little Stint, Whimbrel and Greenshank) in Spring and Autumn. It is also a favoured haunt of Garganey in Spring.

In Summer, the area becomes crowded with holidaymakers and boaters and is probably best avoided unless you wish to catch a boat out to Blakeney Point for

Access details

(Approx. 9.6 miles W of Sheringham).

About two miles W of Blakeney village on A149, Morston Quay is sign-posted on a brown tourist sign. Follow rough track to pay-and-display car park, watching out for some vicious speed humps.

The National Trust watch tower overlooks the marsh and creeks, but unfortunately this is locked in Winter, as are the toilets. However, a balcony on the tower provides a good

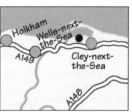

vantage point to watch raptors and geese coming in to roost. For those wishing to stretch their legs, footpaths run east to Blakeney and west to Stiffkey from the car park along the raised sea wall (slightly raised grass bank would be a better description).

the seal and tern colonies (highly recommended).

In summary, this is an excellent place for a quiet hour's birding on a fine Winter's evening and it should produce one or two goodies. It would be even better if the National Trust

opened the observation tower more often to allow us to get out of the biting wind.

Other nearby sites

NWT Cley Marshes, Felbrigg Hall, Holkham NNR, Holkham Park, Salthouse Beach, Stiffkey Fen, NOA Walsey Hills.

Key points

- **Access at all times.**

- **Park sensibly – all roads heavily used by gravel lorries.**

- **Be careful of heavy trucks in the bridge area.**

- **Telescope very useful.**

- **Best to arrive early in Summer, as the Leisure Park area is busy with holidaymakers.**

- **Viewing the Leisure Lake is from the road, so wheelchair access is good.**

VIEWS OF THIS working gravel pit – renowned for its breeding Little Ringed Plovers, Sand Martins and Nightingales – can be obtained from a public footpath alongside the River Nar. At other times of year, common waterfowl dominate the scene. The lakes at the Pentney caravan site hold common waterbirds, including Egyptian Geese, which can be scanned from the road.

Target birds *All year* – Common wildfowl (100%). *Summer* – Sand Martin (100%), Little Ringed Plover (50%), Nightingale (hear 30%, see 5%). *Spring/Autumn* – Passage waders.

Other likely bird species

All year	Sky Lark	Winter thrushes
Great Crested Grebe	Pied Wagtail	
Cormorant	Common scrub birds	*Spring/Autumn*
Egyptian Goose	Corvids	Ringed Plover
Common wildfowl	Bullfinch	Little Stint
Common waterbirds	Other common finches	Curlew Sandpiper
Sparrowhawk	Yellowhammer	Ruff
Kestrel		Whimbrel
Common gull species	*Summer*	Greenshank
Kingfisher	Common Tern	Green Sandpiper
Green Woodpecker	Hirundines	Wood Sandpiper
Great Spotted Woodpecker	Warblers	Common Sandpiper
		Black Tern
	Winter	Yellow Wagtail
	Goldeneye	
		Occasional
		Hobby

Background information and birding tips

A CASUAL glance might suggest Pentney Pits has little to offer birdwatchers, but it is worth a diversion off the A47 at all times of year.

The main workings can be viewed from the track running east from High Bridge along the road between Wormegay and Blackborough. The gravel workings are home to breeding Little Ringed Plovers and Sand Martins. The pits also attract passage waders such as Dunlin, Ruff, Green and Curlew Sandpipers in Spring and Autumn.

Throughout the year, the pits are home to many species of common wildfowl (including Egyptian Geese), waterbirds, and hundreds of gulls (which feed on nearby Blackborough tip). The path alongside the River Nar can be muddy at all times of year. The river may produce common wildfowl and Kingfisher to liven up the walk.

The pit by the Leisure Lakes can be viewed from the verge opposite the track to Ashwood Lodge. In

Contacts

None

Summer look out for Little Ringed Plovers and Sand Martins as well as the commoner House Martins, Swallows and Swifts. Egyptian Geese breed here as do many common waterbirds (Coots, Moorhens, Mallards, etc). The field between the verge and lake can be good for finches and buntings, especially in Winter, as can the hedgerows all along the road.

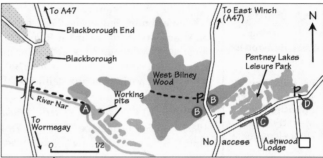

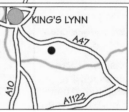

In Winter the lake holds Tufted Duck, Pochard, Goldeneye, Shoveler, etc and in Autumn keep an eye on the muddy edges for passage waders such as Greenshank, Green and Common Sandpipers. Yellow Wagtails also frequent the pool's edges on passage.

This area is best visited early in the morning before the holiday-makers have stirred from their caravans. Be warned that lorries use this road at all times of the day, and travel at a fair rate of knots.

Nightingales are declining here but there were still nine singing males found during the last full survey taken in 1999. One was also reported to be singing in April 2002. The trick is to drive slowly along the road – from late April to late May – listening for their beautiful song.

In recent years I have heard them from the thick bushes around the entrance to the Leisure Park, and around the car park (lay-by) for West Bilney Wood (see grid reference in

Key
A Viewpoint for working pits
B Cover for Nightingales
C Hedgerows along roadside
D Viewpoint for Pentney Lakes
   (suitable for wheelchairs)

Access details

(Approx. 5.5 miles SE of King's Lynn).

WORKING PITS: Take A47 Norwich road from King's Lynn, and after 2.5 miles turn right at Middleton, sign-posted Blackborough. Follow signs for the delightfully-named Wormegay, through Blackborough End and Blackborough.

Half a mile outside Blackborough, park in the lay-by by the bridge over the River Nar. Walk E for half a mile along a rough, muddy track to view Pentney gravel workings.

CARAVAN SITE LAKES: Take A47 Norwich road from King's Lynn and after about 4.5 miles take the minor

road off to the right following the brown tourist signs for 'Pentney Lakes'. Follow to the entrance of Pentney Lakes Leisure Park. The area of bushes just before this entrance used to be good for Nightingales, as did the area around the sandy pull-in for West Bilney Wood (TF 699133).

To view the pits, go past the Leisure Park entrance and turn left at the sharp bend by the house (straight on is access for lorries only). After one mile, park on the left-hand verge opposite track to Ashwood Lodge (if you reach the ancient cross on the right you have gone too far). View the pits from the verge but beware of heavy lorries.

Access panel above). The walk from this lay-by, through the pine forest, is also good for Goldcrest, Siskin, Coal Tit, Tawny Owl, Great Spotted Woodpecker, Treecreeper and other common woodland species.

Other nearby sites

Dersingham Bog, Gypsy Lane, NWT Holme Dunes, NOA Holme Observatory, Hunstanton, King's Lynn Docks, NOA Redwell Marsh, Roydon Common, Sandringham, RSPB Snettisham, RSPB Titchwell.

Key points

- **Free parking near Ranworth Staithe.**

- **No toilets on site – use block opposite the Maltster pub (wheelchair accessible).**

- **Level terrain, fully wheelchair accessible.**

- **Visitor centre open April to October (10am-5pm), trail open at all times.**

- **Groups should book in advance.**

- **No cycling or dogs.**

- **Electric boat from Ranworth Staithe to the visitor centre.**

- **Play area, book sales, sightings board, snacks at centre.**

Contacts

Norfolk Wildlife Trust
01603 625540

Broadland Conservation Centre, Ranworth
01603 270479

General Broads Authority
01603 610734

VISIT NWT Ranworth Broad for a pleasant diversion on a boating holiday on The Norfolk Broads. There is an impressive visitor centre at Ranworth, accessed through an area of wet woodland, excellent for many common species. The reserve is a designated SSSI. You may also wish to take a trip from the staithe to the visitor centre on the electric boat.

Target birds
All year - Cetti's Warbler (hear 60%, see 10%). *Summer* - Common Tern (100%), Marsh Harrier (15%). *Winter* - Common wildfowl (100%).

Other likely bird species

All year	Kingfisher	Hirundines
Great Crested Grebe	Great Spotted Woodpecker	Summer warblers
Cormorant (large roost)	Common scrub birds	*Winter*
Egyptian Goose	Marsh Tit	Wigeon
Shelduck		Gadwall
Common wildfowl	Common woodland birds	Teal
Common waterbirds	Common finches	Shoveler
Sparrowhawk	Reed Bunting	Pochard
Common gull species	*Summer*	*Occasional*
	Cuckoo	Lesser Spotted Woodpecker

Background information and birding tips

PART of the Bure Marshes National Nature Reserve, Ranworth Broad, managed by Norfolk Wildlife Trust, is a good site for wheelchair users to observe birds, insects and flora as the 500 yard trail is a boardwalk throughout.

The visitor centre, where Ranworth Broad can be viewed through the windows, is easily accessed by wheelchair users, though the upstairs viewing area can only be reached by steps.

There is a sightings board near the entrance so you can see what you missed on the way in. An ice cream goes down a treat here while you are watching the Common Terns rearing their young on the nesting platforms near the centre. In June 2002, an Osprey could be viewed from the visitor centre as it sat in trees on the Broad.

Once you have found the reserve (sign-posting from the car park could be improved), it provides a very pleasant stroll through wet woodland (known as carr) where you may encounter many common species, plus Cetti's Warblers singing from the thick cover.

In Winter, NWT Ranworth Broad attracts a large number of wildfowl but the centre itself is closed. This sometimes means viewing can be uncomfortable from the boardwalk

Access details

(Approx. 8 miles NE of Norwich).

BY CAR: From B1140 (Acle to Wroxham road), follow signs into South Walsham village. In village centre take the road N to Ranworth. Follow road for 1.1 miles to a junction of roads at The Maltster public house (pub on left, Granary Stores straight ahead). Turn right here, following signs to the Conservation Centre car park about 30 yards down on the right, indicated by a brown tourist sign.

Walk back to the pub and Ranworth Staithe. Look for a Norfolk Wildlife Trust sign indicating the start of the walk to the Conservation Centre (the electric boat to the visitor centre also leaves from this area). Follow boardwalk (adjacent to the road, running west) towards church to its end. Turn immediately right (do not go straight on to the church) and follow for 0.2 miles

to reserve entrance on the right (opposite a large white house). Follow the boardwalk through the alder carr to the visitor centre.

BY BOAT: Head W from Wroxham along River Bure, through Horning, and moor up at Ranworth Staithe. The reserve notice board is on the right near the shop. Follow the directions above to the visitor centre or catch

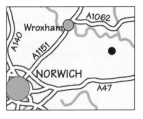

the electric boat from the staithe (small fee payable).

due to the lack of shelter, but can be worth the effort. The Broad is usually swarming with common water birds such as Pochard, Shoveler, Teal, Tufted Ducks and Great Crested Grebes.

All in all, there is something here for everyone. The reserve is also good for butterflies and dragonflies in Summer and a visit is usually an enjoyable one, though the trip might be made more endurable by

using insect repellent at this time of the year.

Probably the most exciting sight for birdwatchers is the roost of more than 400 Cormorants throughout the year.

Other nearby sites

Breydon Water, Buxton Heath, NWT Cockshoot Broad, Great Yarmouth Beach, NWT Hickling Broad, NWT Hoveton Great Broad, How Hill Trust, RSPB Strumpshaw Fen, NWT Upton Fen, Winterton Dunes.

Key points

- **Access for NOA members only.**
- **Access by key only (£5 deposit at the NOA Holme Observatory).**
- **Fully boardwalked for wheelchair access.**
- **Telescope useful.**
- **Fieldguide in hide for reference.**
- **Sightings book in hide.**

EVEN THOUGH access to the new hide overlooking Redwell Marsh is for Norfolk Ornithologists' Association members only, this part of the Holme complex is well worth making the effort to visit as Redwell has become *the* place to see Wood and Green Sandpipers in Norfolk in Spring and Autumn.

Target birds *All year* – **Barn Owl (90%).** *Spring/Autumn* – **Green Sandpiper (60%), Wood Sandpiper (40%).**

Other likely bird species

All year	Corvids	Whitethroat
Egyptian Goose	Common finches	Blackcap
Common wildfowl		
	Winter	*Spring/Autumn*
Common waterbirds	Brent Goose	Little Ringed Plover
Kestrel	Wigeon	Little Stint
Lapwing	Teal	Ruff
Redshank		Greenshank
Snipe	Other common wildfowl	Common Sandpiper
	Winter thrushes	Yellow Wagtail
Common gull species		
Sky Lark	*Summer*	*Occasional*
Meadow Pipit	Black-tailed Godwit	Hen Harrier
Pied Wagtail	Turtle Dove	Marsh Harrier
	Hirundines	Hobby
Common scrub birds	Sedge Warbler	Avocet
	Lesser Whitethroat	

Background information and birding tips

REDWELL MARSH has only recently been opened up to visitors by the NOA. The organisation has built a new hide and boardwalk to overlook the marsh and the hard work has been rewarded with records of some interesting birds. To gain access to the hide you must first obtain a key from the NOA Holme Observatory (directions on page 107).

The mud of Redwell Marsh proves attractive to many species of wader, including Common Sandpipers.

Contacts

Norfolk
Ornithologists'
Association
01485 525406

In the Spring and Summer of 2001, Redwell attracted numerous Green and Wood Sandpipers along with Common and Curlew Sandpipers, Ruff, Little Stint, Whimbrel and Greenshank. A few Yellow Wagtails regularly visit in Spring and are usually to be found around the hooves of the resident cows.

In Summer, small numbers of Avocets and Black-tailed Godwits may visit the marsh and, overhead, you may be lucky to see a Marsh Harrier or Hobby.

Winter brings an array of common wildfowl to Redwell. Expect to see Wigeon, Tufted Duck, Gadwall, Teal and Mallard. If these species become agitated, scan the marsh for Hen Harrier, Merlin or Peregrine.

At any time of the year, Redwell Marsh is an excellent place to see a Barn Owl. A vigil in the hide for any reasonable length of time should result in superb views of this special bird.

Finally, don't neglect to scan the hedgerow alonside the boardwalk leading to the hide. This can hold several bird species, such as Goldfinch, Greenfinch, Bullfinch, Linnet, Dunnock and Blackbird which may all be encountered at any time of year. They will be joined by Sedge Warbler, Blackcap and Whitethroat in Summer.

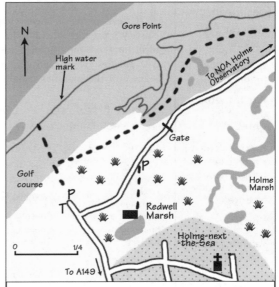

Access details

(Approx. 2 miles North East of Hunstanton).

From Hunstanton head E on A149 to left turn (sign-posted NOA Watchpoint/ NNT Reserve). Continue on this road for about half a mile, then turn right onto a rough track just before you reach the toilet block (note there are no facilities on site). Drive slowly as track is very bumpy. Go to the NOA Holme Observatory (see page 107 for instructions) to obtain a key

and follow their directions for parking.

Be careful not block the gate to the marsh as it will obstruct for wheelchair users. Follow the short boardwalk to the hide.

Other nearby sites

Brancaster Marsh, Gypsy Lane, NWT Holme Dunes, NOA Holme Observatory, Hunstanton, Ken Hill Wood, Sandringham, RSPB Snettisham, RSPB Titchwell Marsh.

Key points

- Free car parking.
- Free 24-hour mooring.
- Public footpath open at all times.
- Access along a rough track, but terrain is flat. Can be muddy after rain.
- One hide.
- Facilities in the pub when open.

Contacts

General Broads Authority
01603 610734

RSPB Strumpshaw Fen
01603 715191

HEAD FOR this pleasant reserve in Broadland if you are keen to see or hear Cetti's Warbler. This is one of Norfolk's premier sites for the skulking species. Rockland is ideal for those on a boating holiday though it is not teeming with rarities. The Broad itself supports many common water birds and the marshes usually attract a Marsh Harrier in Summer.

Target birds *All year* - Cetti's Warbler (hear = 80%, see = 25%). *Spring/Summer* - Marsh Harrier (55%).

Other likely bird species

All year	Meadow Pipit	Lesser Whitethroat
Great Crested Grebe	Pied Wagtail	Whitethroat
Common wildfowl	Common scrub birds	Blackcap
Common waterfowl	Corvids	Chiffchaff
Sparrowhawk	Common finches	Willow Warbler
Kestrel	Reed Bunting	
Common gull species		*Winter*
	Summer	Winter wildfowl
Barn Owl	Common Tern	Winter thrushes
Kingfisher	Turtle Dove	
Green Woodpecker	Cuckoo	*Spring/Autumn*
	Hirundines	Arctic Tern
Great Spotted Woodpecker	Sedge Warbler	Black Tern
Sky Lark	Reed Warbler	Yellow Wagtail
		Occasional
		Hobby

Background information and birding tips

ROCKLAND is a small and mostly overlooked Broad but has many delights to offer the visiting birdwatcher. It is probably my most successful place to see Cetti's Warbler in the county. And yes, I did say *see* Cetti's!

The birding starts in the car park where common species such as Chaffinch, Goldfinch, House Sparrow, Robin, etc can be encountered. In Summer, Sedge and Reed Warblers sing from the vegetation around the staithe car park.

If the area is peaceful, listen out for Kingfisher along the mooring channel. First thing in the morning is best. After about 150 yards, cross the first stile and linger awhile in the area as this is prime Cetti's Warbler territory. Their explosive song is readily heard but patience is needed to catch a glimpse of this notorious skulker.

After the stile, the path runs atop a raised bank. There are a few gaps in the bushes on your left where you can view Rockland Broad. Watch out for terns in the Summer and ducks in the Winter. Common Tern is most numerous here but Black and Arctic Terns pass through occasionally in Spring and Autumn.

The bushes and reeds along the path should also produce Sedge and Reed Warblers and Whitethroat. The marsh on your right is a good place to see Marsh Harriers if you are lucky.

Green and Great Spotted Woodpeckers inhabit the trees at the back of the marsh to your right, and they can sometimes be seen flying along the edges of the wood. Yellow Wagtails may be seen in the fields, especially in Spring.

After about a quarter of a mile there is a second stile and immediately after that there is a hide – managed by the RSPB – overlooking Rockland Broad.

This is the best place to view water birds such as Great Crested Grebe, Coot, Moorhen, Grey Heron, Mute Swan, Tufted Duck, Pochard, Gadwall etc. The windows at either end of the hide look into thick bushes and are excellent places to get a fleeting glimpse of Cetti's Warblers.

From here, the path wends its way through bushes, and continues alongside the marsh up to the River Yare. You may get closer views of Marsh Harrier here.

You can now retrace your steps to the car park or continue along the footpath, which rejoins the minor road at Claxton. You will then have to turn right along the road back to Rockland Staithe.

Personally, I walk to the hide then give up and return to the car. This short walk is about 0.75 miles long in total, the round trip to Yare/Claxton is about four miles.

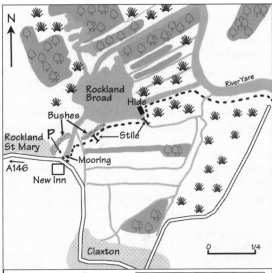

Access details

(Approx. 6.5 miles E of Norwich).

BY CAR: From A47 Norwich bypass, turn onto A146 (sign-posted Lowestoft and Norwich). Head SE on this road (i.e. away from Norwich) for about 100 yards until first set of traffic lights. Turn left to Bramerton. Stay on this minor road to Rockland then follow signs for Claxton (basically you are staying on this minor road throughout). Beyond the houses in Rockland, follow the small sign on left directing you to 'Rockland Staithe Car Park'. If you reach the New Inn, you have gone too far (the car park is almost opposite the pub). Do not park in the pub car park.

From the designated car park follow the path over a small bridge towards the pub. The footpath to the reserve starts after you have crossed the mooring channel and continues to the River Yare.

BY BOAT: The reserve is situated along the River Yare about half an hour's journey SE from the Brundall boat yards. Moor in the channel at Rockland Staithe.

Other nearby sites

Breydon Water, RSPB Buckenham Marshes, Cantley, Great Yarmouth Beach, Hardley Flood, NWT Hickling Broad, Horsey Mere, RSPB Strumpshaw Fen, RSPB Surlingham Church Marshes, Ted Ellis Reserve.

Key points

- SSSI and RAMSAR site.

- National Nature Reserve, managed by NWT.

- No facilities.

- Insect repellent recommended in Summer.

- Open at all times.

- Access along sandy tracks, which can be wet after rain. Mostly level terrain.

- Access very difficult for wheelchair users.

- A torch may be useful on Nightjar trips.

- Telescope essential for watching raptors.

HERE'S A Norfolk Wildlife Trust reserve that is equally good in Summer and Winter. Hen Harriers coming into the raptor roost can be seen from November to March, joined occasionally by a Merlin. In Summer, Nightjars show well at Roydon. The whole reserve is packed with rare and scarce animals, insects and plants, and is a fantastic place for the all-round naturalist to visit.

Target birds *Winter* – Hen Harrier (90%), Merlin (25%). *Summer* – Nightjar (90%), Tree Pipit (60%), Nightingale (10%).

Other likely bird species

All year	Great Spotted Woodpecker	Winter thrushes
Sparrowhawk	Sky Lark	
Kestrel	Meadow Pipit	*Spring*
Grey Partridge	Pied Wagtail	Hirundines
Lapwing	Jay	Warblers
Snipe	Common finches	
Woodcock	Yellowhammer	*Occasional*
Curlew	Reed Bunting	Barn Owl
Stock Dove		Long-eared Owl
Tawny Owl	*Winter*	Short-eared Owl
Green Woodpecker	Jack Snipe	Hobby

Background information and birding tips

THOUGH Roydon Common is a well known raptor roost, in recent years the number of Merlins reported has declined. Hen Harrier totals have remained stable and a visit here in Winter will almost certainly result in sightings of at least two harriers, along with Kestrels, Sparrowhawks and possibly a Merlin.

The standard procedure is to turn up an hour before dusk between late October and early March (though I have found December through to February to be the optimum period) and scan the Common. The harriers can appear as if out of nowhere, so be alert.

Keep a close eye on Carrion Crows as any raptors approaching is usually welcomed with a mass mobbing by these corvids. Hen Harriers normally head towards the back of the Common and fly around before landing on the ground to roost. I recorded three here in February 2001, including a fine male which came very close before landing in full view, hassled by Crows and a Kestrel.

Good numbers of Jack Snipe are present in Winter but unfortunately, you will not see them because the area they favour involves a trek in freezing cold water up to your knees !

In Summer, NWT Roydon Common is a good place to see Nightjars and in 2001, 14 *'churring'* males were counted on the reserve.

Contacts

Norfolk Wildlife Trust
Tel 01603 625540

Access details

(Approx. four miles E of King's Lynn).

FOR RAPTORS: From the King's Lynn bypass, take A148 towards Cromer. After approx. 300 yards turn right (sign-posted to Grimston and Congham Hall Herb Garden). After 0.6 miles, take the sandy track on the right (with the wooden public footpath sign). Park in gravel car park after 250 yards. From car park, walk through the new gate then along the sandy track for about 100 yards. Take the first track on your left (blocked by a huge log) which opens out onto a flat, grassy area that overlooks the Common.

FOR NIGHTJARS: (Also general access to the heath and bog) follow directions as above but after the new gate, take second track on your left (by the NWT Roydon Common noticeboard). Nightjars can be seen anywhere from this track. This track passes through the reserve then on to Grimston Warren, a newly acquired NWT reserve that is being restored to bog (currently no access but can be viewed from the fence).

FOR NIGHTINGALE: (TF 697228) Follow instructions as for raptors (above) but instead of using car park, travel further along the Grimston road to just before the road junction. There is a small car park on the right that is not easy to see (if you reach the road junction sign-posted to Roydon, you have gone too far). The bushes around the car park and the nature trail that starts from this car park used to be very good for Nightingales.

[Map showing To King's Lynn (A47), Gate, P, Pig field, Raptor watch point, Open area for Nightjar, Roydon Common, Nightingale area, Main track, Old railway line, Grimston Warren, Gate, Roydon, Pott Row, N, scale 0 – 1/4]

[Map showing KING'S LYNN, A149, A148, A47]

Take the main track onto the Common, but you do not have to go very far as the Nightjars can usually be seen as close as the junction of the two main tracks, approximately 300 yards from the car park.

During the day in Summer, Tree Pipits can be found on the Common. They are best looked for during May or early June as they give themselves away with their parachuting display flight.

One word of warning: the track down to the car park would have tested Rommel's tanks to the limit so those of a nervous disposition should park closer to the Grimston road and walk down to view the Common.

This used to be an excellent site for wheelchair users to see a raptor roost in action, but alas no more. The new layout has meant that cars cannot get to the flat grassy area which used to be so good for looking out over the Common, though it can still be reached on foot.

Nightingales used to be recorded regularly from the car park near the Roydon village turn-off, further down the Grimston Road, but are declining rapidly here.

All in all, this is one of the top 500 nature reserves in the country. You wouldn't believe the work that goes into maintaining the habitat for all kinds of flora and fauna. The result of all this hard work is that Roydon Common, as well as being an excellent site for raptors and breeding birds in general, is also host to an amazing number of rare plants, dragonflies and moths.

143

Key points

- **Free access at all times.**

- **Marsh can be viewed from the road so suitable for wheelchair users.**

- **Terrain is level along shingle bank.**

I**N RECENT** Winters, Salthouse has established itself as one of the most reliable places to see Snow Buntings in Norfolk, more often than not joined by a Shore Lark or two. The flood pools along the access road give the visiting birdwatcher the chance to obtain close views of common wader species, while the shingle seawall is a handy place from which to seawatch.

Target birds *Winter* - Barn Owl (65%), Seabirds (40%), Snow Bunting (25%), Winter raptors (20%), Shore Lark (10%). *Spring/Autumn* - Passage waders, passage seabirds, Lapland Bunting (5%). *Summer* - Marsh Harrier (80%), Little Tern (80%).

Other likely bird species

All year	Common Scoter	Temminck's Stint
Cormorant	Goldeneye	Curlew Sandpiper
Kestrel	Red-breasted Merganser	Ruff
Common waders		Whimbrel
Common gull species	Hen Harrier	Greenshank
Sky Lark	Merlin	Green Sandpiper
Meadow Pipit	Peregrine	Wood Sandpiper
Pied Wagtail	Guillemot	Common Sandpiper
Reed Bunting	Razorbill	Skuas
	Winter thrushes	Arctic Tern
Winter		Yellow Wagtail
Divers	*Spring/Autumn*	Wheatear
Grebes	Shearwaters	
Brent Goose	Gannet	*Summer*
Wigeon	Garganey	Sandwich Tern
Long-tailed Duck	Little Ringed Plover	Common Tern
	Little Stint	

Background information and birding tips

S**ALTHOUSE**, to all intents and purposes, is an extension of NWT Cley Marsh reserve, thus the range of species to be seen is similar to its larger, more illustrious neighbour.

In Winter, if you walk west towards Cley, you pass the area favoured by Snow Buntings and Shore Larks, known as the Little Eye (the small hump visible from the car park). Both species are regularly seen but neither can be guaranteed. If you are lucky, a Lapland Bunting may also be present in this area, though they are more usually seen on Autumn passage. The pools to your left should be scanned for common wader species, which may be joined by one or two Avocets in Spring and Summer.

Further west, look out for Barn Owl and Marsh Harrier. Up on the shingle sea wall, seawatching can be productive at all times of year. The terns, divers, grebes, ducks, shearwaters and skuas listed for

Contacts

None

Cley can all be seen at sea from Salthouse, at the right time of year.

To the east, you may follow the Peddars Way footpath along the shore to Sheringham, via Gramborough Hill and Weybourne, birdwatching all the way.

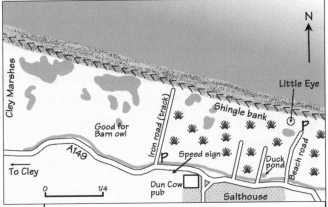

The road to the beach is an excellent area to watch birds at close range, but it is important to stay in your car to avoid disturbance. Waders can be very close to the road here, particularly, in Autumn. Little Stints are a speciality in September, while Green, Wood and Curlew Sandpipers can all give superb views. Redshanks are present all year round, possibly joined at migration times by a Greenshank or two. Whimbrels are regular visitors in Spring.

Winter produces Brent Geese and Wigeon in the fields along the approach road. Yellow Wagtails can be seen here in Spring and Autumn and don't forget to watch out for one of the rarer races (Blue-headed, Syke's etc) among them.

Some birders prefer to park in the Iron Road car park and walk down to the Little Eye and seawall. This is generally a quieter route (less people, not less birds!) than from the beach car park, but is essentially the same walk.

In between the Iron Road

Access details

(General area: approx. five miles W of Sheringham).

BEACH ROAD: On A149, heading to Sheringham, you will pass the Dun Cow pub (on right) then the duck pond (on left) after leaving Salthouse village. Take the next road left, (0.4 miles past the pub) signposted 'Beach Road', and follow this down to the shingle car park, scanning fields from your car to avoid disturbing the birds. If available, use a small lay-by just after you have turned off the A149 for scanning.

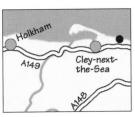

IRON ROAD: Park in very small car park off A149, 1.2 miles E of Cley NWT visitor centre (approaching from Cley, if you reach the 40mph signs as you enter Salthouse, you have gone too far). Walk down the track to the shingle seawall.

and Beach Road car parks, along the A149, is a small duck pond. This usually holds a few loafing gulls, predominantly Black-headed, and common ducks which love to be fed by children of all ages! Occasionally, a Mediterranean Gull joins the throng. This is also a good place to stop as you can feed yourself in the pub or shop and no, you can't count all the feral geese on your list!

Other nearby sites

Blakeney Point, NWT Cley Marshes, Felbrigg Hall, Kelling Heath, NOA Kelling Quags, Salthouse Heath, Sheringham, Swanton Novers, NOA Walsey Hills, Weybourne.

145

Key points

- **Access at all times.**

- **Park sensibly.**

- **The only walking necessary is along level Tarmac roads.**

BETWEEN MAY and August, head for the heath at dawn or dusk as this site probably holds the best watched Nightjars and Nightingales in the county. It is especially good for wheelchair-bound birdwatchers as all target birds may be seen from the road.

Target birds *Summer* - Nightjar (85%), Tree Pipit (May display flight 80%), Nightingale (hear 80%, see 40%), Wood Warbler (5%).

Other likely bird species

Summer		
Hobby	Great Spotted Woodpecker	Common woodland birds
Woodcock	Hirundines	Warblers
Cuckoo	Common scrub birds	Yellowhammer
Tawny Owl		

Background information and birding tips

THE NAMES of the two most noteworthy species to be seen at Salthouse Heath give a clue to their habits. 'Night' suggests that both species, Nightingale and Nightjar, are only to be found during darkness. This is not strictly true of course, but it is necessary to be on site at dawn or dusk for the best chance of locating either of these evocative species.

Nightingales arrive from about April 17, but I suggest you visit the Heath from a week later to be sure of connecting with one. I prefer to arrive around dawn on a mild day and listen for their beautiful, far-carrying song. It doesn't usually take long to locate a singing Nightingale, but seeing it is another matter!

The most promising place to look is in bushes lining the triangle of roads west of the crossroads where you park (see map). In early May 2001, I listened for an hour to a bird singing continually from thick cover three yards in front of me

without catching a glimpse of the little devil. Even more annoying was the fact that it kept moving from bush to bush and I still didn't see it! Eventually, I obtained good views, demonstrating the benefits of patience.

There are stories of more than one Nightingale singing in full view on trees that haven't yet developed their leaves (in April), but this is something I have never experienced. Yet. The junction of the triangle of roads at TG 071422 is supposed to be a good place for this.

Nightingales do sing through the day, especially on warm Spring ones, and in the evenings. This means you can turn up an hour before dark, listen to the Nightingales, then head back along the road for the chorus of Nightjars.

The Nightjars on Salthouse Heath are probably the most watched (listened to) in Britain. On most nights there are several people standing around waiting

Contacts

None.

for the first *'churrs'* of these birds. They arrive in mid to late May and entertain visiting birdwatchers until August.

Once parked, you need go no further. Male Nightjars should start *'churring'* on the Heath north and south of the road just as it is getting dark. If you are really lucky, you may see one perched in a bare tree while it does its vocal impression of a distant moped. This is probably more likely on the north side of the road, the bird being silhouetted against the sunset. What better way to end a day in Norfolk?

As the light dims, flying Nightjars can usually be seen over the road and a close encounter with a one is certainly a life-enhancing experience!

Please remember that both Nightingale and Nightjar are sensitive to disturbance so please do not chase after them or tape-lure them. If you see bad behaviour at this site, please remonstrate with the perpetrator.

Tree Pipits breed on the heath, but usually become elusive after they have settled down with a mate. However, during May they are easy to locate, thanks to their display song. Listen out for a song that ends with a distinct, descending *'seeer, seeer, seeer'.*

Finally, in late April to early May, listen out for the distinctive 'spinning coin' song of Wood Warbler. One or two may stop off in the wood here on passage, but they are not recorded every year.

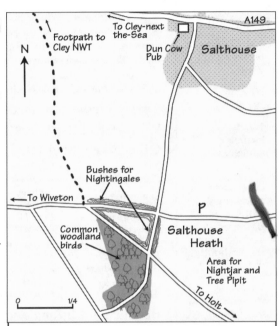

Access details

(Approx. 6 miles W of Sheringham).

From A149 turn inland (S) at the Dun Cow pub. After one mile, you reach a crossroads. Turn left and park on the verge wherever you can find a space. This is the area to hear and see Nightjars. For Nightingales, walk back to the crossroads and listen for their loud song. For either species, it should not be necessary to enter the heath.

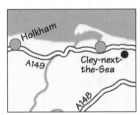

You may also walk from Cley NWT/Walsey Hills to Salthouse Heath (or vice versa) along the public footpath, signposted from A149.

Other nearby sites

Blakeney Point, NWT Cley Marshes, Felbrigg Hall, NOA Kelling Quags, Salthouse Beach, Swanton Novers, NOA Walsey Hills, Weybourne.

147

Key points

- **Some trails can be closed in Winter.**

- **Free car parking.**

- **Toilets, including wheelchair access.**

- **Level terrain along rough paths or roads. Nightjars along a rough sandy track, slightly uphill.**

- **Shop, restaurant and tea-room.**

- **Plants for sale.**

- **Children's play area.**

- **Picnic site.**

- **Bird hide (not accessible to wheelchair users).**

Contacts

Public Enterprises, The Estate Office,
01553 772675
www.sandringhamestate.co.uk
E-mail: enquiries@ sandringhamestate.co.uk

FAMOUS as the Winter home of the Royal Family, Sandringham is also the Summer home to Nightjar, and permanent home to many common woodland species of birds. The expanse of ancient woodland with easy access, coupled with several non-birding attractions, make this an ideal place for the whole family to visit.

Target birds *All year* – Lesser Spotted Woodpecker (25%), Crossbill (15%). *Summer* – Nightjar (90%).

Other likely bird species

All year	Sky Lark	*Summer*
Common wildfowl	Goldcrest	Cuckoo
Common waterbirds	Nuthatch	Hirundines
Sparrowhawk	Treecreeper	Warblers
Kestrel	Coal Tit	Spotted Flycatcher
Woodcock	Marsh Tit	
Tawny Owl	Willow Tit	*Spring/Autumn*
Green Woodpecker	Jay	Redstart
Great Spotted Woodpecker	Siskin	Wood Warbler
	Redpoll	Pied Flycatcher
	Other finches	

Background information and birding tips

SANDRINGHAM'S magnificent mixed woodland is home to many birds. A maze of footpaths through the woods can be accessed from the many parking places along the minor road to the main car park. The pines around the main car park are excellent for Crossbills. Be prepared to stand for a while (or sit in your car), listening out for their loud *'chip chip'* calls. Early mornings are best, when they may come down to drink from the puddles in the car park. I find the Jays are tamer here than anywhere else I know.

Along the approach road, look out for feeders hanging from the trees: these are great places to see woodland birds at close range, especially in Winter.

The colour-marked trails, (blue is one mile long, yellow two miles long), start from the children's play area to the left of the Sandringham shop. They weave in and out of the woods and are excellent walks to see common woodland species. All three woodpecker species are present but Lesser Spotted Woodpeckers are scarcest, especially when the trees are in full leaf. The best time to find them is in late March/early April when they are displaying.

The yellow trail splits from the blue one and leads to a hide overlooking a small pool. A few minutes here should produce good views of many common species and possibly a Crossbill flock coming down to drink.

The trails can be tricky to follow as the yellow and blue paint marks on tree trunks is sometimes hard to see. The arrows are sometimes ambiguous, too. If you go more than 100 yards without seeing a coloured spot on a tree, I suggest you retrace your steps.

The trails may prove difficult for wheelchairs to negotiate, but no matter, as there is a scenic drive that follows the general route of the trails and all species can be seen in this manner. There are also several flat 'rides' that pass between the trees and a tractor that carries tourists around the estate for a small fee.

From the end of May to the end of August, Sandringham is one of the best places in Norfolk to see Nightjars. My favourite area is accessed from a small, muddy lay-by at approximately TF 679273. Park here and take the path left for about 300 yards. You know when you have reached the right area because there are some telephone wires crossing the path. Nightjars like to perch on these wires!

If you cannot find my little pull-in, don't worry, most of the clearings in the area hold this evocative species. The area around the Camping & Caravan Club site is the best place to see and hear them. Follow the brown tourist signs to the entrance of the camp site and park in any of the pull-ins in the area.

Other nearby sites

Dersingham Bog, Gypsy Lane, NWT Holme Dunes, NOA Holme Observatory, Hunstanton, Ken Hill Wood, King's Lynn Docks, RSPB Snettisham, RSPB Titchwell Marsh, Wolferton.

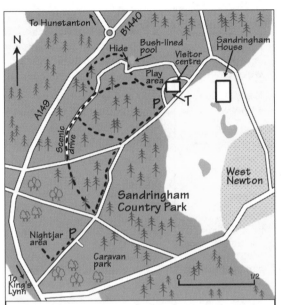

Access details

(approx. 6 miles N of King's Lynn)

The Sandringham Estate is well sign-posted from A149 (about six miles N of King's Lynn town centre).

Follow minor road down to the main car park (1 mile) or pull off wherever takes your fancy to walk into the woods. The 'Scenic Drive' is sign-posted off on the left of the access road.

FOR NIGHTJARS:
From King's Lynn take the 2nd right turn after the one to West Newton. The pull-ins on the right give access to prime Nightjar areas. You can also carry on down the road and turn right (sign-posted to the caravan site).

After half a mile, pull in to the verge on the right (with

a wooden barrier across the track). Walk through the barrier, turn left and follow the sandy track up to where it meets some telephone wires. The track on the right here is excellent for Nightjars.

From Hunstanton, turn off A149 left at the Sandringham brown camping site signs. The pull-ins along this minor road give access to prime Nightjar areas.

Alternatively, continue on road and turn right sign-posted to the caravan site, then follow instructions above.

Key points

- **Many paths accessible by wheelchair.**
- **Many trails to explore.**
- **Trail leaflet available from Forest Enterprise offices in village.**
- **Early mornings best for most species, except Nightjar which can be seen at dusk.**
- **Insect repellent advisable in Summer.**

MANY A HAPPY hour can be spent exploring the woods and clearings of this beautiful area in the heart of Breckland. It is a large area to cover but several sought-after species such as Nightjar, Wood Lark, Golden Pheasant and Hawfinch can be found in the vicinity.

Target birds *All year* – Hawfinch (25%), Lesser Spotted Woodpecker (20%), Golden Pheasant (20%), Crossbill (15%), Goshawk (5%), Long-eared Owl (1%). *Summer* – Nightjar (90%), Tree Pipit (75%), Wood Lark (75%).

Other likely bird species

All year	Goldcrest	Cuckoo
Sparrowhawk	Marsh Tit	Hirundines
Kestrel	Coal Tit	Whitethroat
Woodcock	Nuthatch	Garden Warbler
Stock Dove	Treecreeper	Blackcap
Tawny Owl	Jay	Other warblers
Kingfisher	Siskin	Spotted Flycatcher
Green Woodpecker	Redpoll	
Great Spotted Woodpecker	Yellowhammer	*Occasional*
Sky Lark	*Summer*	Firecrest (breeds occasionally)
Meadow Pipit	Turtle Dove	Hobby

Background information and birding tips

MANY OF THE scarce birds on offer here, for example Crossbill, Goshawk and Hawfinch, can be very elusive, due to the size of the area. However, Nightjars and Wood Lark can be very easy to locate.

I have given directions to the St. Helen's picnic site near Santon Downham, but many species can be seen from any suitable pull-in along the roads and tracks in the forest. St. Helen's picnic site, however, gives easy access to to many of the birds and has a few facilities, with more in nearby Santon Downham village.

The orange-marked trail from St. Helen's car park is a circular route, about a quarter of which is in Suffolk. Walk out of the car park on the entrance road and turn left towards the small church. The track bears left and goes under the railway line via a tunnel. Once through the tunnel, you can turn left along a wide track, or follow the orange trail signs almost directly ahead.

You should keep your eyes and ears open for Crossbills in the trees and Golden Pheasants scuttling in the pine forest undergrowth. In Summer, any clearing should be scanned for Wood Larks and Tree Pipits during the day, and Nightjars at dusk. Both tracks described above eventually reach a minor road by the railway line. Here the mixed woodland area on the left should be checked for common species and Lesser

Contacts

Forest Enterprise,
East Anglia Division
01842 810271

High Lodge Forest
Centre
01842 815434

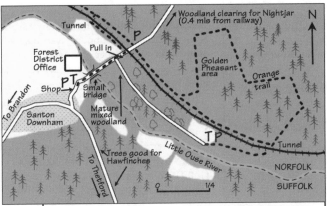

Spotted Woodpecker. Nearby, the bridge over the Little Ouse River is a good place for Kingfisher.

You now have another choice: straight ahead (following the orange trail markers) to more clearings, right along the road for Wood Larks and Nightjars, or left through the Forestry Office car park to the Suffolk side of the walk.

If you choose to go straight ahead, pass through the sandy car park, then through the barrier marked 'Protect Wildlife. Dogs On Lead'. This track continues for several miles alongside the railway line and gives access to many clearings, which are good for both Wood Larks and Nightjars.

You should also scan the sky at regular intervals for the chance of glimpsing a displaying Goshawk. Late February to late April is the best time, but they are very elusive.

If you don't want to walk far along this track, the orange trail bears left through a tunnel, about 400 yards from the barrier. Scan the meadow for Snipe and Lapwing and the creek for the rare Des Moulin's whorl snail. The orange trail then rejoins the road at the river bridge, continuing through Suffolk back to St. Helen's car park.

On the walk up the road

Access details

(Approx. 3.5 miles NW of Thetford).

From Thetford, take the B1107, sign-posted Brandon. Take the first right turn (after approx. 3 miles) signed to Forest Offices. As you drive down this road, keep an eye open for Hawfinch in the lime trees on either side. Follow this road to the Forest Office car park or continue to St. Helen's picnic site car park. For St. Helen's, go past the

offices and continue along the narrow road, cross the small bridge, then turn right immediately after this bridge (if you cross over the railway line you have gone too far). The car park is 0.75 miles down this road.

(right) from the railway line, after half a mile or so you will come across a large clearing either side of the road. This is the best area in Santon Downham for Wood Larks and Nightjars. Early mornings from February to May are best for the former species, and dusk from mid-May to the end of August for the latter. While you are waiting for the Nightjars to show, listen out for the begging calls of young Long-eared Owls, or the squeaks and honks of a roding Woodcock.

If you choose the Suffolk option, (the final third of the orange trail), you may wish to divert along the road to scan the trees for Hawfinch, particularly in Winter. The small churchyard you pass should be searched for Firecrest, though records are now few and far between.

Other nearby sites

Barnhamcross Common, NWT East Wretham Heath, NWT Foulden Common, RSPB Lakenheath, Lynford Arboretum, Wayland Wood, NWT Weeting Heath.

151

Key points

- A sheltered seawatching vantage point.

- Toilet block on the promenade, including disabled toilets.

- Early mornings or evenings seem best.

- Access via footpaths to flat terrace, perfect for wheelchairs.

- Some shelter available on the prom for wheelchair users down a steep ramp.

Contacts

None

I N THE RIGHT weather conditions – strong onshore winds with a bit of mist or rain – seawatchers intent on enjoying the offshore bounty can take advantage of sheltered accommodation. Especially good access for wheelchair users. The target percentages below are for when the conditions are ideal for seawatching.

Target birds *Spring/Autumn* – Arctic Skua (60%), Great Skua (40%), Manx Shearwater (35%), Little Auk in November (10%), Balearic Shearwater (10%), Sooty Shearwater (5%), Grey Phalarope (5%), Pomarine Skua (5%), Long-tailed Skua (3%), Leach's Petrel (2%), Sabine's Gull (1%), Storm Petrel (1%).

Other likely bird species

All year	*Summer*	*Winter*
Fulmar	Gannet	Red-throated Diver
Cormorant	Kittiwake	Wigeon
Common wildfowl	Tern species	Common Scoter
Common waders	Hirundines	
		Red-breasted Merganser
Common gull species		Auks

Background information and birding tips

SHERINGHAM'S Leas area is arguably the best seawatching spot in the county. In the right weather conditions (and sometimes even in seemingly unfavourable conditions), close views can be had of many of the passage seabird specialities.

From late July, Manx Shearwaters should be seen in small numbers with the chance of one or two Balearic Shearwaters passing, too. However, it is in Autumn when this spot can really produce the goods. Unfortunately, the best conditions for seawatching are strong onshore winds with rain or mist, which can make birding very uncomfortable. At Sheringham there is help at hand in the form of a large shelter on the prom with seats: luxury!

From this vantage point, and in the conditions described above, the hardy birdwatcher can settle down to enjoy some excellent seawatching. Anticipated birds include all four skua species, Sooty Shearwater and Sabine's Gull, all of which are seen with some regularity, especially in September.

If you are even luckier you may pick out a Leach's or European Storm-petrel, or something even more special such as a Fea's Petrel!

Tardy Common, Sandwich and Little Terns can be seen, as well as Gannets, Fulmars, Kittiwakes and common gull species. Common wader species are seen daily, and ducks on passage are usually noted too. In truth, the majority of birders here are

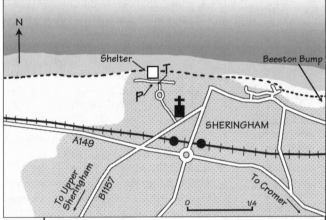

waiting for a biggie to come along (Fea's Petrel, Tropicbird, etc) but you will have to put in many hours to stand a chance of that happening - unless you are extremely lucky.

Late October into early November sees Little Auks passing in variable numbers. 2000 was a poor year, whereas 2001 was a reasonable one.

When seabirds are passing in large numbers, the atmosphere in the shelter can be electric as every few seconds someone picks out something new to test your ID skills. A quick glance at the TV weather charts the previous night should help you decide if an early morning trip to the prom is going to be worthwhile. However, if things do look promising, arrive early as the shelter can get packed full of fellow nutters, erm, I mean seawatching fanatics.

In addition to seawatching, the area to the east of the town, as far as Cromer, has become renowned as a raptor migration hotspot. In Spring and Autumn species can include Buzzard, Marsh Harrier, Sparrowhawk and an occasional Goshawk. A good vantage point is Beeston Bump at TG 168433. This site is also good for visible migration of more common species such as Tree and Meadow Pipits and winter thrushes.

Access details

(General area: Sheringham town centre).

From A149, turn into the town down Church Street, opposite B1157 to Upper Sheringham. Cross railway bridge and follow road to the church (about half a mile). Turn left into The Boulevard where you will find a small roundabout with a cenotaph on it. Take the second exit from the roundabout (dead end) and park by the concrete bridge straight ahead of you. This is

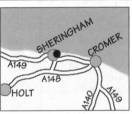

the area known as The Leas.

Walk through the arch onto a terrace, which gives a superb view of the sea. If the weather is poor, go down the steps into a shelter with seats.

Other nearby sites

Blakeney Point, NWT Cley Marshes, Holkham NNR, Salthouse Beach, NOA Walsey Hills, Warham Greens, Wells Woods, Weybourne.

153

Key points

- **Open at all times.**
- **Obey all 'Anglers Only' signs.**
- **Paths can be very muddy in winter.**
- **Three sets of steps to negotiate – otherwise flat terrain.**
- **Disabled drivers can park close to first hide by prior arrangement.**
- **Wader roost best 3-4 days either side of a full moon. Arrive at hide up to 90 minutes before high tide.**
- **To view geese at dawn or dusk avoid 3-4 days either side of a full moon when geese movements become unpredictable.**

VISIT SNETTISHAM at high tide and you will be treated to one of the great avian spectacles of Britain, if not the world. Thousands of waders swarm over The Wash in an ever-changing maelstrom of feathers (if only I were eloquent enough to truly describe the scene to you: you will just have to go and see for yourself!). Many thousands of Pink-footed Geese also roost on The Wash here, and it is a real treat to watch them depart to their feeding grounds at dawn.

Target birds
All year – Wader roost (100%), Barn Owl (60%), Short-eared Owl (10%). *Winter* – Pink-footed Goose (dawn & dusk, 90%), Peregrine (40%), Snow Bunting (30%), Scaup (20%). *Summer* – Avocet (90%), Marsh Harrier (60%). *Spring/Autumn* – Passage waders.

Other likely bird species

All year		*Spring/Autumn*
Cormorant	Red-breasted Merganser	Little Stint
Common wildfowl	Golden Plover	Curlew Sandpiper
Kestrel	Grey Plover	Spotted Redshank
Common waders	Knot	Greenshank
Common gull species	Sanderling	Green Sandpiper
Sky Lark	Black-tailed Godwit	Common Sandpiper
Meadow Pipit	Bar-tailed Godwit	Yellow Wagtail
Pied Wagtail	Winter thrushes	Whinchat
Common finches		Wheatear
Reed Bunting	*Summer*	
	Common Tern	*Occasional*
Winter	Hirundines	Bittern
Brent Goose	Sedge Warbler	Smew
Goldeneye	Reed Warbler	Montagu's Harrier
Hen Harrier	Whitethroat	Hobby
Merlin	Other warblers	Grasshopper Warbler

Background information and birding tips

ENSURE YOU get the best out of Snettisham by checking the time of high tide before visiting. If you catch the place at low tide you could be in for a very miserable visit!

The best time for watching the thousands of waders is at high tide three to four days either side of a full moon. This is because the Wash is a vast area of mud, and the sea only pushes the waders within viewable distances when the tide is at its highest. You should be in position at least 90 minutes before the high tide to get the best experience. The downside of a full moon is that for three to four days either side, geese movements become unpredictable, as the extra light allows them to remain on their feeding grounds throughout the night. Please view the geese from the Rotary hide as they can be disturbed by people standing on the bank.

Catch Snettisham at the right time and the spectacle of thousands of waders swirling through the air will leave you breathless. A number of species roost throughout the year, except in June, with numbers highest in Winter. It cannot be overstated just what a stunning sight they make. I urge you to witness this magnificent avian spectacular and marvel at the sheer number of birds present.

To reach the roost you have to walk nearly two miles through the reserve, though wheelchair users and people with mobility difficulties can take their car up to the first hide – Rotary Hide. This must be arranged with the warden BEFORE you visit.

You will pass several pits on the way to The Wash, which are good for Tufted Duck, Pochard, Goldeneye, Gadwall, Mallard, etc and several fields good for Barn Owl, thrushes and finches. The bushes and hedgerows hold common garden birds throughout the year, joined by Whitethroat and sometimes Grasshopper Warbler in Summer. In the Winter of 2001/02, a Bittern was seen regularly in the reeds surrounding one of the pits near the RSPB car park.

Once on the seawall, follow

Access details

(Approx. five miles S of Hunstanton).

Snettisham reserve is well sign-posted from A149's Dersingham bypass, 6.5 miles N of King's Lynn. Follow brown tourist signs for 'Snettisham Beach and RSPB reserve' down Beach Road. Continue for 1.5 miles to the signed car park on the left. If you arrive before 7.30am or after 9pm, you may have to park near the gate and walk through onto the access road. Follow the new footpath from the car park for 1.5 miles to the hides.

the wide track to the hides or the seats overlooking The Wash. Look out for Snow Bunting on the shingle in Winter. There is also a circular route that cuts across two pits and through a field of rough grass (good for Sky Larks, Meadow Pipits and owls).

The most numerous wader is Knot. In Winter they look plain grey, dumpy birds but if you visit in July/August many will show remnants of their red breeding plumage, whereas others will be grey. This gives the impression of someone

having paved the mud with pretty bricks, but a glance through your binoculars/ telescope will reveal thousands of Knot constantly shifting position as the tide comes in.

Also in the mayhem, you should be able to pick out Bar-tailed Godwit, Dunlin, Sanderling, Turnstone, Grey Plover, Curlew, Ringed Plover and Redshank. And the fun really starts when a bird of prey comes in to try to reduce the throng by one. The waders take to the air in huge, swirling flocks to unsettle the raptor.

- **Continues overleaf.**

155

● **Continued from page 155.**

Key points

● **Essential to check tide times before visiting.**

● **Wader ID charts in some hides, plus sightings sheet.**

● **Free car park for RSPB members, non-members £2. Honesty box situated in post along the path from the car park.**

● **Toilets open all year in beach car park (don't turn in to reserve car park but carry on to the end of road).**

● **Café open in Summer adjacent to car park entrance gate.**

● **Dogs on leads.**

Contacts

Snettisham RSPB Reserve Office 01485 542689

RSPB East Anglia Office 01603 661662

Check the shingle areas in Winter for foraging Snow Buntings.

On very high tide days, many of the waders come in to roost on the southernmost pit, affording excellent views from the hides surrounding the lake. This also give photographers ample opportunity to obtain close-up wader shots.

This pit is good for passage waders too, and in Summer, Black-headed Gulls, Common Terns and one or two pairs of Avocets nest on the islands here. In Winter, this pit is the favoured place for Smew and Scaup.

A Winter walk at Snettisham can be a very cold experience so wrap up warmly. On the sea wall there is no respite from the bitter wind but the old saying 'no pain, no gain' is usually proven to be well-founded. And don't be lulled into thinking Summer will be much warmer either: always be prepared for anything at Snettisham!

A final word about the beach car park area. This is reached by continuing past the RSPB car park turn off, following signs to the 'Beach'. There is no access to the reserve from here but there are many bushes around the car park which attract Grasshopper Warblers, common finches and scrub birds. There is also a good chance of migrants in Spring and Autumn.

In Winter, if you walk north from here, you can usually get views of Wigeon and other wildfowl on the marshy grasslands behind the second sea wall. You may also be treated to a good view of Pink-footed Geese flying over.

If you plan your trip carefully, Snettisham is *the* place in Norfolk, if not Britain, to witness one of the great marvels of the bird world; a mass wader roost. And that's not taking into account the 40,000 Pink-footed Geese flying overhead at dusk or dawn!

Other nearby sites

Dersingham Bog, Gypsy Lane, NWT Holme Dunes, NOA Holme Observatory, Hunstanton, Ken Hill Wood, King's Lynn Docks, NOA Redwell Marsh, NWT Roydon Common, Sandringham, RSPB Titchwell Marsh, Tottenhill Gravel Pits, Wolferton Triangle.

HEAD for these reclaimed gravel pits along the River Wensum if you want to add Grey Wagtail to your Norfolk list, though there are many commoner bird species on site. Local attractions for non-birding family members are the Dinosaur World or the Norfolk Wildlife Park.

Target birds *All year* – Egyptian Goose (95%), Grey Wagtail (65%). *Summer* – Common Tern (95%), Spotted Flycatcher (70%). *Winter* - Goosander (55%).

Other likely bird species

All year	Pied Wagtail	Lesser Whitethroat
Little Grebe	Common scrub birds	Whitethroat
Great Crested Grebe	Marsh Tit	Blackcap
Cormorant	Bullfinch	Chiffchaff
Common wildfowl	Other common finches	Willow Warbler
Common waterbirds	Common woodland birds	*Winter*
Sparrowhawk	Reed Bunting	Goldeneye
Kestrel		Winter thrushes
Common gull species	*Summer*	Siskin
Kingfisher	Oystercatcher	Redpoll
Green Woodpecker	Cuckoo	
Great Spotted Woodpecker	Turtle Dove	*Spring/Autumn*
Sky Lark	Sand Martin	Passage waders
Meadow Pipit	Other hirundines	Yellow Wagtail
	Sedge Warbler	*Occasional*
		Garganey

Background information and birding tips

SPARHAM POOLS is a Norfolk Wildlife Trust reserve, reclaimed from former gravel workings. The pits and surrounding habitats are home to many common species all year round and offer a peaceful alternative to the nearby tourist traps of Dinosaur World and the Norfolk Wildlife Park.

Once you have found the NWT car park, (and it will take you a little while), there is a circular path round the pits. You can't get lost as the path does not veer off, but leads you back to the car park whichever way you choose.

The track takes you through bushes and trees with occasional views over the pools themselves. Scan the islands in the pools for Egyptian Geese, Oystercatchers and Common Terns, which all nest in Summer. You should see plenty of common wildfowl whatever time of year you visit, though numbers increase in Winter. Shoveler, Gadwall, Mallard, Pochard, and Tufted Duck are joined by Goldeneye and Teal in Winter.

In the south-eastern corner of the pools, there is a working

• **Continues overleaf.**

Key points

• **Level terrain along narrow grass and mud paths.**

• **Not suitable for wheelchairs (though Grey Wagtail habitat is viewable from the road).**

• **Paths can be muddy after rain.**

• **Free access at all times.**

• **No facilities other than a car park.**

Contacts

Norfolk Wildlife Trust
Tel 01603 625540

- **Continued from page 157.**

gravel pit which may be worth checking for waders such as Common, Green, Curlew and Wood Sandpipers, Greenshank, Ruff, Little Ringed Plover, etc during migration periods. These new pits seem to be a favourite site for any gulls that may be around, though a telescope may be needed to see them well.

The field adjacent to the road, near the car park, should be scanned for pipits, wagtails and larks especially when wet. The bushes and trees on the reserve should produce many species such as Bullfinch, Marsh Tit, Long-tailed Tit, Siskin, Redpoll, Great Spotted and Green Woodpeckers, etc.

Fifty yards from the entrance to the reserve is the best place to see Grey Wagtail in Norfolk. They are resident around the bridge over the River Wensum, though can go missing for long periods. To view the area, walk to the bridge from the NWT car park, as there is no other parking nearby. In Summer, the wagtails are joined by Spotted Flycatchers around the bridge.

This is a decent site to spend an hour or two wandering around. The mile circular route should reveal many common species of birds, though the more often you can visit, the more you will see. It is the sort of place which turns up a really rare bird once every 20 years, and it is the dedicated 'patch-watcher' who will be rewarded.

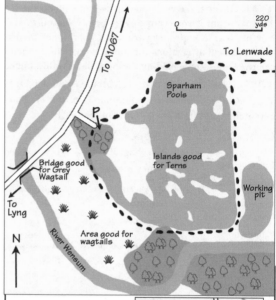

Access details

(Approx: 11.5 miles NW of Norwich).

From the Norwich outer ring road, take A1067 NW for approximately 11 miles (sign-posted Bawdeswell). A mile beyond Lenwade, turn left down Lyng Road (sign-posted Lyng) and continue for 0.8 miles (if you reach the river bridge you have gone too far). Turn down a narrow track on left to the car park (50 yards from the bridge). This is well hidden as the NWT sign is pointing towards Lyng village, so you will probably have to turn around at the bridge and return to find the car park

(look out for the wooden public footpath sign, also well hidden!).

Once in the car park, you can take the path signed with yellow arrows (slightly uphill at 11 o'clock as you drive down the entrance track) or bear right from the access track along a narrow muddy path. Ignore the path with the NWT sign as it doesn't lead anywhere.

Other nearby sites

NWT Alderfen Broad, NWT Barton Broad, Buxton Heath, NWT Great Hoveton Broad, NWT Hickling Broad, How Hill Trust Reserve, NWT Martham Broad, NWT Ranworth Broad, NWT Upton Fen, Winterton Dunes.

THIS AREA of saltmarsh owned by the National Trust produces some interesting birds throughout the year. The bushes and trees running east from the car park are magnets for migrants in Spring and Autumn, and the flooded fields further east (known as Stiffkey Fen) attract interesting species all year round.

Target birds *Winter* – Hen Harrier (75%), Barn Owl (60%), Rock Pipit (40%), other raptors (25%). *Spring/ Autumn* – Passage waders, passage migrants.

Other likely bird species

All year	*Winter*	Redstart
Cormorant		Whinchat
Shelduck	Brent Goose	Wheatear
Common wildfowl	Wigeon	Winter thrushes
	Merlin	Barred Warbler
Common waterbirds	Peregrine	Goldcrest
Kestrel	Golden Plover	Spotted Flycatcher
Common waders	Grey Plover	Pied Flycatcher
	Winter thrushes	
Great Spotted Woodpecker		*Summer*
Sky Lark	*Spring/Autumn*	Breeding waders
Meadow Pipit	Garganey	Breeding gulls
Pied Wagtail	Little Stint	Terns
	Ruff	Sedge Warbler
Common scrub birds	Whimbrel	Reed Warbler
Corvids	Greenshank	Other warblers
Common finches	Green Sandpiper	
Reed Bunting	Wood Sandpiper	*Occasional*
	Common Sandpiper	Marsh Harrier
	Yellow Wagtail	Pink-footed Goose

Background information and birding tips

THE VILLAGE of Stiffkey is surrounded by a variety of habitats that attract many bird species. The most obvious of these habitats is the extensive saltmarsh, with views out to Blakeney Point, which is home to a few species of breeding wader (Curlew, Lapwing, Redshank, Snipe, etc) and Black-headed Gull.

In Winter, the marsh is regularly visited by raptors and sometimes a Short-eared Owl. Dusk is probably the best time to see most of these raptors, especially Hen Harriers and Merlins which roost at Warham Greens, not far to the west of Stiffkey. Barn Owls may be encountered on the marsh at any time of year.

The footpath leading straight out from the car park across the marsh is a good one to find Rock Pipit in Winter. Twite and Snow Buntings are also sometimes seen.

The footpath running east

• **Continues overleaf.**

Key points

- **Free access at all times.**
- **Do not trespass. Obey all 'Private' signs.**
- **Terrain is level along muddy tracks.**
- **Not suitable for wheelchair users: view marsh from car park.**
- **Telescope useful.**
- **Facilities available in village.**

Contacts

The National Trust, East Anglia Regional Office
01263 733471

● **Continued from page 159.**

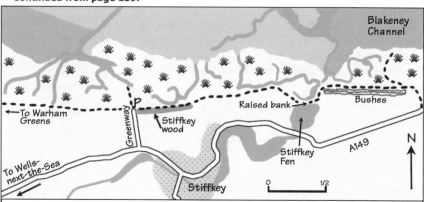

Access details

(Approx. three miles E of Wells-Next-The-Sea).

From A149, turn down Greenway (unadopted road) at the western end of Stiffkey village (first left in Stiffkey if

approaching from Wells). The car park is 500 yards down this track. Walk W to Warham Greens and Wells-Next-The-Sea, or E to Stiffkey Fen and Morston Quay.

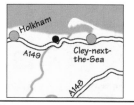

from the car park skirts an area of woodland that comes into its own during migration periods, when the trees and bushes attract migrants of many sorts. Redstarts and Pied Flycatchers are regulars, but rarities such as Yellow-browed Warbler, Red-breasted Flycatcher and Dusky Warbler are distinct possibilities.

About a mile and a half east of the NT car park lies Stiffkey Fen. The fields here regularly flood in Winter, making it ideal habitat for wildfowl such as Brent Geese, Wigeon and Teal and in February 2002, a Slavonian Grebe.

During Spring and Autumn, water levels may drop at Stiffkey Fen to reveal muddy islands that sometimes attract passing Garganey and in May

2002 there was a Red-necked Phalarope. Be sure to scan the muddy edges for passage waders such as Whimbrel, Greenshank, Green Sandpiper and Ruff. If water levels remain low during the Summer, Avocet and Oystercatcher may breed on the islands.

Please only view Stiffkey Fen from the raised sea wall as the whole area is privately owned. From this raised vantage point, you can scan Blakeney Point and Blakeney Channel for terns during the Summer. If you prefer closer views, you will either have to walk out onto the marsh along one of the muddy footpaths or catch a boat from Morston Quay (see Morston site page for details).

The footpath continues to Morston Quay, about a mile

further east. Along the way, scan the gorse bushes for common scrub birds all year round and migrants in Spring and Autumn.

Stiffkey is a fine site to find your own birds, as it doesn't seem to get the coverage of similar sites nearby. However, it can be a very exposed place, especially when standing on the raised sea wall as the wind here is very lazy (it cuts straight through you, doesn't go around). And that's just in Summer!

Other nearby sites

Blakeney Point, NWT Cley Marsh, Felbrigg Hall, Holkham NNR , Holkham Park, Morston Quay, Salthouse Beach, NOA Walsey Hills, Warham Greens.

PATIENCE is a virtue at this popular RSPB reserve which features many different habitats and is excellent all year round for a half or full day's birdwatching. Basically, the longer you stay on the reserve, the more you will see, though some of the sought-after species can be very elusive!

Target birds *All year* – Marsh Harrier (70%), Bearded Tit (70%), Cetti's Warbler (hear 60%, see 15%), Bittern (20%). *Winter* – Hen Harrier (25%) *Summer* – Grasshopper Warbler (hear 40%, see 10%), Hobby (25%), Garganey (25%).

Other likely bird species

All year	Sky Lark	Common Sandpiper
Great Crested Grebe	Meadow Pipit	*Summer*
	Pied Wagtail	
Cormorant	Common scrub birds	Hobby
Common wildfowl		Common Tern
Water Rail	Common woodland birds	Hirundines
Common waterbirds		Sedge Warbler
	Marsh Tit	Reed Warbler
Sparrowhawk	Willow Tit	Garden Warbler
Kestrel		Other warblers
Woodcock	*Winter*	
	Common wildfowl	*Occasional*
Common gull species	Redpoll	Lesser Spotted Woodpecker
Kingfisher	*Spring/Autumn*	Goosander
Green Woodpecker	Osprey	Spotted Crake
Great Spotted Woodpecker	Greenshank	Savi's Warbler (rare)
	Green Sandpiper	

Background information and birding tips

VISITORS to Strumpshaw Fen should be prepared to walk quite a distance if they wish to see everything on offer as it is a large reserve. It is a popular birding venue at all times of year with sought-after species being relatively easy to see – with patience.

Your walk starts at the visitor centre just inside the reserve. This is the only part of the reserve that is truly accessible for the wheelchair user. On view should be common water birds and wildfowl,

plus the chance of a Marsh Harrier. The dead branch protruding across the water to your right is a favoured perch of the resident Kingfisher.

My preferred route then proceeds through a small wood, home to several resident species of common woodland birds, and on to Fen Hide. This hide gives a view over the large reedbed and the main hide. It is also the best place to linger in Winter for any Hen Harriers coming in to roost.

• **Continues overleaf.**

Key points

- **Managed by the RSPB.**

- **Entry is free to RSPB members, £2.50p non-members.**

- **Open from sunrise to dusk every day except Christmas Day.**

- **Only one hide accessible to wheelchairs.**

- **Manned reception hide with updated sightings board.**

- **Toilet block on site.**

Contacts

RSPB Office, Strumpshaw
01603 715191
e-mail: strumpshaw
@rspb.org.uk

• **Continued from page 161.**

Access details

(Approx. seven miles E of Norwich)

Leave A47 Norwich to Great Yarmouth road at the roundabout sign-posted to Brundall. Continue along this minor road for 0.4 miles. Bear left at the sharp bend onto The Street (sign-posted Brundall Station). Negotiate mini-roundabouts and the traffic-calmed area until, after 1.1 miles, you go under a railway bridge. Look for the sign for RSPB Strumpshaw Fen, turning right (Stone Road), then immediately right again (Low Road). Continue to RSPB car park (muddy verge!) by the railway line. Walk across the railway line at the crossing to the reception centre.

OR: **From A47, turn S at signs to Cantley/Beighton (just where the road becomes a dual carriageway) into Lingwood village. In Lingwood, take the left turn (sign-posted to Station/Strumpshaw/Cantley & Freethorpe) along Station road.**

Continue past the station to a T-junction. Turn right to Strumpshaw/Norwich, along Norwich Road. Go into Strumpshaw village and turn left (at signs for Strumpshaw Fen and Household Waste Disposal

Key

A Best bushes for Cetti's
B Tower hide
C Visitor Centre
D Fen hide
E Summer meadow
F Pumphouse

Site) then immediately right down Low Road at the small brown RSPB sign (easily missed). Follow this road down to the RSPB car park.

You should also see Bearded Tit here at any time of year.

If the fancy takes you, you can walk through the wood along the Woodland Trail. This takes you to the River Yare footpath, where you can turn right to join up with the Fen Hide footpath. The walk alongside the Yare should produce Great Crested Grebes and Sedge Warblers in the bushes on the water's edge (summer only). Listen out too

for Cetti's Warbler here, though further along the trail is better.

Half a mile from Fen Hide is the Tower Hide, accessed up a steep flight of steps. The climb is worth the effort though as Tower Hide affords superb views over the whole reserve. Sit here for as long as you can, to increase your chance of seeing the more desirable species.

A long wait in Tower Hide

may produce a flight view of Bittern. This species bred at Strumpshaw in 2001, rewarding the RSPB's hard efforts to attract them. In Winter, the lagoons hold a good selection of common wildfowl, joined in Spring by a Garganey or two.

Once you have had your fill from Tower Hide, continue along the footpath by the River Yare. Very soon, this path bears right to run alongside a

Often heard, Cetti's Warblers can be hard to see.

Key points

- **Hearing Loop installed at reception centre for hard of hearing visitors.**

- **Terrain is level along muddy paths.**

- **Steep steps to Tower Hide.**

small stream called the Lackford Run. The hide that used to overlook a fine wader scrape has disappeared, but you can still see the scrape from the path. Be careful not to flush the birds.

The bushes along the Lackford path hold common finches, and scrub birds (Dunnock, Wren, etc) and also Cetti's and Grasshopper Warblers. In the Summer of 2001 and 2002, this was the best place to sit and listen at dusk to the strange call of a Spotted Crake or two.

Further along this path, you enter an area of what can only be described as a swamp, accessed along a boardwalk. This area, stretching a couple of hundred yards to the railway crossing, is the best place to try and see the Cetti's Warblers. They are easy to hear but

do like to hide in the thick cover. Be patient! Look out, too, for Willow Tit here.

Once you have crossed the railway line, take the wide track to the right back to the car park (past a cottage). This completes a long, circular route, which produces many common and scarce species no matter what time of year you visit. You should encounter at least a couple of the target species, but you may be unlucky and see nothing. The longer you stay, the more chance you have of seeing the birds.

Strumpshaw Fen is also an excellent place for other wildlife. In Summer, many species of dragonfly and butterfly can be seen along with many scarce plants.

Other nearby sites

Breydon Water, RSPB Buckenham Marshes, Buxton Heath, Cantley Beet Factory, Great Yarmouth Beach, Great Yarmouth Cemetery, Hardley Flood, Rockland Broad, RSPB Surlingham Church Marshes, Ted Ellis Reserve.

Key points

- £2 fee for non NWT members.

- Access road can be very muddy or flooded. Getting a wheelchair onto the viewing bank is impossible, but birds may be viewable from the end of the access road.

- NWT visitor centre closed in Winter, though toilets usually open.

THE BEST PLACE in the country to see Cranes in Winter, and Norfolk's leading site to see Merlin, Hen and Marsh Harriers is simply a slightly raised mud bank where you can stand to get panoramic views of the favourite roosting site of these four sought-after bird species.

Target birds
Winter - Marsh Harrier (99%), Crane (85%), Hen Harrier (85%), Merlin (75%).

Other likely bird species

Winter		
Pink-footed Goose (in flight)	Woodcock	Pied Wagtail
Wigeon (in flight)	Common gull species	Common scrub birds
Sparrowhawk	Barn Owl	Winter thrushes
Kestrel	Sky Lark	Jay
Lapwing	Meadow Pipit	Common finches

Background information and birding tips

HARDY birdwatchers are virtually guaranteed to see Cranes in Winter at this famous site, the only area in Britain where this is possible. It is also an excellent place to see Merlin, and Hen and Marsh Harriers as they come in to roost.

Arrive at the raptor watchpoint at least an hour before dusk and regularly scan the fields. The harriers and Merlins seemingly appear from nowhere so keep your eyes peeled! In 2001, up to 11 Cranes, 17 Marsh Harriers, six Merlins, and four Hen Harriers were recorded here, but my maxima were four, seven, two and two respectively. Also seen on a regular basis are one or two Barn Owls.

If it is raining it is probably worth postponing your visit. The birds still fly in to roost but I have found that they tend to hunker down quickly in wet weather. Apart from that, there is no shelter here so you get wet too! If it is foggy forget it!

If the weather is fine, the raptors quarter the fields in search of a last meal before roosting. I have noted that Hen Harriers tend to

Stubb Mill is a good site for Marsh Harriers coming in to roost.

Contacts

The Warden, Hickling Broad National Nature Reserve 01692 598276

Norfolk Wildlife Trust 01603 625540

come in later than the other birds so do not despair if it is getting late and you still haven't seen one. The Merlins will quite often be seen mobbing the harriers and, if you are lucky, you may see one land on a fence post in reasonable light.

Once on the ground, the Cranes can be surprisingly difficult to see. This sounds impossible for a four foot tall, three foot long shaggy mop but it is remarkable how they melt away into the tall grass when feeding.

This is a fantastic way to end a day's birding in this corner of Norfolk. What could be better than listening to the evocative '*cronk, cronk*' of the Cranes as they fly over two species of harrier being mobbed by a lightning-fast Merlin?

Other species seen from the watchpoint include Jay, Fieldfare, Redwing, Kestrel and an occasional Woodcock.

One cautionary note: in the Winter of 2001 to 2002, the road to the mill was flooded and I thought I was going to have to hire a Broadland cruiser to get down to the watchpoint. Take your wellies!

Also look out for the Chinese Water Deer, a small introduced species.

Other nearby sites

Breydon Water, RSPB Buckenham Marshes, Burgh Castle, Great Yarmouth Beach, Haddiscoe Marshes, NWT Hickling Broad, Horsey, NWT Martham Broad, RSPB Strumpshaw Fen.

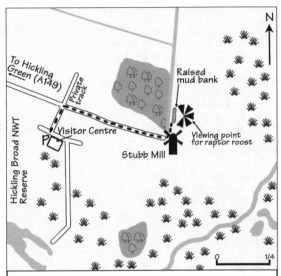

Access details

(approx. 14 miles NE of Norwich)

From A149, about one mile south of Potter Heigham, turn NE at the sign-post to Hickling. Follow all the way to Hickling Green, then turn right at The Greyhound public house.

Follow the brown duck signs to the Norfolk Wildlife Trust's car park. DO NOT DRIVE DOWN TO THE MILL. Disabled drivers should phone the warden for permission to drive closer to the viewing area.

From the car park, retrace your steps down the road. After about 100 yards you will reach an obvious cross roads (straight on is a private farm track). Turn right down the muddy road and walk for about half a

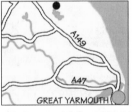

mile down to the disused Stubb Mill. Do not enter the mill and cottage grounds but watch the fields from between the red posts on the obvious raised mud bank where the track ends (TG 437222).

There is free entry to NWT members, but non-members should pay a fee. This is difficult as the visitor centre is closed in Winter and I have never seen a warden on site to issue permits. The raised bank can get crowded at times so get there early to reserve your place.

Key points

- **Open at all times.**

- **Circular route along rough paths. Some shallow steps en route.**

- **Limited free parking by church. Be considerate to church users on Sundays.**

- **Two hides.**

- **Not suitable for wheelchair users.**

- **Boots or Wellingtons advisable.**

- **Keep dogs under control.**

- **Stick to paths at all times.**

- **RSPB notice board at Surlingham church.**

- **Sightings record board in both hides.**

Contacts

RSPB Mid-Yare
Reserves
01603 715191

RSPB East Anglia Office
01603 661662

SOMETIMES REWARDING, sometimes quiet for birds, the Surlingham site is a small RSPB reserve in Broadland that deserves more attention from birdwatchers. It is always worth calling in to see what is around at any time of year.

Target birds *All year* – Bearded Tit (40%), Cetti's Warbler (hear = 60%, see 20%). *Winter* – Hen Harrier (50%). *Spring/Autumn* – Passage waders. *Summer* – Marsh Harrier (30%), Grasshopper Warbler (hear = 50%, see 10%).

Other likely bird species

All year	Kingfisher	Jack Snipe
Great Crested Grebe	Green Woodpecker	Winter thrushes
Cormorant	Great Spotted Woodpecker	*Summer*
Gadwall	Sky Lark	Hobby
Shoveler	Meadow Pipit	Cuckoo
Other common wildfowl	Pied Wagtail	Hirundines
Common waterfowl	Long-tailed Tit	Yellow Wagtail
Sparrowhawk	Corvids	Sedge Warbler
Kestrel	Common finches	Reed Warbler
Water Rail	Reed Bunting	Whitethroat
Snipe	*Winter*	Blackcap
Barn Owl	Winter wildfowl	Chiffchaff
		Willow Warbler

Background information and birding tips

SURLINGHAM Church Marshes is one of the lesser known RSPB reserves. It is quite difficult to find but is worth the effort. Though quite a small area (68ha), it holds some desirable species for the visiting birdwatcher.

My suggested route starts from Surlingham Church. Follow the reserve sign-post straight down the grassy track past the cottage. This runs downhill along a bush-lined path to a dyke. The hedgerow is good for common scrub birds (Robin, Blackbird, Dunnock, etc) and common finches. The path soon reaches the River Yare and runs adjacent to it all the way to the two hides.

While on the grass path by the river, listen out for Cetti's and Grasshopper Warblers in the thick bushes: neither species is easy to see. Common birds on the river itself include Coot, Moorhen, Grey Heron and Great Crested Grebe, with a good chance of Kingfisher.

Both hides are reached by short grass paths to your right (on your left if approaching from the Ferry House pub). The hides overlook a large pool, which holds breeding Gadwall and Shoveler. In front of the hides you should see Reed and Sedge Warblers in Summer and Bearded Tits all year.

Cetti's Warblers may also show

in the bushes around the hides all year round. If the water level in the pool is low, watch the muddy edges for the resident Water Rails and passage waders such as Green and Common Sandpipers.

In Summer, Marsh Harriers may patrol the reserve and in Winter, Hen Harriers are seen regularly from the hides at dusk. In Winter, the pools become flooded and attract decent numbers of common wildfowl such as Tufted Duck, Pochard and Shelduck.

After the hides, you can either retrace your steps to the car or boat, or complete the circuit of the reserve. As the river bends to the left, the footpath bears right and skirts a marshy field that is good for Snipe, Lapwing and Pied Wagtail, with Yellow Wagtails regularly recorded in Spring.

You will then reach a T-junction of public footpaths. You should turn right along a narrow, muddy path towards the gun club. The marshes are regularly hunted, but only on Sundays and Thursdays after 10 am.

After the gun club, the path becomes a rough farm track. Follow this for another quarter of a mile back to the car park, scanning the bushes and small wood for common woodland birds and finches.

Other nearby sites

Breydon Water, RSPB Buckenham Marshes, Cantley Beet Factory, Great Yarmouth Beach, Hardley Flood, How Hill Trust Reserve, Rockland Broad, RSPB Strumpshaw Fen, Ted Ellis Reserve, NWT Upton Fen.

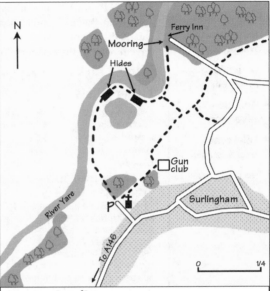

Access details

(Approx. five miles E of Norwich)

BY CAR: From A47 Norwich bypass, turn onto A146 (sign-posted to Lowestoft & Norwich). After 100 yards, turn left to Bramerton and Kirby Bedon at first set of traffic lights.

After 2.5 miles you will reach a green with the Bramerton village name-post on it. Turn left here (not sign-posted anywhere) and continue all the way into Surlingham.

Take a left turn in Surlingham village down Church Lane (a dead end), sign-posted to the Church and park there. The reserve is sign-posted either straight on or to the right by the cottage (circular route).

BY BOAT: Moor up at the Ferry House pub, which is about half way between Norwich and Rockland Broad on the River Yare.

There is a permissive footpath running south to the RSPB reserve. Follow this until you reach a small wooden bridge. The reserve starts immediately after the bridge, marked by the RSPB sign. The first hide is on the left just after the bridge.

167

Key points

- **No access to woods.**
- **No walking involved.**
- **Donation asked for.**
- **Telescope recommended.**
- **No facilities.**

THIS RESERVE provides a viewpoint over Swanton Great Wood, Summer home of Buzzards and Honey Buzzards. There is no access to the wood, so you will just have to wait in the car park for the raptors to appear.

Target birds Buzzard (80%), Honey Buzzard (40%).

Other likely bird species

Spring/Summer		
Sparrowhawk	Sky Lark	Blackcap
Kestrel	Hirundines	Corvids
Hobby	Common scrub	Common finches
Lapwing	birds	Yellowhammer
	Whitethroat	

Background information and birding tips

THIS SITE IS owned by the Astley Estate but is managed by English Nature. Honey Buzzards have nested in Swanton Great Wood since 1989, joined by Buzzards a couple of years later. More than 50 species of birds nest in the woods but access is by permit only: and no, you won't get one, so don't bother asking!

The owners ask for donations from visitors, which they put towards the renovation of the church in Swanton Novers. The donation box is situated at the entrance gate. There is usually an English Nature warden on hand for advice and a friendly chat.

Honey Buzzards arrive around mid-May, and by June should be incubating eggs. This means they become more elusive until July/August if nesting has been successful. Even on a good day during their visit, the Honey Buzzards can be out and about for long periods so patience is a requirement you'll need in abundance.

Scan the whole area at regular intervals as the HBs (as they are

Contacts

English Nature
01603 620558

Site Manager
01485 543044

Honey Buzzards have been established in the Breckland area for some time.

commonly known) can appear as if out of thin air. Luckily, there are usually several other hopeful telescopes trained to the skies at this site.

While waiting, Buzzards entertain the crowd at regular intervals, each sighting usually bringing a debate as to whether it is a Honey or not (raised wings = Common, flat wings = Honey is the general rule).

Yellowhammers can be seen coming and going to nests nearby, and they have been known to nest in the car park itself (I nearly had the embarrassment of running over a nest a few years ago).

Also, keep an eye on the bird table in the bottom right hand corner of the car park field as this is kept topped up with seed for the Greenfinches, Goldfinches, etc to feed on (and the occasional Tree Sparrow in Winter).

In 2002, Honey Buzzards could be seen more regularly at a watchpoint near Great Ryburgh, a few miles from Swanton Novers (TF 971256).

Great Ryburgh is four miles south east of Fakenham. To reach the watchpoint, take Mill Road, which runs south of the church in Great Ryburgh. Follow this road for 1.25 miles and park on the right, just beyond the disused railway bridge.

Look east over Sennowe Park Wood, where the Honey Buzzards have shown well at regular intervals. In early June 2002 a Black Stork was seen from this watchpoint for three days, as well as one or two Hobbies.

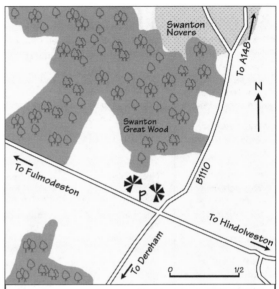

Access details

(Approx. 5 miles E of Fakenham).

At the roundabout in Holt, on the A148 King's Lynn to Cromer road, turn off onto B1110 to East Dereham. After about five miles, cross the B1354 (you need to turn right then immediately left, sign-posted Guist). After a further two miles, turn right at the crossroads to Fulmodeston.

The raptorwatch car park is 0.4 miles on the right: turn into the field at the wooden signposts. Park in the field and view the surrounding woods.

If approaching from Fakenham on the A148, take the turning off right after

the Fakenham bypass, sign-posted "Fulmodeston 2 miles" (opposite the Kettlestone Road crossroads – if you reach The Green Man pub you have gone too far). Follow through to Fulmodeston where you go straight over at the crossroads down Hindolveston Road.

Follow the road down to the raptorwatch car park on the left after 3.3 miles (turn into the field at the brown sign – if you reach the B1110 crossroads you have gone too far).

Other nearby sites

Blakeney Point, Cley NWT, Holkham Park, Kelling Heath , Kelling Quags, Salthouse Heath, Walsey Hills NOA.

169

Key points

- **Free parking and access every day but please give generously at donations box.**

- **Small visitor centre and toilets.**

- **Very limited wheelchair access (the hide/visitor centre is accessible).**

- **Hide is full of info boards plus drawing paper for children.**

- **Terrain is level, along muddy tracks, boardwalks, and uneven grass paths.**

- **Keep to paths at all times.**

- **Use insect repellent.**

- **No dogs.**

Contacts

Ted Ellis Nature Reserve 01508 538036 (warden David Nobbs). www.tedellistrust.org.uk

Friends of the Ted Ellis Trust, 4 The Pippins, Blundeston, Lowestoft, NR32 5AE

HERE is a beautiful reserve hidden in the southern part of the Norfolk Broads that offers a pleasant stroll at any time of year to see many common and scarce bird species, plus many other types of wildlife.

Target birds *All year* – Cetti's Warbler (hear = 75%, see 20%), Bearded Tit (30%), Lesser Spotted Woodpecker (March/April = 60%, rest = 10%). *Summer* – Marsh Harrier (50%).

Other likely bird species

All year	Green Woodpecker	*Winter*
Great Crested Grebe	Great Spotted Woodpecker	Winter thrushes
Common wildfowl	Pied Wagtail	*Summer*
Common waterbirds	Common scrub birds	Cuckoo
Sparrowhawk	Reed Warbler	Sedge Warbler
Kestrel	Marsh Tit	Other warblers
Common gull species	Common woodland birds	Hirundines
Barn Owl	Reed Bunting	*Occasional*
Kingfisher		Bittern
		Hobby
		Osprey

Background information and birding tips

TED ELLIS was a well-known writer and broadcaster who died in 1986. This reserve, sometimes known as Wheatfen Broad, is owned by the Ted Ellis Trust and is a wonderful memorial to a respected naturalist and countryman.

It is a well hidden reserve near Surlingham, but once you have found it I predict you will return again and again to stroll along the three miles of paths. The trails pass through many different habitats, all of which can hold several desirable species. Cetti's Warblers seem to show themselves frequently, particularly in the bushes by Wheatfen Broad.

Lesser Spotted Woodpeckers inhabit the woods but as they can be secretive, try visiting on a fine day in March when they will be drumming and displaying. Also in Spring, you should get excellent views of the resident Bearded Tits in the extensive reedbed. In Summer they are joined by good numbers of Reed Warblers at Wheatfen.

In Summer, after strolling along the path through the reeds hoping for a glimpse of the Marsh Harriers, you can walk to the River Yare. From here you can see Great Crested Grebe, Coot, Moorhen and quite probably Kingfisher as you wave to the passing boats. However, be warned that this path can be closed, even in Summer, as the reserve can be very wet underfoot.

This is a superb site for the

all-round naturalist. There are some excellent birds to be seen (including an occasional Bittern) but the place is also alive with scarce and rare plants, butterflies and dragonflies.

You are guaranteed a very friendly welcome from the staff who are only too pleased to tell you what is around for you to see and the current warden, David Nobbs, is one of the friendliest chaps you could wish to meet.

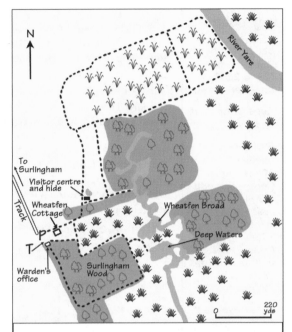

Other nearby sites

Breydon Water, RSPB Buckenham Marshes, Burgh Castle, Buxton Heath, Cantley Beet Factory, Great Yarmouth Beach, Haddiscoe Marshes, Hardley Flood, NWT Rockland Broad, NWT Sparham Pools, RSPB Strumpshaw Fen, RSPB Surlingham Church Marshes, NWT Upton Fen.

Access details

(Approx. six miles E of Norwich).

From A47 Norwich bypass, turn onto A146 (sign-posted Lowestoft). Head SE for about 100 yards until first set of traffic lights, where you turn left to Bramerton and Kirby Bedon.

After 2.5 miles you reach a junction with the Bramerton village name-post on a patch of grass. Turn left (not sign-posted anywhere!) and continue all the way into Surlingham.

In Surlingham, go through the village to a small pond. Take the next left turn (The Green). Follow for half a mile and turn right down

The Covey (sign-posted to the Ted Ellis reserve).

This road becomes a rough track and the reserve is well sign-posted at the end of this track.

The trail to the hide is straight on as you enter the car park, access to the wood is behind the small wooden warden office. Pick up a leaflet before you enter the reserve for more detailed trail directions.

Key points

- Car park free to RSPB members, (£3 in 2002 for non-members).

- Reserve open at all times.

- Visitor centre opening times: 10am – 4pm (Mon – Fri) and 9.30am – 5pm (Sat – Sun) in Winter. 10am – 5pm (Mon – Fri), 9.30am-5.30pm (Sat – Sun) in Summer.

- Café closes half an hour earlier than visitor centre.

- Toilet block in car park, including disabled access.

- Regular guided walks.

- Visitor centre sells books, clothes, binoculars etc.

- Binoculars for hire (£2).

NO VISIT to Norfolk is complete without an outing to Titchwell, one of the jewels in the RSPB crown. This is my favourite bird reserve in Britain, as there is always something to see here and most species give close views as you quietly walk along the footpath to the beach.

Target birds

All year – Black-winged Stilt (85%), Bearded Tit (60%), Little Egret (60%). *Winter* – Spotted Redshank (70%), Red-throated Diver (65%), seaduck and grebes (65%), Purple Sandpiper (60%), Black Brant (60%), raptors (40%), Twite (35%), Water Pipit (25%), Shore Lark (20%), Snow Bunting (20%). *Spring* – Avocet (99%), Marsh Harrier (75%). *Summer* – Avocet (99%), Marsh Harrier (95%), Mediterranean Gull (25%). *Autumn* – Passage seabirds, passage waders.

Other likely bird species

All year	Hen Harrier	Blackcap
Little Grebe	Merlin	Chiffchaff
Cormorant	Peregrine	Lesser Whitethroat
Shelduck	Golden Plover	Willow Warbler
Eider	Grey Plover	
Common Scoter	Knot	*Autumn*
Velvet Scoter	Woodcock	Shearwaters
Common wildfowl	Guillemot	Gannet
Sparrowhawk	Razorbill	Garganey
Kestrel	Stonechat	Hobby
Water Rail		Avocet
Common waders	*Spring*	Little Ringed Plover
Barn Owl	Garganey	Little Stint
Great Spotted Woodpecker	Little Ringed Plover	Curlew Sandpiper
Sky Lark	Black-tailed Godwit	Ruff
Meadow Pipit	Whimbrel	Whimbrel
Pied Wagtail	Greenshank	Greenshank
Long-tailed tit	Little Gull	Green Sandpiper
Corvids	Sand Martin	Wood Sandpiper
Bullfinch	Yellow Wagtail	Common Sandpiper
Linnet		Grey Phalarope
Reed Bunting	*Summer*	Skuas
	Black-tailed Godwit	
Winter	Sandwich Tern	*Occasional*
Brent Goose	Common Tern	Bittern
Pintail	Little Tern	Hobby
Goldeneye	Hirundines	Short-eared Owl
	Sedge Warbler	Spotted Crake
Red-breasted Merganser	Reed Warbler	
	Whitethroat	

Background information and birding tips

THE BEAUTY of Titchwell is that there is *always* something to see, no matter what the weather conditions, no matter what time of year you visit. You are guaranteed half a day's birding at least, and at certain times of the year a whole day can be spent tootling around. This really is a five star reserve that deservedly draws big crowds, so if you like your privacy see Gypsy Lane site page 84.

Birdwatching starts in the car park. The surrounding bushes are full of common birds eager to share your food and Chaffinches and Robins often come to take crumbs off your wing mirror.

Before leaving the car park you should have 'ticked off' Blackbird, Robin, Dunnock, Song Thrush, Long-tailed Tit, Blue Tit, Great Tit, Greenfinch, Goldfinch, House Sparrow, Woodpigeon, Collared Dove, and if lucky a Bullfinch or two, or a wintering Chiffchaff or Blackcap. In Summer Willow Warbler and Blackcap join the throng.

After a quick look in the shop to check the 'What's Around' board, the feeders near the visitor centre should be checked for Great Spotted Woodpecker and other common birds, or even a glimpse of a Brown Rat. In Winter and Spring watch the feeders and surrounding trees for Bramblings or Tree Sparrows.

The main reserve lies either side of a 1km track down to the sea. The only deviations allowed are down the short paths to the

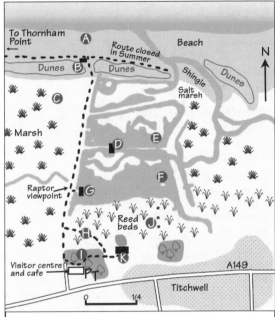

Key

A Pill box (good for Purple Sandpiper
B Viewing platform
C Bare ground (good for buntings/finches
D Parrinder Hide
E Lagoon

F Lagoon
G Island Hide
H Meadow Trail
I Feeding tables
J Dead trees (good for Marsh Harriers
K New Fen Hide

Access details

(Approx : five miles E of Hunstanton).

The reserve is sign-posted off A149, between the villages of Thornham and Titchwell. There is a large car park on site. The reserve is accessed via a public footpath, which is open at all times.

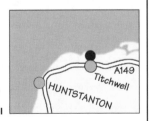

hides, though unless it is raining heavily it is hardly necessary to enter them as birds seem unperturbed by our constant comings and goings on the main track.

The first hide is the new Fen Hide, which is reached along a 250 metre long boardwalk from the visitor centre. This hide affords excellent views across the
• **Continues overleaf.**

173

Key points

- **Footpath generally level, but wheelchair users may need assistance at one point.**

- **All hides wheelchair accessible.**

- **Dogs allowed on the main path but not in hides or along Fen Trail.**

- **Picnic site adjacent to car park.**

Contacts

Titchwell RSPB Reserve
01485 210779

RSPB East Anglia Office
01603 661662

• **Continued from page 173.**

reeds for breeding Marsh Harriers in Summer and roosting Hen Harriers in Winter. Bearded Tits should be encountered here, but are seen much better from the main track. If you are really patient you may catch sight of a Bittern.

Rejoin the main track via the boardwalk, and scan the fields to your left. These are good for Barn Owl (mornings and evenings best) all year round, and Golden Plover and Lapwing flocks in Winter. Look to your right in the ditches for Water Rail (best in Winter) or a flyover Woodcock at dusk.

Follow the track and check the reeds on your right for Bearded Tits (windless days are best). I have found Autumn the best time to get close views, as the adults feed their noisy young right next to the path.

Marsh Harriers regularly quarter the reeds for prey in Spring and Summer, often chased by a Lapwing or two. In Summer, the reedbed is alive with Reed Warblers and Reed Buntings, while Wrens and Sedge Warblers sing from the small bushes and trees.

Look over the bank to your left at regular intervals for raptors and geese in Winter. Redshanks take flight at the slightest thing, and are often your indicator that a raptor is in the vicinity. Also on the marsh in Winter, you should see Snipe, Curlew and Wigeon feeding in the grass. Brent Geese are guaranteed in Winter and Spring (sometimes up until May), and for the last five Winters they have been joined by a Black

Brant, their American cousin. This is also a good place to look for Little Egret at any time of the year. They occasionally fly over the path giving excellent views, especially at dusk.

Two paths lead off to your right, the first to Island Hide and the second to Parrinder Hide, both of which overlook lagoons. The former is good for spotting Bearded Tits and Water Rails, and in recent Autumns this area has regularly attracted a Spotted Crake.

A good selection of ducks can also be seen from Island Hide during the year, along with common wader species. If you are lucky, you may be able to pick out a Mediterranean Gull from the swirling throng of noisy Black-headeds. This hide also gives a good view over the reedbed for Marsh Harrier and possibly Bittern. In Spring, this hide is the best place to observe Little Gull, usually flying at the back of the lagoon.

Parrinder Hide is good for viewing breeding Avocets and close views of Autumn waders such as Little Stint and Curlew Sandpiper. In Winter, Pintail can be seen from here, often at the back of the lagoon and Water Pipits are sometimes seen on the islands.

The lagoons attract longer-legged waders such as Spotted Redshank, Black-tailed and Bar-tailed Godwits, and don't forget Sammy the, Black-winged Stilt, who has been resident here for more than eight years now. The islands in the lagoons attract waders such as Ringed Plover, Dunlin and Ruff, joined by Little Ringed Plover in Summer and Little Stint and Curlew Sandpiper in Autumn.

Where the track ends at a boardwalk onto the beach, there is an area of bare ground to the left. In recent Winters, this has been an excellent area for feeding Twite, Shore Lark, Goldfinch and Linnet. If the birds are not here, try walking east (right) along the beach. The area of pebbles around here is another good place for all the above species and Snow Bunting, though none can be guaranteed as they tend to roam along the beach as far as Hunstanton and Holkham. Each Winter is different, so check recent records to ensure you are not disappointed (2002 was very poor). To avoid disturbing birds, only take this route in Winter and do not attempt to walk onto the salt marsh, which can be dangerous.

To view the sea/beach you can either sit on the wooden viewing platform (good for wheelchair users, but too bouncy for easy telescope use) or settle down out of the wind on the beach. Winter should produce large numbers of waders on the beach and an unpredictable number of sea duck/grebes/divers out to sea. High tide is best as all birds are closer to the viewer at this time.

The old pill box is an excellent place to see regular Purple Sandpiper in Winter as well as Turnstone. Sanderling, Dunlin, Ringed Plover, Bar-tailed Godwit and Oyster-catcher are usually present all year. Grey Plover and Knot join the party in the Autumn and remain into late Spring.

Common Scoters can be present all year round, though they range as far as Hunstanton so cannot be guaranteed. Some years up to 3,000 can be seen and in other years (2000 - 2002) hardly any. Also watch out for the white wing-flashes of Velvet Scoter among the Commons.

Winter sea enthusiasts can have their days enlivened by regular Red-throated Divers and, if lucky, the not so regular Black-throateds or Great Northern Divers. Long-tailed Ducks are unpredictable in their numbers as are Slavonian and Red-necked Grebes. One or two Guillemots and Razorbills are regularly seen in Winter. The onset of Spring is heralded in late March by the return of Sandwich Terns, joined by Little and Common Terns in May.

Autumn seawatching, preferably in a strong onshore wind, can be very good from the beach at Titchwell. Skuas are regularly seen, with Great and Arctic being the commonest but Pomarine and Long-tailed are occasionally spotted. Manx Shearwaters can virtually be guaranteed from August to October and look out for the rarer shearwaters (Sooty, Balearic, Great and Cory's). Little Auks pass by in November.

Titchwell has an excellent record for turning up rarities. A few years ago a Franklin's Gull and a Laughing Gull were seen together and I have seen two Penduline Tits here (not at the same time), the second only minutes after I had seen a Rough-legged Buzzard fly over the unsuspecting Black-winged Stilt! Obviously, this does not happen every time you visit but there is usually a rare or scarce bird to be seen whenever you decide to drop in.

I cannot praise this reserve enough. Hardened twitchers mix with beginners and so-called dudes without any problems: beginners ask the 'telescope brigade' questions without being pooh-poohed and this is how it should be.

All in all, you will be very lucky to catch up with everything on the list for the relevant time of year, but you will see a high percentage of them if you look hard enough. It is very rare to have a disappointing trip to Titchwell.

Other nearby sites

Brancaster Marsh, Choseley Barns, Dersingham Bog, Gypsy Lane, NWT Holme Dunes, NOA Holme Observatory, Holkham Hall, Holkham NNR, Hunstanton, Ken Hill Wood, King's Lynn Docks, Sandringham, RSPB Snettisham, Swanton Novers, NOA Redwell Marsh, NWT Roydon Common, Wolferton Triangle.

Key points

- **The pits can be viewed at all times from the road.**

- **Do not enter the fenced-off areas.**

- **No walking necessary.**

- **Wheelchair users may find pits obscured by bushes.**

THIS FLOODED gravel pit has become a traditional wintering site for Smew in varying numbers, and it can be viewed from the road. Rumours of Nightingales present in the thick bushes along the roadside are unsubstantiated by me. The pits are private and you must not enter the site.

Target birds   *Winter* - Smew (65%), Willow Tit (65%).

Other likely bird species

Winter	Other common wildfowl	Long-tailed Tit
Great Crested Grebe	Sparrowhawk	Other common woodland birds
Cormorant	Common gull species	Common finches
Common waterfowl		Reed Bunting
Wigeon	Great Spotted Woodpecker	
Gadwall	Pied Wagtail	*Early Spring*
Teal		Sand Martin
Shoveler	Common scrub birds	Swallow
Goldeneye		House Martin

Background information and birding tips

IN RECENT YEARS, Tottenhill has become the most reliable place to see Smew in the county as they are easily viewed from the small lay-by. Birds are usually present in small numbers through the Winter into Spring (November to March, though one male was seen here as late as April in 2001).

While scanning the lake, you should also see more common ducks such as Wigeon, Tufted Duck, Pochard and Goldeneye. By March, you will be able to watch the comical head-tossing

Wigeon are regularly among the wildfowl species using the flooded pit at Tottenhill in Winter.

Contacts
None.

courtship displays of the drake Goldeneye as they try to impress the females who are usually more occupied with feeding.

Great Crested Grebes should also be present and coming into their resplendent breeding plumage by February. Look out or their elaborate courtship rituals, including the famous 'weed dance' and synchronised head bobbing and shaking.

Several species of common woodland birds frequent the trees, the most notable being Willow Tit. This species is becoming increasingly more difficult to find in the county, but they remain regular visitors here. By the end of March, you should also encounter the first Chiffchaffs, Blackcaps, and Sand Martins of the year as they pour in from their African wintering grounds.

In the Summer months the bushes along the road completely obscure the view of the pits. Besides, bird activity is confined to very common species which are readily seen elsewhere, so a visit is probably only advised while the Smew are in residence, unless you wish to investigate reports of Nightingales in the area.

The large pit on the left of the A10, just past the junction with the A134, attracts a large number of common wildfowl but do not be tempted to stop on either road as they are very busy at all times.

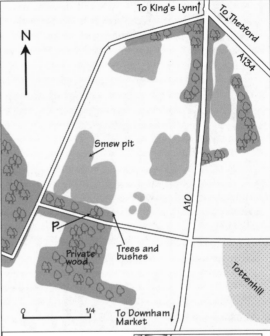

Access details

(Approx. 4 miles S of King's Lynn).

From King's Lynn, take A10 S towards Downham Market. Ignore the turn-off to Thetford (A134) after four miles, but a mile after this junction there is a crossroads.

Take the minor road to the right, then park on the right

after another half a mile in the very small pull-off. The gravel pits can be viewed from the road here.

Other nearby sites

Flitcham Abbey Farm, Hunstanton, Ken Hill Wood, NWT Roydon Common, Sandringham, RSPB Snettisham, WWT Welney, Wolferton Triangle.

177

Key points

- Site is a designated SSSI.

- Phone NWT warden before going on to the reserve.

- Small car park, otherwise no facilities.

- Trail not suitable for wheelchairs.

- Terrain is level along muddy, grass paths and a short boardwalk.

- Walking boots (at least) recommended.

Contacts

Norfolk Wildlife Trust
01603 625540

General Broads Authority
01603610734

UPTON FEN is very hard to find, but once on site, you'll discover it is a fantastic place for the all-round naturalist, with plenty of bird species to please those visitors only interested in feathered wildlife!

Target birds
All year – Cetti's Warbler (hear 50%, see 5%), Lesser Spotted Woodpecker (March 40%, rest 5%). *Summer* – Marsh Harrier (65%), Hobby (40%), Grasshopper Warbler (hear 50%, see 5%).

Other likely bird species

Spring/Summer		
Sparrowhawk	Sky Lark	Blackcap
Kestrel	Meadow Pipit	Chiffchaff
Water Rail	Hirundines	Willow Warbler
Woodcock	Common scrub birds	Goldcrest
Turtle Dove	Sedge Warbler	Marsh Tit
Cuckoo	Reed Warbler	Long-tailed Tit
Green Woodpecker	Lesser Whitethroat	Reed Bunting
Great Spotted Woodpecker	Whitethroat	*Very Occasional*
	Garden Warbler	Savi's Warbler

Background information and birding tips

THIS Norfolk Wildlife Trust reserve is perhaps best known for its dragonfly populations but it has much to offer the birdwatcher as well. There is a blue, way-marked trail around the reserve, consisting of muddy grass paths and boardwalks.

You should see Sky Lark, Yellowhammer, Goldfinch, Linnet, etc along the hedges and in the fields as you approach the car park.

The walk starts at the Turf Ponds, small pools just inside the reserve entrance. This is an excellent area for dragonflies, but birds can include Garden Warbler, Blackcap, Chiffchaff, Kestrel, Sparrowhawk, Swallow, Swift and House Martin. Listen out for the explosive song of Cetti's Warbler.

Follow the marked trail straight ahead into a wet woodland.

Migrants include Willow Warbler, Blackcap, Garden Warbler and Chiffchaff. Goldcrest and Marsh Tit are seen regularly. Common woodland birds are seen and heard here too.

The wood opens out to a cleared area, which is an excellent place to see Whitethroats and Sedge Warblers. There is usually a Grasshopper Warbler reeling from cover at the back of the clearing.

Green and Great Spotted Woodpeckers are sometimes seen flying along the edge of the woodland. Look out for elusive Lesser Spotted Woodpeckers here too. The best times are March and early April when they are in display flight. This spot is also a good place to see Swallowtail butterflies.

The trail then splits into two at

a blue marker. The right fork takes you along a dyke to the viewpoint. The left hand path is a short cut back to the car park. On the way to the viewpoint, you should see Reed Warblers and Reed Buntings. The path opens out to a marsh, which is an excellent place to stand and wait for Hobbies pursuing hirundines and dragonflies, as well as Marsh Harriers as they scour the ditches for prey.

The path rejoins the main track after about a quarter of a mile. You should turn right towards the Turf Ponds and car park, listening and watching for warblers and scrub birds in the bushes along the way.

A combination of birdwatching, dragonfly and butterfly watching and plant finding will guarantee a successful visit to this first-rate little site. As well as the excellent birds - a Savi's Warbler took up residence in 2000 - this is a superb place for rare butterflies (Swallowtail), dragonflies (Norfolk Hawker) and plants (Marsh Fern).

Walking boots are recommended at all times and you really need that insect repellent; the mosquitos here are the most vicious I have found anywhere in the world! I forgot my repellent in June 2001 and was fortunate to escape with all limbs intact. It was very satisfying to watch a Norfolk Hawker devour one of these mozzies back-end first, giving it a taste of its own medicine. Isn't nature wonderful!

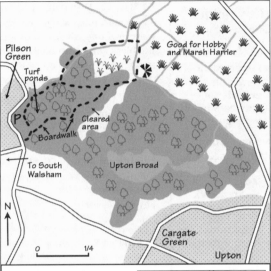

Access details

(Approx. ten miles NE of Norwich).

Upton Fen can be a devil to find! Basically, you are heading for Pilson Green, NE of South Walsham. From the B1140 (Wroxham to Acle road), follow signs for South Walsham/Ranworth. In the village, keep heading E, past the church, then take the left turn sign-posted to Pilson Green/Fairhaven Water Gardens.

Take second left turn (ignoring the one signed to 'Broad') sign-posted 'Upton

1 mile'. Once past the houses, take the first left down Low Road, which is a dead end.

The small reserve car park is approx. 200 yards on the right, just before the house. If you have made it this far, you deserve to see everything on the reserve!

Other nearby sites

Breydon Water, Buxton Heath, Cantley Beet Factory, NWT Cockshoot Broad, Great Yarmouth Beach, NWT Hickling Broad, NWT Hoveton Great Broad, How Hill Trust, NWT Ranworth Broad, RSPB Strumpshaw Fen, Ted Ellis Reserve, Winterton Dunes.

Key points

- **Open dawn to dusk every day.**

- **Report to visitor centre on arrival. Non-members need a permit.**

- **Small visitor centre accessed up steep steps (sells books and bird reports).**

- **Some paths level, some steep but all are narrow.**

- **Warden usually present to tell you what is around.**

- **Telescope very useful to scan Cley marshes.**

- **Wheelchair users will not be able to obtain panoramic views over Cley Marshes.**

Contacts

Norfolk Ornithologists'
Association
01485 525406

THE VIEWPOINT at Walsey affords an excellent panoramic view over Cley Marshes. Even though the reserve is tiny, the thick bushes are home to many breeding warblers and scrub birds. I feel it is a special place just to sit to see what comes into view.

Target birds   *All year* – Barn Owl (60%), Bittern (5%).
Spring/Autumn – Passage migrants. *Winter* – Water Pipit (60%), raptors (15%). *Summer* – Marsh Harrier (99%), Lesser Whitethroat (65%), Grasshopper Warbler (hear 50%, see 5%).

Other likely bird species

All year		*Spring/Autumn*
Little Grebe	Reed Bunting	Passage migrants
Egyptian Goose		Redstart
Other common wildfowl	*Winter*	Whinchat
	Brent Goose	Wheatear
Sparrowhawk	Winter thrushes	Winter thrushes
Kestrel		Barred Warbler
Common waders (distant)	*Summer*	
	Hobby	Yellow-browed Warbler
Common gull species	Turtle Dove	Firecrest
	Cuckoo	Pied Flycatcher
Common scrub birds	Hirundines	Red-backed Shrike
	Sedge Warbler	
Common finches	Reed Warbler	
	Other warblers	

Background information and birding tips

THERE IS always something to see on or from this reserve. Though it is small (12 acres, owned by the Norfolk Ornithologists' Association) it is covered by thick bushes and gorse, ideal for attracting migrants in Spring and Autumn. These have included Yellow-browed Warbler, Hume's Leaf Warbler, Barred and Icterine Warblers, Red-backed, Woodchat and Great Grey Shrikes, Firecrest, Wryneck etc.

The extensive area of gorse at the top of the hill is usually closed, but if a rarity is found, the warden opens up the footpath.

There are two narrow paths cutting through the bushes. I recommend pausing at regular intervals to see what pops out of cover as the bushes really are quite thick on this reserve.

Another feature of Walsey Hills is the panoramic views of the NWT Cley reserve, affording the chance to obtain distant telescope views of some of Cley's specialities. For instance, Bitterns sometimes are seen flying across the reeds. Water Pipits can be seen around the channel opposite the reserve car park in Winter and 'scope views of Avocets, Brent Geese and various species of ducks can be obtained at appropriate times of the year.

Good views of Cley marshes produce regular raptor sightings, including Hen, Marsh and (occasionally) Montagu's Harriers. Merlin, Peregrine, Kestrel and Sparrowhawk are also seen regularly. Barn Owls are noted on a daily basis.

In Summer, an array of warblers breed on the reserve. These include the locally scarce Lesser Whitethroat, along with the more common Blackcap, Whitethroat, Willow Warbler, Chiffchaff, and Garden Warbler. Grasshopper Warblers are often heard from the car park but seldom seen. Also on the reserve in Summer, warm days can produce sightings of Adder, Slow Worm and Common Lizard as well as a wide range of butterflies.

In summary, this is an excellent reserve to spend a while wandering around the paths looking for migrants or the commoner breeding birds. Alternatively, you could spend an hour or two basking in the sun while eating your sandwiches, looking out over Cley marshes. The bird feeder below the visitor centre is worth keeping an eye on as well. Don't mind the regular swarm of flies in Summer, they don't bite!

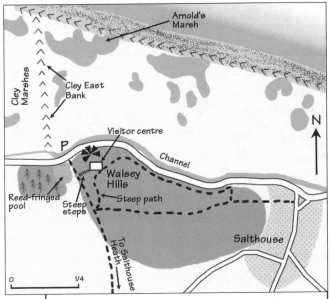

Access details

(General area: six miles W of Sheringham.

Head E from Cley on A149 towards Sheringham. About half a mile after passing the NWT Cley Marsh visitor car park on right, turn onto the rough lay-by on the right signed 'NOA Watchpoint' (virtually opposite Cley East Bank).

All visitors should enter the

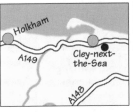

reserve via the path leading from the car park and report to the small visitor centre up the steep steps on the left.

The reserve is open from dawn to dusk every day. The friendly warden is always game for a birdy chat, too.

You can walk from here to Salthouse Heath along a public footpath (just over one mile) or vice versa if you wish.

Other nearby sites

Blakeney Point, NWT Cley Marsh , Felbrigg hall, Kelling Heath, NOA Kelling Quags, Morston Quay, Salthouse Beach, Salthouse Heath , Sheringham, Stiffkey, Swanton Novers, Weybourne.

181

Key points

- **Part of the Holkham National Nature Reserve.**

- **Narrow, rough access roads.**

- **Small car parks.**

- **Terrain is level along grass paths. Narrow, muddy paths to marsh.**

- **Wheelchair users may get a view of raptors from the car parks, but the paths are definitely not accessible.**

- **Avoid walking onto the marsh to prevent disturbance to birds.**

THIS expanse of saltmarsh holds populations of some scarce Norfolk breeders and has gained a reputation in recent years as a passage migrant hotspot, especially in Autumn. In Winter, Hen Harriers come in to roost at dusk, sometimes accompanied by a Merlin or two.

Target birds

Winter - Hen Harrier roost (75%), Rock Pipit (40%), Merlin roost (30%). *Spring/Autumn* - Passage migrants (e.g. Wheatear, Whinchat, Garden Warbler, Barred Warbler, etc). *Summer* - Breeding waders (60%), Marsh Harrier (20%).

Other likely bird species

All year		*Summer*
Shelduck	Greenshank	Terns
Lapwing	Green Sandpiper	Hirundines
Snipe	Wood Sandpiper	Sedge Warbler
Curlew	Common Sandpiper	Whitethroat
Redshank	Wryneck	Blackcap
Kestrel	Yellow Wagtail	Chiffchaff
Grey Partridge	Bluethroat	Willow Warbler
Black-headed Gull	Black Redstart	
Barn Owl	Redstart	*Winter*
Sky Lark	Whinchat	Brent Goose
Meadow Pipit	Wheatear	Wigeon
Pied Wagtail	Ring Ouzel	Seaduck
Starling	Winter thrushes	Short-eared Owl
Reed Bunting	Barred Warbler	Stonechat
	Lesser Whitethroat	Twite
Spring/Autumn	Blackcap	Snow Bunting
Little Stint	Goldcrest	
Dunlin	Firecrest	*Occasional*
Whimbrel	Pied Flycatcher	Hobby

Background information and birding tips

WARHAM GREENS is part of Holkham National Nature Reserve. It first came to my notice when I heard of a strange harrier in the fields here, rumoured to be a Pallid Harrier. After spending an hour trying to find the place, the bird turned out to be a Montagu's, but was still thrilling to see. Since then, Warham has produced several Barred Warblers and a Blyth's Reed Warbler to mention but a few goodies.

Summer is the quietest period, though Shelduck, Snipe, Curlews, Redshanks and Black-headed Gulls all nest on the marsh. The hedgerows around the car parks hold Whitethroats, Blackcaps and Chiffchaffs and common scrub species and the bushes along the edge of the marsh attract breeding Sedge Warblers. Marsh Harriers occasionally hunt over the marsh but are more easily seen elsewhere.

Contacts

English Nature
01603 620558

The main attraction in Winter is the raptor roost. Hen Harriers are seen daily between December and February, appearing from about an hour before dark. Merlins are also regularly seen here but are never guaranteed. I didn't see any during two trips here in the Winter of 2001 but saw harriers both times.

Sharing the marsh in Winter are varying numbers of Brent Geese and Wigeon. A Short-eared Owl is occasionally seen but Barn Owls are noted more regularly. A few Twite may be among the flocks of Goldfinches, Linnets, Greenfinches etc and if you are really lucky maybe even a Snow Bunting or two. Rock Pipits also Winter in small numbers but can be hard to locate.

Warham's reputation as a migrant trap, particularly in Autumn, is well formed. The bushes running east and west from the car parks can hold species such as Redstart, Chiffchaff, Willow Warbler, Blackcap, Pied Flycatcher, Garden Warbler, etc. Be alert, too for something a little special, such as Firecrest or Barred Warbler.

If you walk west from the main car park, check the small, bush-lined hollow on the left after about 400 yards, rather grandly called 'the quarry'. This is a nice sheltered, sun-trap, ideal for attracting migrants.

The marsh and bushes around the edges of the marsh should be checked for migrant Wheatears and Whinchats etc, but don't ignore the sky for a passing Honey Buzzard or, more likely, migrating thrushes, hirundines, etc.

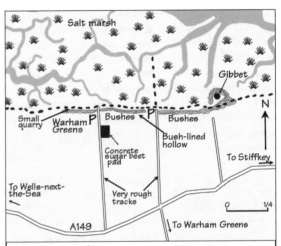

Access details

(Approx. 1.5 miles E of Wells-Next-The-Sea).

Head E from Wells along A149 towards Sheringham. To find the most convenient Warham car park turn N onto a very rough track opposite the turn-off to Warham Greens (look for a small, partly hidden sign-post). The track is signed 'not suitable for vehicles'. If you worry about the suspension on your car, park here and walk the rest of the way. If not, drive slowly to a small car park at the end (about half a mile).

From here walk straight ahead onto the marsh, or to the left or right to view the bushes during passage periods. Raptors can be seen

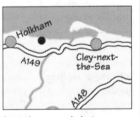

from the car park, but particularly recommended is the area surrounding The Gibbet, a strange metal structure on a concrete base, 500 yards to the right.

A smaller car park is at the end of an even rougher track about a quarter of a mile W of this one. Do not park on concrete sugar beet pad used by farmers and large farm vehicles. Do not block access for any farm vehicles.

The pools and creeks on the marsh may attract passage waders such as Greenshank, Whimbrel, Little Stint, etc along with Yellow Wagtails in Spring.

Other nearby sites

Blakeney Point, NWT Cley Marsh, Felbrigg Hall, Holkham Park, Holkham NNR, Salthouse Beach, Sheringham, Stiffkey, NOA Walsey Hills, Wells Woods, Weybourne.

Key points

- **Free access at all times**

- **An ancient wood managed by Norfolk Wildlife Trust.**

- **Site is a designated SSSI.**

- **Car parking.**

- **Early morning and dusk are best.**

- **Terrain is level, mainly along uneven grass paths.**

- **Can be wet at all times. Muddy in Winter.**

- **Never leave paths to see Golden Pheasants.**

- **Too boggy for Wheelchairs, but birds can occasionally be seen from car park.**

Contacts

Norfolk Wildlife Trust
01603 625540

THIS beautiful mixed woodland in Breckland is a favoured site for Golden Pheasants and is especially pleasant on a fine Spring morning when the sun-dappled clearings make a perfect backdrop to a stunning dawn chorus.

Target birds *All year* - Willow Tit (70%), Golden Pheasant (60% - Early morning and dusk are best), Lesser Spotted Woodpecker (March 40%, other months 15%).

Other likely bird species

All year	Common scrub birds	Common finches
Sparrowhawk		
Tawny Owl	Long-tailed Tit	*Summer*
Green Woodpecker	Marsh Tit	Cuckoo
	Nuthatch	Hirundines
Great Spotted Woodpecker	Treecreeper	Warblers
	Jay	Spotted Flycatcher
Common woodland birds	Corvids	

Background information and birding tips

SOME SAY small is beautiful, and NWT Wayland Wood is certainly beautiful and small(ish). If you pick the right day and time, as you get out of your car in the car park, the sun will be slicing through the trees to light the grass 'rides' perfectly. To complete the picture you should hear the raucous 'strangled chicken' call of Golden Pheasants!

To see the birds here walk through the metal gate from the car park, then follow the muddy, grass path for approximately 50 yards. You'll then reach a clearing in front of you, with a grass path (or 'ride') to your right.

The best place for the Golden Pheasants is in the thick bushes alongside the right-hand grass path. You can either stand very quietly at the junction of the car park path and grassy ride, or walk quietly along the ride to peer into gaps between bushes. Display some patience and you should be successful. Fortunately, the Golden Pheasants here are very vocal. At other sites they cease calling in June but at Wayland they seem to like the sound of their own voices and I have heard them calling in late August at midday.

Norfolk Wildlife Trust is coppicing some of the thick cover here to improve the habitat for numerous species of birds. Hopefully, they will be able to attract Nightingales back as I haven't heard them here for a few years now.

Stand quietly in the clearing opposite the area recommended for Golden Pheasants and you will be surrounded by Marsh Tits, Willow Tits, Nuthatches, Great Spotted Woodpeckers and Jays, as well as Great, Blue and Long-tailed Tits and other common species.

Lesser Spotted Woodpeckers

have been seen in these woods but are always elusive. A Summer visit to Wayland should produce numerous warbler species including Blackcap, Goldcrest, Willow Warbler, Chiffchaff and Garden Warbler.

You may wish to follow the NWT way-marked route along a grass 'ride' all the way around the wood but I have found the first patch of wood up to the cleared area the best for all the birds. The way-marked footpath is a circular route that eventually leads back to the clearing near the car park. It is only about a mile in length, if that, and Golden Pheasants can be seen on any of the paths if you remain quiet. To be honest, though, the rest of the walk can be quite unproductive compared to the car park area.

Just one word of caution: some birders have been known to leave the paths to search for pheasants. If you see this happening tell them bluntly that you will not stand for such behaviour. Not only are they disturbing the birds; it is very poor fieldcraft. They may see the rear end of a petrified Goldie hurtling away from them but a pheasant won't be seen again for a few hours after that. Simply standing still should produce views of one scratching contentedly in the leaf litter, dazzling you with their plumage.

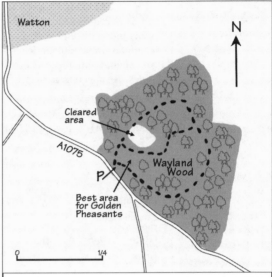

Access details

(Approx. 10.5 miles NE of Thetford).

Turn S off A47 (King's Lynn to Norwich road) at Dereham onto A1075. After approximately seven miles you will pass through Watton village followed by a right turn to 'Thompson 3 miles/Merton 1.5 miles'.

Keep going on A1075 and you will see SLOW signs painted on the road, followed by a public footpath

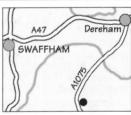

signpost to a track on your left. Immediately after this track there is a narrow entrance to the reserve car park on the left. This entrance is 0.4 miles past the national speed limit signs in Watton.

Other nearby sites

Barnhamcross Common, NWT East Wretham Heath, Fordham, NWT Foulden Common, RSPB Lakenheath, Lynford Arboretum, Santon Downham, NWT Sparham Pools, NWT Weeting Heath.

185

Key points

- Open from April 1 to end of August.
- Site is a designated SSSI.
- Terrain is level along gravel paths.
- Access to hides is up short, steepish wooden ramps.
- Access to one hide is just possible for wheelchair users.
- £2 entrance fee for non-NWT members.

Contacts

Norfolk Wildlife Trust
01603 625540

WEETING is a superb Breckland reserve famous for its breeding Stone Curlews. The hides are accessed along short paths through a pleasant conifer wood, packed with common woodland species. As well as the Stone Curlews, you should obtain excellent views of Wood Larks from the hides. A superb little place!

Target birds *Spring/summer* - Stone Curlew (90%), Wood Lark (70%), Marsh Harrier (45%), Buzzard (45%), Hobby (45%), Little Owl (35%).

Other likely bird species

Spring/Summer		
Sparrowhawk	Meadow Pipit	Corvids
Kestrel	Common scrub birds	Siskin
Lapwing		Linnet
Common gull species	Wheatear	Other common finches
Green Woodpecker	Mistle Thrush	
	Summer warblers	*Occasional*
Great Spotted Woodpecker	Goldcrest	Tree Pipit
	Spotted Flycatcher	Crossbill
Hirundines	Common woodland birds	
Sky Lark	Marsh Tit	

Background information and birding tips

WANT TO SEE Stone Curlew and Wood Lark? Then head for NWT Weeting Heath. There are other sites, of course, but please avoid these so as not to draw attention to them as both species are still the targets of egg collectors.

The return of heathland species to Weeting each Spring depends entirely on the Rabbit population busy nibbling away, keeping the plants low enough for Stone Curlews and Wood Larks to nest. You may see both species from either the east or west hides. Wood Larks usually nest close to the hides, especially the west one.

The Stone Curlews nest further away, sometimes out of sight over the ridge. Patience may be required to see these ground-nesters but they usually show in the end. An early morning or evening visit is best for the Stone Curlews as the heat haze can get quite restrictive during the middle of the day. If you are really lucky, you may even hear the eerie call of the Stone Curlew, a loud, haunting *'tudlooweeet, tudlooweet'* (when you hear it you will know what I mean!).

Recently, Marsh Harriers and Buzzards have started nesting in the area and both species visit Weeting Heath on a regular basis. Scan the trees at the back of the heath for a chance of seeing them. From the west hides, a good scan of the trees and fence posts on your right might reveal a Little Owl.

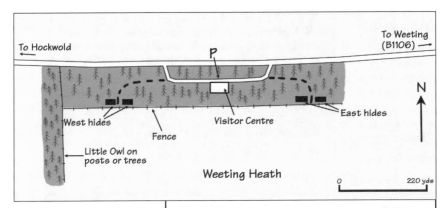

To Hockwold ←

To Weeting (B1106) →

P

N

West hides

Fence

Visitor Centre

East hides

Little Owl on posts or trees

Weeting Heath

0   220 yds

While waiting for the target species to show, you will be entertained by Spotted Flycatchers, sometimes almost entering the hide. Green Woodpeckers root about in the field and Wheatears and Mistle Thrushes will undoubtedly be running around the heath. I have seen the latter species mistaken for a Stone Curlew in extreme heat haze conditions. Lapwings occasionally breed on the heath, too.

In the pine trees surrounding the hide, you will see Long-tailed Tit, Chaffinch, Goldcrest and maybe a Tree Pipit or two. Crossbills occasionally visit and Nightingales usually breed but in areas not open to visitors.

The new visitor centre sells books and hot drinks, and there is also a toilet suitable for wheelchair users. Though the hides are indicated to be wheelchair friendly, the east hides certainly are not, and the west ones can only be entered with a struggle! On my last visit, (June 2001) the bushes outside the low level hide flaps had grown so as

Access details

(Approx. 7.5 miles NW of Thetford).

Head N on A1065 from Brandon towards Swaffham. Immediately after crossing the railway turn left onto B1106, signposted to Weeting.

After about 1.5 miles turn left at the green to Hockwold. After a further 1.5 miles the reserve is sign-posted off to the left. Park in

THETFORD

A11

A134

A134

the car park and obtain your permit from the new visitor centre (NWT members free). The centre is open from April to August.

to partly obscure the view for my friend in a wheelchair. We did, however, both get excellent views of a pair of Stone Curlews with two large young! The area in front of the west hide is also good for Stoats which often chase the Rabbits here.

All in all, this is a first-class little reserve and you are guaranteed a friendly

welcome from the wardens, who are only too happy to spend time with you to show you what is on the reserve.

Other nearby sites

NWT East Wretham Heath, Fordham, NWT Foulden Common, RSPB Lakenheath, Lynford Arboretum, Santon Downham, NWT Wayland Wood, WWT Welney.

187

Key points

- **Large pay and display car park, open dawn until dusk.**

- **Two toilet blocks on site.**

- **Café on site.**

- **Some tracks are wheelchair accessible (after negotiating a tight kissing gate).**

- **Terrain is level along a wide track, but several narrower paths are steep.**

- **Managed by English Nature as part of its Holkham NNR.**

- **Dogs on leads.**

Contacts

English Nature
01603 620558

WELLS WOODS is a superb place to hunt for your own migrants in Spring and Autumn, but be warned, it is a large area to cover, with lots of hiding places for the birds, as it forms part of a huge National Nature Reserve with Holkham Pines.

Target birds *Spring/Autumn* - Passage migrants including: Wryneck, Redstart, Whinchat, Wheatear, Ring Ouzel, Winter thrushes, Barred Warbler, Firecrest, Red-breasted Flycatcher, Pied Flycatcher, etc.

Other likely bird species

Spring/Autumn	Common scrub birds	Treecreeper
Woodcock	Lesser Whitethroat	Jay
Common gull species	Garden Warbler	Other corvids
Green Woodpeckers	Blackcap	Crossbill
Great Spotted Woodpecker	Chiffchaff	Other common finches
Sky Lark	Willow Warbler	Siskin
Meadow Pipit	Goldcrest	Redpoll
Hirundines	Common woodland birds	

Background information and birding tips

THOUGH several species of bird such as Spotted Flycatcher breed in Wells Woods and common woodland birds, plus Crossbill and Jay, can be found all year round, the most productive periods to visit are during Spring and Autumn migration times. I could even go further and say that Autumn is the best time to visit.

Wells Woods is part of the Holkham National Nature Reserve, but I have split this site from Holkham Gap/Pines for ease of coverage. The whole area can provide a superb day searching for grounded migrants, though be warned that it is a huge area to cover thoroughly.

From the beach car park, take the path at the right hand edge of the boating lake. After a few yards the path splits left or straight on; the choice of route is yours and either is good for migrants.

The path straight ahead leads to a toilet block. The berry bushes opposite are excellent for warblers, and it is well worth pausing here for quite some time to see what flits out of the thick cover. If it starts raining there is the added attraction of good shelter offered by the block's roof.

This path continues up a boardwalk into Wells Dell. This is a patch of wood criss-crossed by undulating paths, and is a favoured area for migrants. For instance, in October 2001, a Subalpine Warbler was found here. This area should also be searched thoroughly. Another narrow path skirts the wood on its seaward side and runs the length of the forest to Holkham Gap.

Alternatively, you can take one of several paths behind the toilet block. These all lead to the wide path which you would have reached if you had taken the left fork just past the boating lake. It sounds complicated but you cannot get lost as you either hit the beach on the northern side of the woods or the wide track to Holkham on the southern side. All areas can be good for migrants.

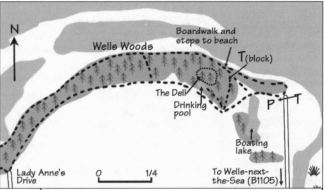

Another area renowned for rare and scarce migrants is the Drinking Pool. This is difficult to find but is best reached by the following route: take the left-hand path after leaving the car park. Follow to a T-junction then turn right along a wide track. Continue on this track when it bends to the left (ignore the wide track into the wood) and carry on for about 150 yards until you see a single pine tree and a single bramble bush on the right of the path, with what looks like a grass lay-by behind them. The drinking pool is reached by continuing beyond the single pine tree, and taking the next path on the right for about 100 yards.

Once you have found the pool (it took me 75 minutes the first time I tried) wait quietly around the edge and see what pops out of the surrounding bushes. This area has an outstanding record of producing rare, scarce and common migrants.

Access details

(Approx. 15 miles E of Hunstanton).

About half way between Sheringham and Hunstanton, turn off A149 at the sign-posts for Wells Quay/Wells Beach. In the town, follow signs for Beach Car Park and Pinewoods Caravan Site. This road runs adjacent to Wells harbour and ends in a large pay and display car park. The path into the wood starts at western end of the car park, behind of the boating lake.

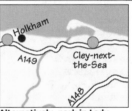

Alternatively, park in Lady Anne's Drive, opposite the main entrance to Holkham Park, and walk east (right) at the bottom. This takes you through Wells Woods and to the car park/ toilets after about a mile and a half.

It is hard to say which species you will see in Wells Woods but bear in mind the following advice to help you find something interesting. I always try to find a sheltered area of berry bushes, hopefully with a bit of sun on them. This usually produces Garden Warbler, Blackcap, Dunnock, Wren and Blackbird and hopefully a Barred Warbler in Autumn.

Another tip is to find a feeding flock of tits (or rather wait for it to find you). Scarce migrants such as Firecrests and Yellow-browed Warblers tend to join these flocks, so scrutinise them carefully.

Wells harbour can be very good for wintering wildfowl especially in harsh weather. A King Eider overwintered here in 2001/2, so watch for its return in subsequent years.

Wells Woods can be a frustrating place. I have wandered around in the rain with just a Redstart and two Garden Warblers to show for three hours birding, but as soon as the sun came out so did the hidden migrants!

Key points

- Permits (£3.50 for non-members of WWT) must be obtained from the visitor centre (open from 10am – 5pm every day (except Christmas Day).

- Wild Birds by Floodlight in Winter (November 7 – February 28 except Mon & Tues) starts from 6.30pm & should be booked in advance.

- The café is open from 10am – 4.30pm.

- Toilets on-site, including disabled facilities.

- Free hire of wheelchairs (one motorised, two self-wheeled).

- Binocular hire (£1).

HIGHLY RECOMMENDED to visit at all times of year, Welney is perhaps most famous for its wildfowl spectaculars, and is indeed the best place to see wild swans in Norfolk. My wife would argue that Welney should be more famous for its heated hide looking out onto the wildfowl lakes! In Summer, many scarce species breed on the reserve, putting it onto my Five-Star-Rated reserve list.

Target birds   *All year* – Whooper Swan (100%),
Bewick's Swans (100%: a few injured birds of both species remain throughout the year), Corn Bunting (60%), Tree Sparrow (20%). *Winter* – Bewick's Swan (100%), Whooper Swan (100%), Pintail (99%), Peregrine (65%), Brambling (10%). *Spring/Summer* – Avocet (95%), Little Ringed Plover (80%), Black-tailed Godwit (80%), Marsh Harrier (65%), Garganey (40%). *Autumn* – Passage waders (40%).

Other likely bird species

All year	Pied Wagtail	Ringed Plover
Great Crested Grebe	Corvids	Little Stint
Cormorant	Common finches	Temminck's Stint
Common wildfowl	Yellowhammer	Curlew Sandpiper
Sparrowhawk	Reed Bunting	Dunlin
Kestrel		Ruff
Red-legged Partridge	*Winter*	Whimbrel
Grey Partridge	Common wildfowl	Greenshank
Lapwing	Winter thrushes	Green Sandpiper
Snipe		Wood Sandpiper
Redshank	*Summer*	Common Sandpiper
	Common Tern	Grey Wagtail
Common gull species	Oystercatcher	Winter thrushes
Barn Owl	Turtle Dove	
Little Owl	Hirundines	*Occasional*
Kingfisher	Yellow Wagtail	Willow Tit
Green Woodpecker	Sedge Warbler	
	Reed Warbler	(Tundra) Bean Goose
Great Spotted Woodpecker	Whitethroat	Pink-footed Goose
Sky Lark	Blackcap	Smew
Meadow Pipit		Hen Harrier
	Passage	Merlin
	Little Gull	Short-eared Owl
	Arctic Tern	Hobby
	Black Tern	

Background information and birding tips

WELNEY is owned by the Wildfowl and Wetlands Trust and is worth a visit at any time of year. It is particularly famous for its Winter birds when the feeding of swans and ducks is a feature of many a family visit. Each evening, under floodlights, a staff member scatters a wheelbarrow load of grain for the wildfowl to feed on.

Personally, I find this spectacle a bit degrading to the birds as they frantically flap over each other for a share of the spoils. This feeding does, however, ensure the continued survival of staggering numbers of ducks and swans. For example, recent Winter counts include 1,150 Mallard, 1,720 Pintail, 7,700 Wigeon, 1,800 Teal, 4,750 Pochard, 3,700 Bewick's Swans and 1,000 Whooper Swans! And one thing is for sure; the Mallards you see here are truly wild birds.

During the day, the wild swans feed on potatoes left out by sympathetic farmers in the surrounding fields and can be hard to locate. Avoid disturbing the swans as any break in feeding could be disastrous for the birds. The heated hide on the reserve gives a much better view of all the species and can be very welcome on a wild, freezing cold day!

The feeders around the visitor centre are alive with finches, sometimes including scarce Bramblings. An added bonus is the fact that you can watch birds filling their stomachs from the feeders while you fill yours in the café! Corn Buntings are usually seen sitting on the 'phone wires along the main road and Tree Sparrows are sometimes seen around the farm near the visitor centre.

Recent Winters have seen the regular occurrence of a small number of Tundra Bean Geese (the smaller race of Bean Goose)

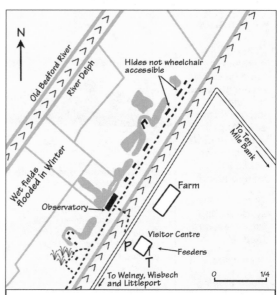

Hides not wheelchair accessible

Access details

(Approx. seven miles S of Downham Market).

From the north: The reserve is off A10, seven miles S of Downham Market ('Ten Mile Bank/Welney' on a brown tourist sign). Follow road for 0.8 miles to a bridge. Turn left then immediately right down Station Road (there is a brown tourist sign but it is difficult to see). Follow Station Road for about 4.5 miles to the reserve car park on the left. Be warned: this road is straight but keep your speed down as there are severe undulations and potholes along the route.

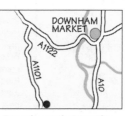

From the south: From Ely, head N on A10 to Littleport. Turn left onto A1101 towards Wisbech. After about four miles the road turns sharply right to run alongside a high bank. At the next sharp left bend, take the minor road straight on. The reserve centre is approximately 1.3.miles further on.

and a Smew or two. Peregrine Falcons regularly hunt the ducks and their presence is generally indicated by mass panic among the wildfowl. If everything goes up in the

air, quickly scan for a Peregrine or other raptor, such as Hen Harrier, Merlin, Short-eared Owl or Sparrowhawk.

Spring sees the arrival of

- **Continues overleaf.**

191

• **Continued from page 191.**

Key points

- **Hearing loop installed in main hide. This means that the hearing-impaired can enjoy the sounds of birds on the marsh, which is a superb idea.**

- **There is a well stocked shop for books, bird food, etc.**

- **Picnic site.**

- **Pond dipping facilities.**

Shovelers are among the common wildfowl species that can be found at Welney all year.

Garganey, Avocet, Little Ringed Plover and Black-tailed Godwit. Garganey appear in late March/early April and usually show well to visitors, but become more elusive as the season wears on. Marsh Harriers have also recently started breeding at Welney. The Little Ringed Plovers usually breed on the island in front of the main hide, giving superb views as they raise their chicks. A useful comparison with the similar Ringed Plover can usually be made as they argue over the best feeding areas.

Avocet chicks can be seen from mid-June along with odd-looking Shelduck youngsters. Several injured Bewick's and Whooper Swans also Summer at the reserve. Turtle Doves often sit on the phone wires along the access road in Summer.

The main hide is the most popular viewpoint, but there are several more hides that overlook the marshes: most are wheelchair accessible, though if there has been a lot of rain, paths may become muddy making access difficult. For those who like to count their Mallard flocks in peace, there are one or two mini-shelters along the track which hold one person; they look like Portaloos but some hardy birders prefer them to the luxurious heated hide.

This is a very good reserve at all times of year. There is usually a warden in the main hide to show the visitor what is around. Most birdwatchers turn up in Winter when the wildfowl are in attendance, but this reserve should not be overlooked in Spring and Autumn – one or two species of wader usually drop in on passage – or Summer.

Other nearby sites

Winter - Denver Sluice, Dersingham Bog, Flitcham Abbey Farm, Ken Hill Wood, King's Lynn Docks, NWT Roydon Common, Sandringham, RSPB Snettisham, Wolferton Triangle.

Summer - Fordham, Foulden Common, RSPB Lakenheath, NWT Weeting Heath.

Contacts

The Wildfowl and Wetlands
01353 860711

THOUGH at first glance, this seems a poor place for birds, as it is merely a grassy cliff-top, Weybourne is an excellent, easy-to-cover area to find migrant birds in Spring and Autumn. The cliff here is a superb seawatching vantage point at all times of year.

Target birds *Winter* – Seabirds. *Spring/Autumn* – Passage migrant passerines, passage seabirds. *Summer* – Sandwich Tern, Roseate Tern (occasional), Common Tern, Arctic Tern, Little Tern.

Other likely bird species

All year	Brent Goose	*Summer*
Cormorant	Eider	Hirundines
Common waders	Common Scoter	Sedge Warbler
Common gull species	Velvet Scoter	Reed Warbler
	Goldeneye	Whitethroat
Sky Lark	Red-breasted Merganser	Blackcap
Meadow Pipit		
Pied Wagtail	Hen Harrier	*Autumn*
Common finches	Merlin	Sooty Shearwater
Reed Bunting	Peregrine	Manx Shearwater
		Balearic Shearwater
Winter	*Spring*	Gannet
Red-throated Diver	Hirundines	Skuas
Great Crested Grebe	Yellow Wagtail	Kittiwake
	Black Redstart	Little Auk
Red-necked Grebe	Whinchat	Black Redstart
Slavonian Grebe	Wheatear	Winter thrushes
Pink-footed Goose	Ring Ouzel	

Background information and birding tips

WEYBOURNE is a site with an excellent track record of attracting migrants in Spring and Autumn. It is also a good seawatching site at all times of year, though Sheringham offers a bit more shelter in bad weather conditions.

Your birding starts in the car park, where to your left, a small area of reeds holds Reed Buntings all year round, and Reed and Sedge Warblers in Summer. The small pond sometimes attracts common wildfowl and waterbirds, mainly Mallard and Coot. The bushes behind you are on private land but you can see into them from the car park to check for migrants.

From the car park, there is a choice: If you choose to walk right (east), go up the slight incline onto the cliff top and follow the grass track. After about half a mile there is a hedgerow near a cottage, which is worth searching for migrants in Spring and Autumn. The extensive grassy area attracts Sky Larks and Meadow Pipits all year, and migrants such as

• **Continues overleaf.**

Key points

• **Pay and display car park.**

• **Steepish incline onto the cliff, then flatish track.**

• **Free access at all times.**

• **A public house and shop close by.**

Contacts
None.

• **Continued from page 193.**

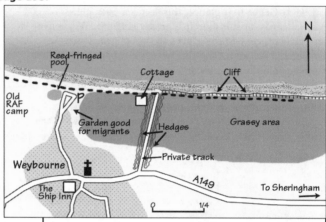

Yellow Wagtails and Ring Ouzels in Spring and Autumn. Rarer species such as Short-toed Lark are a distinct possibility. In Winter, raptors sometimes hunt over this area.

The cliff is a superb place from which to seawatch. In Winter, look out for Great Crested, Red-necked and Slavonian Grebes, all three diver species, Red-breasted Mergansers, Goldeneye, Long-tailed Ducks, Velvet and Common Scoters.

In Spring, you may be able to see incoming migrants make landfall, or Winter visitors such as Fieldfares and Redwings departing for warmer climes. In Autumn, the reverse happens.

Nothing is guaranteed, of course, but watch the weather forecasts to assist you in deciding whether to visit Weybourne at migration times. In Spring, if there is a low pressure system over East Anglia coupled with high pressure over the rest of Europe, then sit and watch the birds stream in! In Autumn, high pressure over Scandinavia with a low pressure system over Britain, and onshore winds is likely to produce the best results.

In Summer, terns will be fishing offshore and, from late July onwards, watch out for species such as Manx Shearwater, all four species of skua, Sabine's Gull etc.

Access details

(Approx: three miles W of Sheringham)

Turn off A149 in Weybourne village opposite The Ship Inn (from Hunstanton this is just before the church, from Sheringham just after the church). Follow this rough road down to a pay-and-display car park at the end.

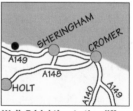

Walk E (right) onto the cliff or W (left) to the disused RAF camp.

If you walk west (left) from the car park, the going is slightly rougher, but there are some good fields and bushes that attract migrants, especially around the disused RAF camp. Ring Ouzel and Black Redstart are specialities around this area. It is possible to walk all the way to Kelling Quags and beyond, to Cley and Blakeney Point if you so desire. On foggy or drizzly Spring and Autumn mornings the whole area can be dripping with newly arrived migrants.

My personal Weybourne triumph came on July 21, 2001 when I decided to do some seawatching before heading up to Kelling Heath for Nightjar. The first bird I saw out to sea, as I stood on the shingle by the car park, was a Caspian Tern!

Other nearby sites

All year – Blakeney Point, NWT Cley Marsh, Felbrigg Hall, NOA Kelling Quags, Salthouse Beach, NOA Walsey Hills.
Summer – Kelling Heath, Salthouse Heath, Swanton Novers.

MANY SCARCE plants, insects, dragonflies and animals are also to be found on the reserve and it is a superb place to find common, scarce and rare migrant birds in Spring and Autumn. In Summer, Little Terns nest on the beach and Nightjars usually show well at dusk by the dunes. In Winter, raptors regularly hunt over the dune system.

Target birds

All year – Marsh Harrier (50%). *Summer* – Little Tern (95%), Nightjar (85%), Grasshopper Warbler (hear 55%, see 10%). *Spring/Autumn* – Passage migrants. *Winter* – Winter raptors (25%), Short-eared Owl (10%).

Other likely bird species

All year	*Winter*	Yellow Wagtail
Sparrowhawk	Seaducks	Bluethroat
Kestrel	Winter thrushes	Redstart
Ringed Plover		Whinchat
Common gull species	*Summer*	Wheatear
	Sandwich Tern	Ring Ouzel
Barn Owl	Common Tern	Winter thrushes
Tawny Owl	Cuckoo	Barred Warbler
Green Woodpecker	Hirundines	Pallas's Warbler
Sky Lark	Warblers	Yellow-browed Warbler
Meadow Pipit		
Pied Wagtail	*Spring/Autumn*	Firecrest
Common scrub birds	Shearwaters	Pied Flycatcher
	Gannet	Red-backed Shrike
Stonechat	Skuas	Ortolan Bunting
Corvids	Long-eared Owl	
Yellowhammer	Wryneck	*Occasional overhead*
Reed Bunting	Richard's Pipit	Crane
	Tawny Pipit	Pink-footed Goose

Background information and birding tips

THE RESERVE is part of an extensive nine-mile-long dune system. In recent years, it has become one of the 'in-places' for birdwatchers to find rare and scarce migrants in Norfolk. In truth, Winterton is much more than a migrant hotspot, with Nightjars and Little Terns on offer in Summer, several raptor species to savour in Winter, and the possibility of some excellent seawatching in Autumn.

After parking in the beach car park (or in the small pull-ins along the beach road) you have a choice of walking north or south through the dune system, though the southerly dunes are really only of interest in Spring and Autumn. At these times the bushes at the bottom of the hill can hold many common (Redstart, Pied Flycatcher, Goldcrest, etc), scarce (Firecrest, Barred and Icterine Warblers, etc) or rare (Pallas's Warbler, Dusky Warbler, etc) migrants.

In Spring and Autumn, all the dunes should be searched thoroughly for anything that

● **Continues overleaf.**

Key points

- **National Nature Reserve and SSSI, managed by English Nature.**

- **Access on foot only.**

- **Avoid Little Tern colony. This is a Schedule 1 species and disturbing them is a criminal offence.**

- **Keep dogs under control.**

- **Keep to paths at all times as there are many rare plants and animals.**

- **Car park closes at 8pm in Summer, 4pm in Winter – DON'T GET LOCKED IN! (if staying late, park in lay-bys).**

- **Toilet block in car park.**

● **Continued from page 195.**

moves! Wheatears, Whinchats, Ring Ouzels, pipits, wagtails, etc, should all be encountered and Wryneck and Red-backed Shrike are regularly reported from here. When I say search the dunes thoroughly, I mean **stay on the paths criss-crossing the site, scanning regularly with your binoculars.** This method usually pays dividends, with the added bonus of not disturbing other rare animals and plants in the process.

If you choose to head north, you may wander for many miles, passing Horsey Gap, Waxham and Sea Palling. All hold the promise of migrants popping up at any time. On the way, about 500 yards from the car park, you will find an object protruding from the sand. This is fancifully called 'The Totem Pole', and is often referred to in bird reports/ bird newslines, etc.

In addition to the migrants, you should encounter many resident species such as Kestrel, Yellowhammer, Meadow Pipit, Reed Bunting, Sky Lark, Green Woodpecker and the delightful Stonechat. Marsh Harriers and Barn Owls regularly hunt over fields to the west of Winterton Dunes (look towards Horsey Mill), with sightings almost guaranteed all year round for the former species.

In Winter, this can seem a barren place, though hardy walkers may be rewarded with sightings of Hen Harrier, Merlin, Peregrine and Short-eared Owl, though none are guaranteed. Skeins of Pink-footed Geese regularly fly overhead, especially in the early mornings and

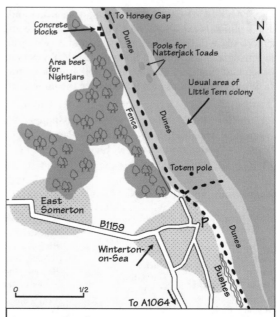

Access details

(Approx. eight miles N of Great Yarmouth).

FROM YARMOUTH: Follow signs for Caister-on-Sea along A1064. After a stretch of dual carriageway near Caister, you reach a roundabout. Take B1159 to Winterton (second exit) and continue for approximately 4.5 miles. As you enter Winterton village, take Hermanus Road on right, sign-posted 'Beach'. Turn right at T-junction (down The Craft), then park in the small lay-bys by the dunes, or in the car park at the end of the road. Walk left (N) or

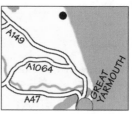

right (S) into the dunes, or straight ahead to the beach.

FROM THE NORTH AND WEST: Enter Winterton village along B1159 and follow signs to The Beach (along The Craft). Park in the small lay-bys alongside the dunes, or in the car park at the end of the road.

evenings. Crane is another species to watch out for around the Winterton area, though they are usually seen more frequently around

Horsey and at Stubb Mill. However, I had two adults and two juveniles fly overhead at Winterton in November 2001 (accompanied by a Sacred

Ibis!), so keep your eyes peeled at all times.

The sea should not be ignored at Winterton either, as Winter can produce reasonable numbers of Red-throated Diver, Red-breasted Merganser, Common Scoter, Long-tailed Duck and other scarce grebes and divers.

In Summer, the main attractions are Nightjars and Little Terns. The tern colony is usually north of the beach car park. Head for, but do not approach too closely, the fenced-off area to watch the comings and goings of this fantastic species.

Also, usually hanging around this area are Oystercatchers, Turnstones and Ringed Plovers. Out to sea, you should see Common and Sandwich Terns busily fishing for food to raise their young at colonies nearby.

For Nightjars, take the main track north following the fence on your left, with trees at the back. Nightjars can be anywhere in this fenced-off area, though I have found the best spot to be about half a mile from the beach road, by the concrete blocks at the northern entrance to the reserve. Green Woodpeckers continually 'laugh' at waiting birders, while a Tawny Owl occasionally shows itself. If you wait quietly, Nightjars will come and perch on fence posts at the edge of the main track.

Winterton Dunes is frequented by one or two pairs of Grasshopper Warblers in Summer, though they are extremely difficult to see. You will more likely hear them 'reeling' from the bushes dotted around the dunes. They may also join Natterjack Toad, Nightjar, Green Woodpecker, Woodcock and Tawny Owl in the dusk chorus for an uplifting end to the birdwatching day!

Key points

- **Terrain generally level along wide, rough, sandy tracks. Difficult wheelchair access.**

- **Do not touch any strange objects on the beach — unexploded missiles turn up occasionally!**

Nightjars usually show well at dusk by the dunes at Winterton.

Other nearby sites

NWT Alderfen Broad, NWT Barton Broad, Breydon Water, Burgh Marshes, Great Yarmouth Beach, Great Yarmouth Cemetery, NWT Hickling Broad, How Hill Trust Reserve, NWT Martham Broad, NWT Ranworth Broad, Ted Ellis Reserve.

Contacts

English Nature, Norfolk Office
01603 620558

Key points

- **Woods are private – do not enter.**

- **No need to even get out of your car.**

- **Access at all times.**

- **Do not impede the progress of local traffic – keep checking the rear view mirror as you crawl along.**

- **Do not run over any pheasants!**

THOUGH generally devoid of other interesting species, Wolferton is England's prime site to see the beautiful Golden Pheasant. As suggested by the site title, it is a triangle of roads, bordered by thick bushes. The pheasants occasionally emerge from these bushes to feed along the grass verges.

Target birds   *All year* - Golden Pheasant (60%).

Other likely bird species

All year	Common woodland birds	*Winter*
Pheasant	Long-tailed Tit	Pink-footed Goose (overhead)
Tawny Owl	Goldcrest	
Great Spotted Woodpecker	Common finches	*Occasional*
		Lesser Spotted Woodpecker
Common scrub birds	*Summer*	
	Warblers	

Background information and birding tips

WOLFERTON TRIANGLE is a site of limited interest as regards species numbers, but is the best site in the country for Golden Pheasants. Patient birdwatchers should be rewarded with good views of these gaudy introductions as long as certain rules are followed.

Though present all year round, I have found early mornings and late afternoons in Winter and Spring provide the best chances of seeing a Goldie. The most important thing to remember is to never get out of your car or the pheasants will scuttle into the undergrowth.

Simply cruise very slowly around the triangle of roads keeping an eye on the grass verges for the birds. Please note that the small muddy lay-bys have now been fenced off so if you do stop, it will have to be on the road. Be prepared for a few sinister glances from the local constabulary when the Royal Family are in residence at Sandringham.

In my experience, the area at approx. TF 673277 is the most productive stop-off. From the road here, you can see into a clearing in the wood where the Golden Pheasants can sometimes be seen scratching for food in the leaf litter. This verge has recently been replanted so the clearing may not be viewable for long!

While waiting for the Golden Pheasants to show, you can amuse yourself by watching some commoner bird species (Robin, Wren, Blackbird) or Grey Squirrels

Other nearby sites

Dersingham Bog, Flitcham Abbey Farm, Gypsy Lane, NWT Holme Dunes, NOA Holme Observatory, Hunstanton, NOA Redwell Marsh, Ken Hill Wood, NWT Roydon Common, Sandringham, RSPB Snettisham, RSPB Titchwell Marshes.

Contacts

None

198

which sometimes approach the car. Great Spotted Woodpeckers are regular visitors to the wood and Lesser Spotted Woodpeckers have been recorded in recent years.

The chance of connecting with Golden Pheasants is quite good though there are horror stories of people visiting more than 100 times without success. I must admit that I have never struggled; if I haven't seen them after half an hour's unsuccessful cruising I'll move on and revisit 'The Triangle' in the evening.

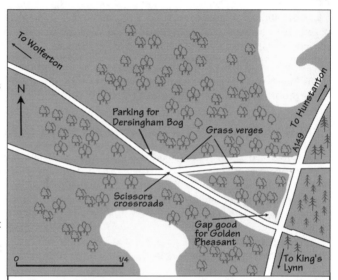

To Wolferton

N

Parking for Dersingham Bog

Grass verges

To Hunstanton

A149

Scissors crossroads

Gap good for Golden Pheasant

To King's Lynn

0   1/4

Access details

(Approx. five miles N of King's Lynn).

Between Hunstanton and King's Lynn off A149. Wolferton is sign-posted opposite the turn-off for Sandringham. Once off the A road, follow the triangle of minor roads (about one mile in 'circumference') skirting the dense bushes.

A149

A148

KING'S LYNN

A47

The Wolferton Triangle is the best site in the country for Golden Pheasant although they are never easy to see.

ACCESS TO SITES

THIS IS A quick-reference chapter to show the various ways you can reach your chosen destination. For instance, if you are relying on public transport, turn to the relevant page to see which reserves are available to you. You can then turn to the Site Guide page for more details (sites listed in alphabetical order). Simple!

Take it as read that all reserves are accessible by car, with the exceptions of Berney Arms Marsh (see Halvergate Marshes), which can only be reached by train and Hoveton Great Broad, which can only be reached by boat.

SITES FULLY ACCESSIBLE TO WHEELCHAIRS

The sites listed on this page are ones I consider to be accessible by wheelchair users, and several have been field-tested by a disabled friend. However, I strongly advise that you check with the contact number listed on the Site Guide page for specific guidance before you visit. I apologise profusely now if you turn up at a site and it is not accessible to you. Please let me know if this happens and I will amend the details for future editions.

BARTON BROAD
CHOSELEY BARNS (view from the road or car).
COCKSHOOT BROAD
EAST WRETHAM HEATH (very pitted, wide track runs alongside the reserve).
FLITCHAM ABBEY FARM
FORDHAM
HADDISCOE MARSH
HICKLING BROAD (most of the reserve is accessible).
HUNSTANTON
KING'S LYNN DOCKS
LYNFORD ARBORETUM
RANWORTH BROAD
REDWELL MARSH (need key to hide from NOA)
SALTHOUSE HEATH
SHERINGHAM
STUBB MILL (restricted view of raptor roost)
SWANTON NOVERS
TITCHWELL MARSH (rough track. May struggle on last third of path)
TOTTENHILL GRAVEL PITS (view from car)
WELNEY (most of the reserve is accessible).
WOLFERTON TRIANGLE

ACCESS TO SITES

SITES PARTLY ACCESSIBLE FOR WHEELCHAIR USERS.

Listed on this page are sites where I consider some sections can be reached by wheelchair users, together with a short description of the accessible area. Please check with the contact number listed on the Site Guide page before you visit.

BRANCASTER MARSH (marsh viewable from the road and beach car park).
BUCKENHAM MARSH (view along very wet, very rough access track).
BURGH CASTLE (marsh and Breydon Water viewable from the Angles Way footpath).
CANTLEY BEET FACTORY (access up to the railway crossing. Good for Cetti's Warbler).
CLEY MARSHES (western end of the reserve from the visitor centre).
FELBRIGG HALL (some of the woodland trail).
FOULDEN COMMON (should at least hear Nightingale from the car park).
GREAT YARMOUTH BEACH (Med Gulls from piers, Black Redstart from road).
GREAT YARMOUTH CEMETERY (some paths in churchyard).
HICKLING BROAD (most of the reserve).
HOLKHAM HALL (trees viewable from estate roads. Tawny Owl track probably too muddy).
HOLKHAM NNR (Washington Hide, Lady Anne's Drive, woods from sandy track. Not saltings).
HORSEY (Mere viewable from 'Easy Access' track. Fields visible from the road).
HOW HILL TRUST (a few paths may be accessible. Check before you go).
KELLING HEATH (limited views over heath from small car parks).
KELLING QUAGS (access down a very rough track. Ask the NOA's opinion).
MORSTON QUAY (limited view of saltmarsh from the car park).
PENTNEY GRAVEL PITS (Leisure Lake viewable from the road, but of limited interest).
ROYDON COMMON (access down rough tracks, which can be wet. Ask the NWT first).
SALTHOUSE BEACH (fields visible from the road, including Snow Bunting area).
SANDRINGHAM (several tracks and roads, plus part of the trails).
SANTON DOWNHAM (several wide sandy tracks and tarmac roads).
SNETTISHAM (Rotary hide. Phone RSPB warden before you visit).
STIFFKEY (saltmarsh viewable from the NT car park).
STRUMPSHAW FEN (main hide, plus track to railway crossing, good for Cetti's Warbler).
WALSEY HILLS (lower path only. Narrow and muddy, but level).
WARHAM GREENS (very limited view of saltmarsh from car park).
WAYLAND WOOD (may catch a glimpse of Golden Pheasant from car park).
WEETING HEATH (west hide accessible with a struggle).
WELLS WOODS (some wide, slightly rough tracks).
WELNEY (most of the reserve).

ACCESS TO SITES

PUBLIC TRANSPORT

If you are relying on public transport to reach birding sites in Norfolk, I pity you! Norfolk is not an easy county to get around by train or bus. If you want to visit more than one site in a day, the task is near impossible. It is worth noting that if you travel to a NWT reserve on public transport, you only pay half price for a permit.

The following is a very rough guide, gleaned from the excellent 'Norfolk County Transport Guide' leaflet, but as timetables can change at any time, I recommend you check the details very carefully before attempting your journey. Contact the Passenger Transport Unit, Norfolk County Council, County Hall, Martineau Lane, Norwich NR1 2SG (08456 020 121 or 01603 223 800).

Your mission, should you choose to accept it...

BARNHAMCROSS COMMON (train to Thetford then walk S for just over a mile).
BLAKENEY POINT (train to Sheringham then bus 36 to Blakeney. Boat to Point).
BRANCASTER MARSH (train to King's Lynn, bus 36 to Brancaster).
BREYDON WATER (train to Yarmouth, walk to N shore via Asda car park).
RSPB BUCKENHAM MARSH (train to Buckenham Station).
CANTLEY BEET FACTORY (train to Cantley Station).
CHOSELEY BARNS (train to King's Lynn, bus 36 to Titchwell. Walk one mile up hill).
CLEY MARSH (train to Sheringham then bus 36 to NWT Cley Marsh visitor centre).
DENVER SLUICE (train to Downham Market, then 3½ mile walk alongside the channel).
DERSINGHAM BOG (train to King's Lynn then bus 412 to Wolferton).
EAST WRETHAM HEATH (train to Thetford then bus X20 to reserve entrance).
FELBRIGG HALL (train to Cromer then bus 16 or 18).
FLITCHAM ABBEY FARM (train to King's Lynn then bus 27 or 419 to Flitcham).
FORDHAM (train to Downham Market then bus 37 to near Fordham. 15 min walk to canal bridge).
FOULDEN COMMON (train to Downham Market then bus 12 to Foulden).
GREAT YARMOUTH BEACH (train to Great Yarmouth, then 15 min walk to beach).
GREAT YARMOUTH CEMETERY (train to Great Yarmouth, then 15 min walk).
GYPSY LANE (train to King's Lynn then bus 36 to Titchwell).
HADDISCOE MARSH (train to Haddiscoe Station).
HALVERGATE MARSHES (train to Berney Arms Station).
HICKLING BROAD (nearest bus stop is two miles away at Hickling Green).
HOLKHAM HALL (train to King's Lynn then bus 36).
HOLKHAM NNR (train to King's Lynn then bus 36).
HOLME SITES (train to King's Lynn then bus 36).
HOW HILL TRUST (train to Wroxham. Bus 12 passes within a mile of reserve, near Ludham).
HUNSTANTON (train to King's Lynn then bus 36, plus others).
KELLING SITES (train to Sheringham then bus 36).

ACCESS TO SITES

KEN HILL WOOD (train to King's Lynn then bus 36 or 31 to Snettisham).

KING'S LYNN DOCKS (train to King's Lynn then 10 minute walk).

LAKENHEATH (train to Lakenheath Station).

LYNFORD ARBORETUM (train to Brandon then bus 151 to Mundford. 10 minute walk).

MARTHAM BROAD (train to Yarmouth then bus 603 or 604 to West Somerton).

MORSTON QUAY (train to Sheringham then bus 36).

RANWORTH BROAD (train to Wroxham then bus 29 to Ranworth).

REDWELL MARSH (train to King's Lynn then bus 36 to Holme-Next-The-Sea).

ROYDON COMMON (train to King's Lynn then bus 429).

SALTHOUSE SITES (train to Sheringham then bus 36)..

SANDRINGHAM (train to King's Lynn then bus 31 or 36).

SANTON DOWNHAM (train to Brandon then bus 130 or 200).

SHERINGHAM (train to Sheringham then walk to seafront).

SNETTISHAM (train to King's Lynn then bus 31 or 36).

SPARHAM POOLS (train to Norwich then bus 56 to Lyng).

STIFFKEY (train to Sheringham then bus 36).

STRUMPSHAW FEN (train to Norwich then bus 706 to Strumpshaw village).

SURLINGHAM CHURCH MARSHES (train to Norwich then bus 1).

SWANTON NOVERS (train to Norwich then bus 24 to Stiffkey. Get off just after Hindolveston).

TED ELLIS RESERVE (train to Norwich then bus 1 to Surlingham. One mile walk).

TITCHWELL MARSH (train to King's Lynn then bus 36).

TOTTENHILL GRAVEL PITS (train to King's Lynn then bus 1 or 37 to Tottenhill).

UPTON FEN (train to Norwich or Yarmouth then bus 705 to near Pilston Green).

WALSEY HILLS (train to Sheringham then bus 36 to Cley. One mile walk to reserve).

WARHAM GREENS (train to Sheringham then bus 36).

WAYLAND WOOD (train to Thetford then bus 3 to Watton).

WEETING HEATH (train to Brandon then bus R1 to Weeting. One and a half mile walk).

WELLS WOODS (train to Sheringham then bus 36).

WELNEY (very difficult. Nearest bus stop is 5.5 miles away at Ten Mile Bank).

WEYBOURNE (train to Sheringham then bus 36).

WINTERTON DUNES (train to Yarmouth then bus 603 or 604 to Winterton village).

WOLFERTON TRIANGLE (train to King's Lynn then bus 412 to Wolferton).

ACCESS TO SITES

BROADLAND BOAT MOORINGS

These sites have mooring facilities at or close to the reserve, and these make for ideal stop-offs during your Norfolk Broad holiday. A river map is an essential aid to planning your holiday, and I can recommend the one produced by GEOprojects (UK) Ltd, 9-10 Southern Court, South Street, Reading RG1 4QS (0118 939 3567) as being the best.

BARTON BROAD (moor at Gay's Staithe and walk to reserve, about half a mile).
BREYDON WATER (moor on River Bure and walk past train station to view Breydon Water).
BURGH CASTLE (moor at Burgh Castle Marina and walk north for half a mile).
CANTLEY BEET FACTORY (moor at The Red House. Two minute walk to security cabin).
COCKSHOOT BROAD (moor in channel at reserve entrance).
GREAT YARMOUTH BEACH (moor on River Bure. 15 minute walk to beach).
GREAT YARMOUTH CEMETERY (moor on River Bure. 15 minute walk).
HALVERGATE MARSHES (moor in Yarmouth, then train to Berney Arms, then walk).
HARDLEY FLOOD (moor on River Chet near the Flood).
HICKLING BROAD (nearest mooring is at Hickling Sailing Club, over a mile away).
HORSEY (moor at Horsey Mill).
HOVETON GREAT BROAD (moor on River Bure at reserve entrance).
HOW HILL TRUST (moor on River Ant at reserve entrance).
MARTHAM BROAD (moor at West Somerton on the River Thurne).
RANWORTH BROAD (moor at Ranworth village and walk 500 yards).
ROCKLAND BROAD (moor at Rockland staithe on the River Yare).
SURLINGHAM CHURCH MARSHES (moor at Ferry House and walk half a mile).

THE NORFOLK BIRD LIST

**Deserted beaches along the Norfolk coast prove
attractive to breeding Little Terns.**

NORFOLK BIRD LIST

THIS IS a run down of all species of birds which have been seen in Norfolk, detailing when and where to see them. This is mainly aimed at beginners who may not be aware of when and how often some species are present in the county. The list can be used as a checklist as there are boxes to record your Norfolk life list and an individual year.

I have to stress that these notes are from my personal experiences of the birds in Norfolk and many folk will disagree with my verdicts! For instance, I made 25 trips to Norfolk in 2001 and saw Marsh Harrier every single time, hence my assessment that they are common. Obviously, they aren't common in the true sense but you can't argue with a 100% strike rate! Also included are several races of species which are sometimes mentioned in bird magazines, and which may be given full species status in future (indicated by italics).

I have assigned all species to one of the following categories.

COMMON
Very abundant, or very easy to see even if there aren't many of them around.

SCARCE
Not very common, or hard to see in the field even if fairly abundant in numbers. Not likely to be seen by a casual visitor unless they are specifically looking for a particular species (eg. Hawfinch). See specific site pages for more detail of when to visit and how likely you are to see the target species.

MODERATELY RARE
Hardly any seen during the year, and certainly almost never by the casual visitor.

RARE
Probably only a handful of records, or several records many years ago. You will not see this species unless alerted to a new sighting by a pager or birdline service.

EXTREMELY RARE
Probably only one record in the history of record-keeping! Probably more chance of winning the National Lottery than seeing one of the species in this category on a casual visit. Only intrepid birders looking for rare birds will find one of these in a lifetime, or twitchers travelling to see these rarities are likely to see them.

NORFOLK BIRD LIST

Bird	Scientific Name	Description
Red-throated Diver	*Gavia stellata*	Relatively common at sea in Winter. Rare inland.
Black-throated Diver	*G. arctica*	Fairly rare at sea in Winter. Rare inland.
Great Northern Diver	*G. immer*	Fairly rare at sea in Winter. Rare inland.
White-billed Diver	*G. adamsii*	Extremely rare.
Pied-billed Grebe	*Podilymbus podiceps*	Extremely rare.
Little Grebe	*Tachyaptus ruficollis*	Fairly common on inland waters.
Great Crested Grebe	*Podiceps cristatus*	Common at sea in Winter. Breeds on inland waters, stronghold in The Broads.
Red-necked Grebe	*P. grisegena*	Scarce at sea in Winter.
Slavonian Grebe	*P. auritus*	Scarce at sea in Winter.
Black-necked Grebe	*P. nigricollis*	Mainly seen on passage on inland waters.
Fulmar	*Fulmarus glacialis*	Relatively common resident. Hunstanton is the best place, or any seawatching site.
Zino's/Fea's Petrel	*Pterodroma madeira/fea*	Extremely rare.
Black-capped Petrel	*P. hasitata*	Extremely rare.
Cory's Shearwater	*Calonectris diomedia*	Rare passage sea bird. Late Summer to October.
Great Shearwater	*Puffinus gravis*	Extremely rare passage seabird. Late Summer to October.
Sooty Shearwater	*P. griseus*	Moderately rare passage seabird. Early Autumn off seawatching sites.
Manx Shearwater	*P. Puffinus*	Scarce (but most common shearwater) passage seabird. Late Summer to October at seawatching sites.
Balearic Shearwater	*P. mauretanicus*	Moderately rare passage seabird. Late Summer at seawatching sites.
Little Shearwater	*P. assimilis*	Extremely rare.
Storm Petrel	*Hydrobates pelagicus*	Moderately rare seabird, from late July – late September.
Leach's Petrel	*Oceanodroma leucorhoa*	Moderately rare seabird. Autumn.
Gannet	*Morus Bassanus*	Relatively common passage seabird. Autumn best.
Cormorant	*Phalacrocorax carbo*	Common resident at coastal sites plus inland waters.
Shag	*P. aristotelis*	Moderately rare passage seabird at seawatching points.
Bittern	*Botaurus stellaris*	Extremely secretive, scarce resident. Look over reedbeds at Hickling, Cley, etc. Best seen in icy weather when they may feed in open areas, but more often seen briefly flying over reedbeds.
Little Bittern	*Ixobrychus minutus*	Extremely rare.
Night Heron	*Nycticorax nycticorax*	Rare.
Squacco Heron	*Ardeola ralloides*	Extremely rare.
Little Egret	*Egretta garzetta*	Scarce but increasing records. Marshes all year, Titchwell a Favoured site.
Great White Egret	*E. alba*	Rare.
Grey Heron	*Ardea cinerea*	Common resident at all wetlands.
Purple Heron	*A. purpurea*	Rare.
Black Stork	*Ciconia nigra*	Extremely rare.
White Stork	*C. ciconia*	Rare.
Glossy Ibis	*Plegadis falcinellus*	Extremely rare.
Spoonbill	*Platalea leucorodia*	One or two regularly seen each year: Titchwell, Holkham NNR and Breydon Water.
Mute Swan	*Cygnus olor*	Common resident on all wetlands.
Bewick's Swan	*C. columbianus*	Localised Winter resident. Best at Welney.
Whooper Swan	*C. cygnus*	Localised wnter resident. Best at Welney.
(Tundra) Bean Goose	*Anser fabalis rossicus*	Moderately rare Winter visitor, mainly at Welney.
(Taiga) Bean Goose	*A.f. fabalis*	Up to 300 winter at Buckenham Marshes, Nov – Feb
Pink-footed Goose	*A. brachyrhynchus*	Thousands winter in Norfolk. Snettisham, Horsey and Holkham favoured sites. Seen in flight or on fields almost anywhere on north coast.
White-fronted Goose	*A. albifrons*	Winter resident, best at Holkham and Buckenham.
Lesser White-fronted Goose	*A. erythropus*	Extremely rare Winter visitor.
Greylag Goose	*A. Anser*	Common resident, feral population on all wetlands.
Snow Goose	*A. caerulescens*	Rare Winter visitor. Probably all escapes!
Canada Goose	*Branta canadensis*	Common resident on all waters.
Barnacle Goose	*B. leucopsis*	Moderately rare Winter visitor. Try Holkham.
(Pale-bellied) Brent Goose	*B. bernicula*	Moderately rare Winter visitor amongst dark-bellied flocks.
(Dark-bellied) Brent Goose	*B.b. hrota*	Very common Winter resident on all north coast marshes.
Black Brant	*B.b. nigricans*	Moderately rare Winter visitor amongst dark-bellied Brent flocks. Titchwell and Cley are best bets.
Red-breasted Goose	*B. ruficollis*	Rare Winter visitor. Scan Brent goose flocks.

NORFOLK BIRD LIST

	Species	Scientific name	Notes
........|......	Egyptian Goose	*Alopochen aegyptiacus*	Increasingly common feral resident on many Broadland rivers and coastal marshes.
........|......	Ruddy Shelduck	*Tadorna ferruginea*	Extremely rare, Recent records due to escapes?
........|......	Shelduck	*T. tadorna*	Common resident mostly on coastal marshes.
........|......	Mandarin	*Aix galericulata*	Rare.
........|......	Eurasian Wigeon	*Anas penelope*	Common Winter resident, all marshes. One or two stay for Winter.
........|......	American Wigeon	*A. americana*	Rare.
........|......	Gadwall	*A. strepera*	Common resident all waters.
........|......	Teal	*A. crecca*	Common Winter resident. A few over-Summer.
........|......	Green-winged Teal	*A. carolinensis*	Rare.
........|......	Mallard	*A. platyrhynchos*	Very common resident.
........|......	Pintail	*A. acuta*	Fairly common Winter resident. Try Welney, with smaller numbers at Titchwell.
........|......	Garganey	*A. querquedula*	Scarce on passage, plus a few pairs breed: Cley, Hickling or Welney.
........|......	Blue-winged Teal	*A. discors*	Extremely rare.
........|......	Shoveler	*A. clypeata*	Common resident.
........|......	Red-crested Pochard	*Netta rufina*	Extremely rare.
........|......	Pochard	*Aythya ferina*	Common Winter resident all waters, some breed.
........|......	Canvasback	*A. valisineria*	Extremely rare.
........|......	Ring-necked Duck	*A. collaris*	Rare.
........|......	Ferruginous Duck	*A. nyroca*	Rare.
........|......	Tufted Duck	*A. fuligula*	Common Winter resident all waters, some breed.
........|......	Scaup	*A. marila*	Scarce Winter visitor. Try Snettisham RSPB pits.
........|......	Common Eider	*Somateria mollisima*	Scarce sea duck. Try Titchwell all year round.
........|......	King Eider	*S. spectabilis*	Extremely rare.
........|......	Steller's Eider	*Polysticta stelleri*	Extremely rare.
........|......	Long-tailed Duck	*Clangula hyemalis*	Scarce Winter sea duck. Coast between Hunstanton and Horsey.
........|......	Common Scoter	*Melanitta nigra*	Up to 3000 off the north coast. Hunstanton, Holme and Titchwell.
........|......	Surf Scoter	*M. perspicillata*	Extremely rare.
........|......	Velvet Scoter	*M. fusca*	Scarce sea duck in with Common Scoters – scan flock for white wing patches (see above).
........|......	Bufflehead	*Bucephala albeola*	Extremely rare.
........|......	Goldeneye	*B. clangula*	Fairly common Winter visitor. At sea or on inland pits.
........|......	Smew	*Mergellus albellus*	Scarce Winter visitor. Best at Tottenhill Pits, also Hickling and Snettisham.
........|......	Red-breasted Merganser	*M. serrator*	Fairly common at sea in Winter. North coast sites.
........|......	Goosander	*M. merganser*	Scarce in Winter. Try Denver Sluice, Sparham Pools.
........|......	Ruddy Duck	*Oxyura jamaicensis*	Scarce, but increasing, resident. Try East Wretham.
........|......	Honey Buzzard	*Pernis apivorus*	Rare breeder (possibly 2 pairs). Swanton Novers and Great Ryburgh mid May to mid September.
........|......	Black Kite	*Milvus migrans*	Extremely rare.
........|......	Red Kite	*M. milvus*	Rare. Flitcham Abbey Farm has recent records.
........|......	White-tailed Eagle	*Haliaeetus albicilla*	Rare Winter visitor.
........|......	Marsh Harrier	*Circus aeruginosus*	Common in Summer on all marshes. Scarce in Winter, Horsey area best.
........|......	Hen Harrier	*C. cyaneus*	Scarce Winter visitor. Roosts at Stubb Mill and Roydon Common are best. Get there about an hour before dark.
........|......	Montagu's Harrier	*C. pygargus*	Rare breeder. Details not given at request of RSPB. Try any watchpoint or marsh. Sometimes seen on migration at Snettisham or Cley.
........|......	Goshawk	*Accipiter gentilis*	Scarce breeder. Try any vantage point in Thetford Forest from late Feb to early May for displaying birds.
........|......	Sparrowhawk	*A. nisus*	Common resident in virtually all woodland.
........|......	Buzzard	*Buteo buteo*	Moderately rare resident. Try Swanton Novers and Great Ryburgh.
........|......	Rough-legged Buzzard	*B. lagopus*	Usually one in the county in Winter. Listen to telephone newslines for current site.
........|......	Golden Eagle	*Aquila chrysaetos*	Extremely rare.
........|......	Osprey	*Pandion haliaetus*	Scarce on passage. May and September best months.
........|......	Kestrel	*Falco tinnunculus*	Common resident everywhere.
........|......	Red-footed Falcon	*F. vespertinus*	Moderately rare Spring vagrant.

NORFOLK BIRD LIST

....	**Merlin**	*F. columbarius*	Scarce Winter visitor. Most marshes but best at Stubb Mill roost.
....	**Hobby**	*F. subbuteo*	Scarce but increasing Summer visitor. Hickling and Weeting Heath best.
....	**Gyrfalcon**	*F. rusticolus*	Extremely rare.
....	**Peregrine Falcon**	*F. peregrinus*	Scarce Winter visitor, most marshes. Holkham NNR and Buckenham Marshes seem favoured spots.
....	**Red-legged Partridge**	*Alectoris rufa*	Common resident. Scan any field.
....	**Grey Partridge**	*Perdix perdix*	Declining resident in fields. Roydon Common best.
....	**Quail**	*Coturnix coturnix*	Present most Summers in wheat fields. Bird newslines will tell you best place but they are rarely seen.
....	**Pheasant**	*Phasianus colchicus*	Common resident everywhere.
....	**Golden Pheasant**	*Chrysolophus pictus*	Scarce resident. Wolferton Triangle and Wayland Woods.
....	**Water Rail**	*Rallus aquaticus*	Secretive resident. More commonly seen in Winter. Try Cley and Titchwell.
....	**Spotted Crake**	*Porzana porzana*	Moderately rare Autumn visitor. Titchwell is a favoured haunt.
....	**Little Crake**	*P. parva*	Extremely rare.
....	**Baillon's Crake**	*P. pusilla*	Extremely rare.
....	**Corncrake**	*Crex crex*	Moderately rare passage migrant. Usually seen when flushed from Blakeney Point.
....	**Moorhen**	*Gallinula chloropus*	Common resident, all waters.
....	**Allen's Gallinule**	*Porphyrula alleni*	Extremely rare.
....	**Coot**	*Fulica atra*	Common resident, all waters.
....	**Common Crane**	*Grus grus*	Small population resident in Horsey/Hickling area.
....	**Little Bustard**	*Tetrax tetrax*	Extremely rare.
....	**Great Bustard**	*Otis tarda*	Extremely rare.
....	**Oystercatcher**	*Haematopus ostralegus*	Common coastal resident.
....	**Black-winged Stilt**	*Himantopus himantopus*	A single bird has taken up residence at Titchwell for last nine years.
....	**Avocet**	*Recurvirostra avosetta*	Fairly common breeder. Cley, Titchwell, Welney. Winter flock on Breydon Water as well as other seasons.
....	**Stone Curlew**	*Burhinus oedicnemus*	Moderately rare but increasing breeder. Weeting Heath, April to September.
....	**Cream-coloured Courser**	*Cursorius cursor*	Extremely rare.
....	**Collared Pratincole**	*Glareola pratincola*	Rare.
....	**Oriental Pratincole**	*G. maldivarum*	Extremely rare.
....	**Black-winged Pratincole**	*G. nordmanni*	Extremely rare.
....	**Little Ringed Plover**	*Charadrius dubius*	Moderately rare breeder. Welney best place, April to late August.
....	**Ringed Plover**	*Charadrius hiaticula*	Common coastal resident, plus inland scrapes.
....	**Kentish Plover**	*C. alexandrinus*	Moderately rare Spring vagrant. Favours Breydon Water.
....	**Greater Sandplover**	*C. leschenaultii*	Extremely rare.
....	**Caspian Plover**	*C. asiaticus*	Extremely rare.
....	**Dotterel**	*C. morinellus*	Moderately rare passage migrant.
....	**American Golden Plover**	*Pluvialis dominica*	Extremely rare.
....	**Pacific Golden Plover**	*P. fulva*	Extremely rare.
....	**Golden Plover**	*P. apricaria*	Common Winter visitor. Snettisham or Titchwell best.
....	**Grey Plover**	*P. squatarola*	Fairly common Winter visitor. Any coastal wader site.
....	**Sociable Plover**	*Vanellus gregarius*	Extremely rare.
....	**Lapwing**	*V. vanellus*	Common resident all marshes.
....	**Knot**	*Calidris canutus*	Common Winter visitor. Snettisham at high tide.
....	**Sanderling**	*C. alba*	Common on beaches in Winter.
....	**Semipalmated Sandpiper**	*C. pusilla*	Rare.
....	**Red-necked Stint**	*C. ruficollis*	Extremely rare.
....	**Little Stint**	*C. minuta*	Scarce passage wader. Autumn at Titchwell and Cley.
....	**Temminck's Stint**	*C. temminckii*	Passage wader. Cley in May is best.
....	**White-rumped Sandpiper**	*C. fuscicollis*	Rare.
....	**Baird's Sandpiper**	*C. bairdii*	Rare.
....	**Pectoral Sandpiper**	*C. melanotos*	Moderately rare vagrant, usually September.
....	**Sharp-tailed Sandpiper**	*C. acuminata*	Extremely rare.
....	**Curlew Sandpiper**	*C. ferruginea*	Passage wader, Titchwell in September is best.
....	**Purple Sandpiper**	*C. maritima*	Scarce Winter visitor. One on the beach by the old pill box at Titchwell, a few by the ski-ramp at Hunstanton all at high tide.

NORFOLK BIRD LIST

Dunlin	*C. alpina*	Common resident wader. All pits and coast.
Broad-billed Sandpiper	*Limicola falcinellus*	Rare. Favours Breydon Water.
Stilt Sandpiper	*Micropalama himantopus*	Extremely rare.
Buff-breasted Sandpiper	*Tryngites subruficollis*	Rare. Usually in September.
Ruff	*Philomachus pugnax*	Fairly common resident, scarcer in Winter. Cley, Holme, Titchwell, Snettisham, etc.
Jack Snipe	*Lymnocryptes minimus*	Moderately rare Winter visitor. Very secretive. Surlingham, Holme, Cley, Roydon Common.
Snipe	*Gallinago gallinago*	Common resident on all marshes and pits.
Great Snipe	*G. media*	Extremely rare.
Long-billed Dowitcher	*Limnodromus scolopaceus*	Rare.
Woodcock	*Scalopax rusticola*	Common but secretive resident. Dusk at Buxton Heath and Holkham Park, Winter from the Fen Hide boardwalk at Titchwell.
Black-tailed Godwit	*Limosa limosa*	Relatively scarce at all times of year. Try Breydon Water and Cley in Winter, Welney and Cley in Summer.
Bar-tailed Godwit	*L. lapponica*	Relatively common all year. Any wader hotspot in Winter (Titchwell, Snettisham) and Titchwell in Summer.
Little Whimbrel	*Numenius minutus*	Extremely rare.
Whimbrel	*N. phaeopus*	Scarce on passage. Try Blakeney Point, Cley, Breydon Water and Salthouse Beach.
Curlew	*N. arquata*	Common in Winter, all marshes, scarcer in Summer. Breeds at Roydon Common, Warham Greens.
Spotted Redshank	*Tringa erythropus*	A few Winter at Titchwell. Passage best at Snettisham.
Redshank	*T. totanus*	Common on all pits and marshes all year.
Marsh Sandpiper	*T. stagnatilis*	Extremely rare.
Greenshank	*T. nebularia*	Scarce on passage. Cley, Breydon Water, Snettisham, Cantley, Holme, etc.
Greater Yellowlegs	*T. melanoleuca*	Extremely rare.
Lesser Yellowlegs	*T. flavipes*	Rare.
Solitary Sandpiper	*T. solitaria*	Extremely rare.
Green Sandpiper	*T. ochropus*	Common passage wader. Holme and Cantley are good but all scrapes should have some.
Wood Sandpiper	*T. glareola*	Scarce passage wader. Cley, Holme, Cantley, Salthouse Beach are all favoured areas.
Terek Sandpiper	*Xenus cinereus*	Rare.
Common Sandpiper	*Actitis hypoleucos*	Relatively common on passage. See Green and Wood Sandpipers for favoured sites
Spotted Sandpiper	*A. macularia*	Rare.
Turnstone	*Arenaria interpres*	Common resident on coast.
Wilson's Phalarope	*Phalaropus tricolor*	Extremely rare.
Red-necked Phalarope	*P. lobatus*	Cley in May is a traditional stop-over. Moderately rare.
Grey Phalarope	*P. fulicarius*	Moderately rare from seawatching points in Autumn.
Pomarine Skua	*Stercorarius pomarinus*	Moderately rare seabird. Autumn best but sometimes seen in Winter.
Arctic Skua	*S. parasiticus*	Scarce on Autumn passage. From late July harassing terns at sea.
Long-tailed Skua	*S. longicaudus*	Moderately rare seabird. Autumn best.
Great Skua	*S. skua*	Scarce seabird. Best from August to October harassing birds at sea.
Mediterranean Gull	*Larus melanocephalus*	Moderately rare breeder. Best seen on Great Yarmouth beach.
Laughing Gull	*L. atricilla*	Rare.
Franklin's Gull	*L. pipixcan*	Rare.
Little Gull	*L. minutus*	Scarce on passage at Titchwell, Breydon Water, Kelling Quags etc. May is best.
Sabine's Gull	*L. sabini*	Moderately rare Autumn seabird at seawatching points.
Bonaparte's Gull	*L. philadelphia*	Extremely rare.
Black-headed Gull	*L. ridibundus*	Very common breeder and resident. All waters and marshes.
Slender-billed Gull	*L. genei*	Extremely rare. Favours Cley.
Ring-billed Gull	*L. delawarensis*	Rare.
Common Gull	*L. canus*	Relatively common resident.
Lesser Black-backed Gull	*L. fuscus*	Relatively common resident. All waters and marshes.
Herring Gull	*L. argentatus*	Common resident on coast.

NORFOLK BIRD LIST

.... (Yellow-legged Gull)	*L. michahellis*	Scarce Summer visitor. Cley is best.
.... (Caspian Gull)	*L. cachinnans*	Rare vagrant, usually Summer.
.... Iceland Gull	*L. glaucoides*	Moderately rare Winter visitor. Phone bird newslines for details.
.... Glaucous Gull	*L. hyperboreus*	Moderately rare, usually Winter, visitor. Favours King's Lynn Docks.
.... Great Black-backed Gull	*L. marinus*	Common on all waters and coast.
.... Ross's Gull	*Rhodostethia rosea*	Extremely rare.
.... Kittiwake	*Rissa tridactyla*	Relatively common seabird at all watchpoints. From late July to October best.
.... Ivory Gull	*Pagophila eburnea*	Extremely rare.
.... Gull-billed Tern	*S. nilotica*	Rare.
.... Caspian Tern	*S. caspia*	Moderately rare Summer vagrant. Any tern colony/roost.
.... Lesser Crested Tern	*S. bengalensis*	Extremely rare.
.... Sandwich Tern	*S. sandvicensis*	Common Summer visitor. From April to September at all seawatching points. Colonies at Blakeney Point.
.... Roseate Tern	*S. dougallii*	Moderately rare Summer visitor. Cley scrapes are a favoured site but look out at Blakeney Point and Breydon Water
.... Common Tern	*S. hirundo*	Common Summer visitor. From April to September at all seawatching points. Colonies at Blakeney Point. Breed inland on platforms on some Broads.
.... Arctic Tern	*S. paradisaea*	Moderately rare Summer visitor. Breeds on Blakeney Point. Also on passage on any water, The Broads in April/May is best.
.... Sooty Tern	*S. fuscata*	Extremely rare.
.... Little Tern	*S. albifrons*	Common Summer visitor. From May to September at all seawatching points. Colonies at Blakeney Point and Yarmouth Beach.
.... Whiskered Tern	*Chlidonias hybridus*	Rare.
.... Black Tern	*C. niger*	Scarce on Spring and Autumn passage. Lakenheath is a favoured site, on the flashes, but watch all Broads.
.... White-winged Black Tern	*C. leucopterus*	Rare passage vagrant.
.... Guillemot	*Uria aalge*	Scarce at seawatching points.
.... Razorbill	*Alca torda*	Scarce at seawatching points.
.... Black Guillemot	*Cepphus grylle*	Moderately rare, Winter.
.... Little Auk	*Alle alle*	Scarce during strong onshore winds in November. All seawatching points. Numbers vary from year to year.
.... Puffin	*Fratercula arctica*	Moderately rare. Pot luck at any seawatching point Spring/Autumn.
.... Pallas' Sandgrouse	*Syrrhaptes paradoxus*	Extremely rare.
.... Rock Dove	*Columba livia*	Descendant of Feral Pigeon. Pure birds now only found on Scottish islands
.... Stock Dove	*C. oenas*	Relatively common resident.
.... Woodpigeon	*Columba palumbus*	Very common everywhere.
.... Collared Dove	*Streptopelia decaocto*	Common in all villages.
.... Turtle Dove	*S. turtur*	Declining Summer visitor. Still common in The Broads, The Brecks and Flitcham Abbey Farm.
.... Rufous Turtle Dove	*S. orientalis*	Extremely rare.
.... Ring-necked Parakeet	*Psittacula krameri*	Rare. Probably all escapes!
.... Great Spotted Cuckoo	*Clamator glandarius*	Rare.
.... Cuckoo	*Cuculus canorus*	Common Summer visitor. Best seen in May when displaying. Foulden Common good to actually see, rather than hear Cuckoos.
.... Barn Owl	*Tyto alba*	Common resident. Any marsh or field at any time of day, but dawn and dusk preferred.
.... Scops Owl	*Otus scops*	Extremely rare.
.... Snowy Owl	*Nyctea scandiaca*	Extremely rare.
.... Little Owl	*Athene noctua*	Scarce resident. Best seen at Flitcham Abbey Farm or Weeting Heath
.... Tawny Owl	*Strix aluco*	Common resident. More often heard than seen, but a Winter roost at Holkham Hall is a good bet to spot one.
.... Long-eared Owl	*Asio otus*	Scarce resident. Breeds in extensive woodlands but rarely seen. Listen out for the squeaks of the young during April/May at Dersingham Bog, Thetford forest etc. Possible on passage at Holme or Winterton Dunes.

NORFOLK BIRD LIST

Short-eared Owl	*A. flammeus*	Scarce resident. Best seen in Winter on any marsh but pot luck which one. Best places seem to be Breydon Water at dusk or Halvergate/Berney Marshes.
Tengmalm's Owl	*Aegolius funereus*	Extremely rare.
Nightjar	*Caprimulgus europaeus*	Common Summer breeder. Mid May to the end of August at Salthouse Heath, Roydon Common, Dersingham Bog, Winterton, etc.
Common Swift	*Apus apus*	Common in Summer. From May to August everywhere, but best at Titchwell where they often fly below you as you stand on the footpath.
Pallid Swift	*A. pallidus*	Rare.
Pacific Swift	*A. pacificus*	Extremely rare.
Alpine Swift	*A. melba*	Rare.
Kingfisher	*Alcedo atthis*	Scarce resident. Try Strumpshaw, Flitcham Abbey Farm.
Bee-eater	*Merops apiaster*	Moderately rare Spring vagrant. Usually in flight.
Roller	*Coracias garrulus*	Rare.
Hoopoe	*Upupa epops*	Moderately rare. Can turn up at any time of year.
Wryneck	*Jynx torquilla*	Scarce passage vagrant. Winterton, Holkham and Holme dunes best bets, usually in Autumn.
Green Woodpecker	*Picus viridis*	Common resident in most woods, parks etc. Listen out for its loud, laughing call.
Gt Spotted Woodpecker	*Dendrocopos major*	Common resident in all woodland.
Lr Spotted Woodpecker	*D. minor*	Hard-to-see resident. Supposedly Common but best at Holkham Park in March, where they display by drumming and fluttering like a butterfly!
Calandra Lark	*Melanocorypha calandra*	Extremely rare.
White-winged Lark	*M. leucoptera*	Extremely rare.
Short-toed Lark	*Calandrella brachydactyla*	Moderately rare passage vagrant.
Woodlark	*Lullula arborea*	Increasingly common in suitable areas. Weeting Heath best, but any clearing in Thetford Forest.
Skylark	*Alauda arvensis*	Common resident all marshes and fields.
Shorelark	*Eremophila alpestris*	Scarce Winter visitor. Bird newslines will tell you the favoured areas but usually Titchwell, Salthouse Beach or Holkham Gap.
Sand Martin	*Riparia riparia*	Common Summer visitor. On passage at all coastal sites plus all Summer at Pentney Gravel Pits, Cley etc.
Swallow	*Hirundo rustica*	Common Summer visitor, everywhere.
Red-rumped Swallow	*H. daurica*	Rare.
House Martin	*Delichon urbica*	Common Summer visitor everywhere.
Richard's Pipit	*Anthus novaeseelandiae*	Moderately rare Autumn passage migrant. Try Blakeney Point, Winterton or Holme.
Blyth's Pipit	*A. godlewskii*	Extremely rare.
Tawny Pipit	*A. campestris*	Moderately rare passage migrant. Declining records, try sites for Richard's Pipit.
Olive-backed Pipit	*A. hodgsoni*	Rare, Autumn.
Tree Pipit	*A. trivialis*	Scarce Summer breeder. Dersingham Bog, Roydon Common, Thetford Forest. Also on passage on coast.
Meadow Pipit	*A. pratensis*	Common resident, all marshes.
Red-throated Pipit	*A. cervinus*	Rare passage migrant.
Rock Pipit	*A. petrosus*	Localised Winter resident. Breydon Water, Blakeney Point.
Water Pipit	*A. spinoletta*	Scarce Winter resident. The Serpentine at Cley always holds a few up to March.
Yellow Wagtail	*Motacilla flava flavissima*	Scarce migrant plus Summer breeder. Cley (east bank), Buckenham Marshes, Kelling Quags etc
(Blue-headed Wagtail)	*M.f. flava*	Moderately rare Spring migrant. Try Cley east bank.
(Black-headed Wagtail)	*M.f. feldegg*	Rare.
(Grey-headed Wagtail)	*M.F thunbergi*	Rare.
(Syke's Wagtail)	*M.f. beema*	Rare.
Citrine Wagtail	*Motacilla citreola*	Rare.
Grey Wagtail	*M. cinerea*	Scarce resident. Best in harsh weather on ice free waters. Try Sparham Pools.
Pied Wagtail	*M. yarellii*	Common resident everywhere. A large roost in Norwich city centre is a spectacular sight!
(White Wagtail)	*M. alba*	Scarce Spring migrant on coast.
Bohemian Waxwing	*Bombycilla garrulus*	Scarce Winter visitor, not every year. Watch any berry bush carefully plus listen to bird newslines.

NORFOLK BIRD LIST

....	**Dipper**	*Cinclus cinclus*	A Black-bellied race occasionally Winters in the county. Listen to telephone newslines for details.
....	**Wren**	*Troglodytes troglodytes*	Common resident everywhere.
....	**Dunnock**	*Prunella modularis*	Common resident everywhere.
....	**Alpine Accentor**	*Prunella collaris*	Extremely rare.
....	**Robin**	*Erithacus rebecula*	Common resident everywhere.
....	**Thrush Nightingale**	*Luscinia luscinia*	Extremely rare.
....	**Nightingale**	*L. megarhynchos*	Scarce and declining. End of April to early June best at Salthouse Heath and Foulden. Very skulking, more often heard than seen.
....	**Bluethroat**	*L.a svecica*	Scarce on passage, usually Spring. Blakeney Point, etc.
....	**Red-flanked Bluetail**	*Tarsiger cyanurus*	Extremely rare.
....	**Black Redstart**	*Phoenicurus ochruros*	Scarce on passage, usually Spring. Usual migrant hotspots. Moderately rare breeder.
....	**Redstart**	*P. Phoenicurus*	Relatively common on passage: try Holme, Holkham Pines, Wells Woods, Yarmouth Cemetery. Scarce breeder.
....	**Whinchat**	*Saxicola rubetra*	Scarce passage migrant. Holme, Winterton, Holkham Pines, Wells Woods, etc.
....	**Stonechat**	*S. torquata*	Scarce Resident at Horsey Gap. Winter at Cley, Titchwell etc.
....	**(Siberian Stonechat)**	*S. stejnegeri*	Moderately rare passage migrant.
....	**Isabelline Wheatear**	*Oenanthe isabellina*	Extremely rare.
....	**Wheatear**	*O. Oenanthe*	Common on passage at coastal sites.
....	**Pied Wheatear**	*O. pleschanka*	Rare.
....	**Black-eared Wheatear**	*O. hispanica*	Extremely rare.
....	**Desert Wheatear**	*O. deserti*	Rare.
....	**Rock Thrush**	*Monticola saxatilis*	Extremely rare.
....	**White's Thrush**	*Zoothera dauma*	Extremely rare.
....	**Siberian Thrush**	*Z. sibirica*	Extremely rare.
....	**Ring Ouzel**	*Turdus torquatus*	Scarce passage migrant. Coastal watchpoints plus Choseley Barns.
....	**Blackbird**	*T. merula*	Common resident everywhere.
....	**Black-throated Thrush**	*T. fuficollis*	Extremely rare.
....	**Fieldfare**	*T. pilaris*	Relatively common Winter resident everywhere.
....	**Song Thrush**	*T. philomelos*	Relatively common resident everywhere.
....	**Redwing**	*T. iliacus*	Relatively common Winter resident everywhere.
....	**Mistle Thrush**	*T. viscivorus*	Common resident, especially in coniferous woods.
....	**Cetti's Warbler**	*Cettia cetti*	Scarce resident. Very skulking, but gives its presence away by singing very loudly from thick cover. Ted Ellis Reserve, Cantley, Rockland Broad seem best to actually see one. Widespread around other Broads.
....	**Pallas' Grasshopper Warbler**	*Locustella certhiola*	Extremely rare.
....	**Lanceolated warbler**	*L. lanceolata*	Extremely rare.
....	**Grasshopper Warbler**	*L. naevia*	Heard more often than seen. Try Winterton, Horsey Gap, Upton Fen, Hickling, etc. Relatively scarce.
....	**River Warbler**	*L. fluviatilis*	Extremely rare.
....	**Savi's warbler**	*L. lusciniodes*	Moderately rare breeder. One or two pairs usually present in The Broads. Details not given at request of the RSPB. Can turn up in any reedbed.
....	**Aquatic Warbler**	*Acrocephalus paludicola*	Extremely rare.
....	**Sedge Warbler**	*A. schoenbaenus*	Common Summer breeder. Any marsh or riverside vegetation.
....	**Paddyfield Warbler**	*A. agricola*	Extremely rare.
....	**Blyth's Reed Warbler**	*A. dumetorum*	Extremely rare.
....	**Marsh Warbler**	*A. palustris*	Moderately rare passage migrant. Sings from vegetation anywhere around water. Early June only. Listen to Bird newslines for any details.
....	**Reed Warbler**	*A. scirpaceus*	Common Summer breeder. Any reedbed.
....	**Great Reed Warbler**	*Acrocephalus arundinaceus*	Rare.
....	**Booted Warbler**	*Hippolais caligata*	Extremely rare.
....	**Icterine Warbler**	*H. icterina*	Moderately rare passage migrant, any migration hotspot (Warham Greens, Winterton, Holkham Pines, Holme, Wells Woods, etc).
....	**Melodious Warbler**	*H. polyglotta*	Rare.
....	**Dartford Warbler**	*Sylvia undata*	Rare.
....	**Subalpine Warbler**	*S. cantillans*	Rare.

....	**Sardinian Warbler**	S. melanocephala	Rare.
....	**Ruppell's Warbler**	S. rueppelli	Extremely rare.
....	**Desert Warbler**	S. nana	Extremely rare.
....	**Barred Warbler**	S. nisoria	Moderately rare Autumn migrant. Warham Greens, Blakeney Point, Winterton Dunes, Wells Woods, etc.
....	**Lesser Whitethroat**	S. curruca	Relatively scarce Summer visitor. Likes thick cover to sing from but not as skulking as Cetti's Warbler or Nightingale. Try Holme.
....	**Whitethroat**	S. communis	Common Summer visitor in hedgerows.
....	**Garden Warbler**	S. borin	Common Summer visitor. Lynford Arboretum, The Broads, etc.
....	**Blackcap**	S. atricapilla	Common Summer breeder, increasingly seen in Winter (try Titchwell). Breeds in all woods.
....	**Greenish Warbler**	Phylloscopus trochiloides	Rare.
....	**Arctic Warbler**	P. borealis	Rare.
....	**Pallas' Warbler**	P. proregulus	Moderately rare Autumn vagrant. Wells Woods, Winterton, Yarmouth Cemetery and Holkham Pines seem best. Newslines will have details, best in late Oct, early November.
....	**Yellow-browed Warbler** P. inornatus		Annual but rare Autumn vagrant. See Pallas' sites.
....	**Hume's Yellow-browed Warbler** P. humei		Rare.
....	**Radde's Warbler**	P. schwarzi	Rare.
....	**Dusky Warbler**	P. fuscatus	Rare.
....	**Western Bonelli's Warbler** P. bonelli		Extremely rare.
....	**Wood Warbler**	P. sibilatrix	Moderately rare breeder. Has bred at Kelling Triangle and Felbrigg Hall.
....	**Chiffchaff**	P. collybita	Common Summer breeder, increasingly seen in Winter (try Titchwell). Breeds in all woods.
....	**Willow Warbler**	P. trochilus	Common Summer visitor, most woods.
....	**Goldcrest**	Regulus regulus	Common resident. Any woodland but especially coniferous.
....	**Firecrest**	R. ignicapillus	Scarce passage migrant, some may breed. Try Holkham Pines, Wells Woods, Yarmouth Cemetery, Holme, Winterton etc in October.
....	**Spotted Flycatcher**	Muscicapa striata	Localised breeder. Weeting Heath and East Wretham etc.
....	**Red-breasted Flycatcher**	Ficedula parva	Moderately rare Autumn vagrant. Try Wells Woods, Holme, etc.
....	**Collared Flycatcher**	F. albicollis	Extremely rare.
....	**Pied Flycatcher**	F. hypoleuca	Passage migrant. Holme, Holkham, Winterton, Yarmouth Cemetery, etc.
....	**Bearded Tit**	Panurus biarmicus	Common resident. Most reedbeds, but pick a windless day for best results. Hickling, Cley, Titchwell, Gypsy Lane.
....	**Long-tailed Tit**	Aegithalos caudatus	Common and increasing resident everywhere.
....	**Marsh Tit**	Parus palustris	Common resident around The Broads.
....	**Willow Tit**	P. montanus	Decreasing resident. Tottenhill Gravel Pits and Holkham Park.
....	**Coal Tit**	P. ater	Common resident. Coniferous forests best.
....	**Blue Tit**	P. caeruleus	Common resident everywhere.
....	**Great Tit**	P. major	Common resident everywhere.
....	**Red-breasted Nuthatch**	Sitta canadensis	Only one. Sorry, there won't be another one!
....	**Nuthatch**	S. europaea	Localised resident. Holkham Park best place, but also Ken Hill Wood, Wayland Wood, etc.
....	**Wallcreeper**	Tichodroma muraria	Extremely rare.
....	**Treecreeper**	Certhia familiaris	Localised resident. Secretive. See Nuthatch for sites.
....	**Penduline Tit**	Remiz pendulinus	Rare vagrant but Titchwell has produced regular January records so stay alert by the reedbed!
....	**Golden Oriole**	Oriolus oriolus	Moderately rare breeder. Fordham and Lakenheath. More often heard than seen.
....	**Isabelline Shrike**	Lanius isabellinus	Rare.
....	**Red-backed Shrike**	L. collurio	Moderately rare Autumn vagrant. Usual migrant hotspots.
....	**Lesser Grey Shrike**	L. minor	Rare.
....	**Great Grey Shrike**	L. excubitor	Increasingly rare Winter visitor: none in recent years. telephone newslines will have details of any in the county.
....	**Woodchat Shrike**	L. senator	Rare.

NORFOLK BIRD LIST

	Common Name	Scientific Name	Notes
....	Jay	Garrulus glandarius	Increasingly common resident. Wayland Wood, Holkham Park, Hickling, etc.
....	Magpie	Pica pica	Increasingly common resident. Moving into all areas.
....	Nutcracker	Nucifraga caryocatactes	Extremely rare.
....	Jackdaw	Corvus monedula	Common resident everywhere.
....	Rook	C. frugilegus	Common resident everywhere.
....	Carrion Crow	C. corone	Common resident everywhere.
....	(Hooded Crow)	C.c cornix	Rare Winter visitor to Horsey/Roydon Common.
....	Raven	C. corax	Rare Winter visitor to the Horsey area.
....	Starling	Sturnus vulgaris	Common resident everywhere.
....	Rose-coloured Starling	S. roseus	Rare.
....	House Sparrow	Passer domesticus	Common resident everywhere, especially towns and villages.
....	Tree Sparrow	P. montanus	Moderately rare resident. Try Flitcham Abbey Farm or Welney.
....	Rock Sparrow	Petronia petronia	Extremely rare.
....	Chaffinch	Fringilla coelebs	Common resident everywhere.
....	Brambling	F. montifringilla	Scarce Winter visitor. Try Holkham Park or Welney.
....	Serin	Serinus serinus	Moderately rare vagrant, any time of year.
....	Greenfinch	Carduelis chloris	Common resident everywhere.
....	Goldfinch	C. C.	Common resident everywhere.
....	Siskin	C. spinus	Localised resident. Usually coniferous forests.
....	Linnet	C. cannabina	Common resident everywhere.
....	Twite	C. flavirostris	Scarce Winter resident. Best places include Holkham Gap and Titchwell.
....	Common Redpoll	C. flammea	Moderately rare Winter visitor.
....	Lesser Redpoll	C. cabaret	Scarce resident. Numbers vary year to year. Try East Wretham Heath.
....	Arctic Redpoll	C. hornemanni	Moderately rare Winter visitor.
....	Two-barred Crossbill	Loxia leucoptera	Rare, only in irruption years.
....	Common Crossbill	L. curvirostra	Scarce resident. Numbers vary year to year. Try Lynford Arboretum, Dersingham Bog, Holkham Pines, Wells Woods, etc. Learn their loud 'chip, chip' call.
....	Parrot Crossbill	L. pytyopsittacus	Extremely rare.
....	Common Rosefinch	Carpodacus erythrinus	Passage vagrant. Winterton, Holme, Holkham Pines, Wells Woods, etc. Occasionally breeds.
....	Bullfinch	Pyrrhula pyrrhula	Scarce resident. Try Titchwell car park, Holme (Redwell Marsh hedges) Pentney Gravel Pits.
....	Hawfinch	Coccothraustes Coccothraustes	Scarce and decreasing resident, best seen in Winter. Barnhamcross Common, Lynford Arboretum, Holkham Park. Learn their 'tick, tick' call.
....	Black and White Warbler	Mniotilta varia	Extremely rare.
....	Lark Sparrow	Chondestes grammacus	Extremely rare.
....	White-throated Sparrow	Zonotrichia albicollis	Extremely rare.
....	Lapland Bunting	Calcarius lapponicus	Moderately rare Winter resident. No reliable sites any more, though Halvergate Marshes and Burnham Norton have held birds in the past. Salthouse Beach and Cley eye field are regularly visited by passage birds.
....	Snow Bunting	Pletrophenax nivalis	Localised Winter visitor. Small flocks around Yarmouth Beach, Holkham Gap, and on the coast from Hunstanton to Brancaster. Very mobile!
....	Pine Bunting	Emberiza leucocephalos	Extremely rare.
....	Yellowhammer	E. citrinella	Relatively common resident. Flitcham Abbey Farm, Salthouse Heath, Kelling Heath, Choseley Barns, etc.
....	Cirl Bunting	E. cirlus	Extremely rare. Unlikely to be another one.
....	Ortolan Bunting	E. hortulana	Moderately rare Autumn vagrant. Try Blakeney Point.
....	Yellow-browed Bunting	E. chrysophrys	Extremely rare.
....	Rustic Bunting	E. rustica	Rare.
....	Little Bunting	E. pusilla	Rare.
....	Yellow-breasted Bunting	E. aureola	Extremely rare.
....	Reed Bunting	E. schoeniclus	Common resident, all marshes and waterways.
....	Black-headed Bunting	E. melanocephala	Extremely rare.
....	Corn Bunting	Miliaria calandra	Scarce resident. Try Flitcham Abbey Farm, Welney or Choseley Barns all year round.

DEFINITIONS OF BIRD GROUPS USED IN THIS BOOK.

HERE IS AN explanation of some general terms I have used in the 'Target Birds' and 'Other Likely Species' sections:

Common woodland birds

Woodpigeon, Tawny Owl, Great Spotted Woodpecker, Wren, Dunnock, Robin, Blackbird, Song Thrush, Mistle Thrush, migrant warblers, Goldcrest, Long-tailed Tit, Marsh Tit, Willow Tit, Coal Tit, Blue Tit, Great Tit, Nuthatch, Treecreeper, Jackdaw, Rook, Crow, Chaffinch, Greenfinch, Goldfinch.

Common wildfowl

Mute Swan, Greylag Goose, Canada Goose, Shelduck, Wigeon (usually in Winter), Gadwall, Teal, Mallard, Shoveler, Pochard, Tufted Duck, Goldeneye (in Winter).

Common waterbirds

Little Grebe, Great Crested Grebe, Cormorant, Grey Heron, common wildfowl, Moorhen, Coot.

Common finches

House Sparrow (not strictly a finch, of course), Chaffinch, Greenfinch, Goldfinch, Siskin, Linnet.

Winter thrushes

Blackbird, Fieldfare, Song Thrush, Redwing, Mistle Thrush.

Summer warblers

Lesser Whitethroat, Whitethroat, Garden Warbler, Blackcap, Chiffchaff, Willow Warbler. (Sedge and Reed Warblers are also Summer visitors, but these are specifically mentioned in Other Likely Species where they occur).

Winter raptors

Marsh Harrier (usually seen in Summer, though some over-winter), Hen Harrier, Sparrowhawk, Kestrel, Merlin, Peregrine, Barn Owl, Short-eared Owl (owls included, though not strictly raptors).

Common waders

Oystercatcher, Ringed Plover, Golden Plover, Grey Plover, Lapwing, Knot, Sanderling, Dunlin, Snipe, Bar-tailed Godwit, Curlew, Redshank, Turnstone.

Passage waders

Little Ringed Plover, Ringed Plover, Little Stint, (Temminck's Stint – scarce), Curlew Sandpiper, Dunlin, Ruff, Whimbrel, Spotted Redshank, Greenshank, Green Sandpiper, Wood Sandpiper, Common Sandpiper.

Common gull species

Black-headed Gull, Common Gull, Lesser Black-backed Gull, Herring Gull, Great Black-backed Gull.

DEFINITIONS

Seaducks and Winter seabirds
Red-throated Diver, Black-throated Diver, Great Northern Diver, Great Crested Grebe, Red-necked Grebe, Slavonian Grebe, Wigeon, Eider, Long-tailed Duck, Common Scoter, Velvet Scoter, Goldeneye, Red-breasted Merganser, Guillemot, Razorbill.

Hirundines
Sand Martin, Swallow, House Martin, Swift (not a hirundine but included here to save space).

Passage migrants
Garganey, Little Gull, Black Tern, Hoopoe, Wryneck, Short-toed Lark, Woodlark, hirundines, Richard's Pipit, Tawny Pipit, Tree Pipit, Yellow Wagtail, Bluethroat, Black Redstart, Redstart, Whinchat, Wheatear, Winter thrushes, Ring Ouzel, Icterine Warbler, Barred Warbler, Summer warblers, Yellow-browed Warbler, Goldcrest, Firecrest, Spotted Flycatcher, Red-breasted Flycatcher, Pied Flycatcher, Red-backed Shrike, Great Grey Shrike, Brambling, Common Rosefinch, Ortolan Bunting, and many unmentioned rarities!

Passage seabirds
Divers, grebes, Sooty Shearwater, Manx Shearwater, Balearic Shearwater, Storm Petrel, Gannet, common wildfowl, common waders, Grey Phalarope, Pomarine Skua, Arctic Skua, Long-tailed Skua, Great Skua, Little Gull, Sabine's Gull, Kittiwake, Terns, Guillemot, Razorbill, Little Auk.

Common scrub birds
Wren, Dunnock, Robin, Blackbird, Song Thrush, Mistle Thrush, Summer warblers, Long-tailed Tit, Marsh Tit, Willow Tit, Blue Tit, Great Tit, Common finches.

Terns
Sandwich Tern, Roseate Tern, Common Tern, Arctic Tern.

GLOSSARY/BIRDSPEAK

LIKE ALL OTHER activities, birdwatching has generated a language of its own and I've attempted to explain terms used in the book that may not be familiar to beginners and less experienced birdwatchers.

BIRDRACE: A competition, usually between teams of four people to see how many species of birds can be seen (and heard) in a day.

BRECKLAND: A large area of heathland and pine forest centred around Thetford. Many scarce species of bird breed in the area.

BRECKS: Abbreviation for Breckland (see above).

BROADLAND: A popular holiday area for boat fanatics, made up of former peat diggings. Many broads and rivers make up this area.

BROADS: See Broadland.

GLOSSARY/BIRDSPEAK

BTO: British Trust for Ornithology.

CATEGORY C: A category on the official British bird list containing species that have escaped from captivity in the past, but now have self-sustaining populations (e.g. Canada Goose).

DIP: To go on a 'twitch' and not see the bird you went for.

DIPPER: One who 'dips' - a person who 'twitches' but misses the target bird. Not good!!

DUDE: A person who has all the top birdwatching equipment, but is a very poor birdwatcher (a bit like most politicians: style over content!).

ECLIPSE: Male duck species moult out of breeding plumage in summer, and don a dowdy, female-type plumage known as eclipse.

FALL: A mass grounding of migrating passerines, usually as a result of fog or heavy rain.

FENCE-HOPPER: A bird that has escaped from captivity.

LIFER: A bird species you have never seen before ("that Desert Warbler at Salthouse was a lifer for me!").

LISTER: Someone who keeps a list of everything they see, everywhere they see it! Garden list, life list, world list, county list, year list, birds seen while undergoing open-heart surgery list, etc. Includes me!

LOCAL PATCH: An area regularly covered by a birdwatcher, usually close to home. The feeling when something new turns up on your patch, rare or not, is pathetically exciting, particularly to a 'lister' such as me!

LOWLISTER: Someone who hasn't seen many species of bird.

LBJ: An affectionate term for Little Brown Job, any bird which has dowdy plumage (Dunnock, pipits, Garden Warbler, etc).

LRP: Shortened term for Little Ringed Plover.

NNR: National Nature Reserve.

NOA: Norfolk Ornithologists' Association.

NWT: Norfolk Wildlife Trust.

PLASTIC: Can refer to an escaped cage bird, or to a Category C species.

RAMSAR: A wetland site of international importance as defined at the convention in Ramsar, Iran.

RODING: The display flight of the Woodcock. Usually seen at dawn and dusk.

SSSI: Site of special scientific interest.

STRINGER: A person who misidentifies a bird and sticks to that identification. I have seen people 'string' a Collared Dove for a White's Thrush, a Little Tern for a Lesser

GLOSSARY/BIRDSPEAK

Crested Tern, a Dunnock for a Black-faced Bunting and a tree stump for an Osprey. And one of those was me (thankfully only once)!

TELESCOPE BRIGADE: A term sometimes used by beginners for a group of birdwatchers all huddled in one area peering through 'scopes, usually at a 'twitch'.

TICK OFF: To see a bird. Probably derived from 'listers' seeing a bird then ticking it off on one or more of their lists.

TWITCH: Travel to see a specific bird (usually a rare species) as soon as news of it breaks. Can involve a journey of many miles, or can just be to your 'local patch' to see something you have never seen there before. Has gained a bad name with beginners and birdwatchers who don't 'twitch', but is usually well organised, friendly, and great fun (if you don't 'dip').

TWITCHER: Someone who goes on a twitch. Ardent 'twitchers' set off as soon as news breaks of a rare bird, anywhere in the country. Others go when they can, usually at the weekend after the target bird has flown on the Friday night!

WWT: Wildfowl and Wetlands Trust.

YEARLIST: A record of birds seen (in Britain) from January 1st to December 31st.

YEARLISTER: Someone who tries to see as many species of bird in a year as possible. This has sometimes involved people seeing a rare bird on December 31, then travelling again to see it the next day to get it on two yearlists! The most famous example of this was in 1999/2000, when several birders turned up on January 1st 2000 to 'yeartick' the Ivory Gull, present on Aldeburgh beach on December 31st 1999. Unfortunately, the bird had been scared off the previous night by the Millennium fireworks display!

BIBLIOGRAPHY

Breckland Bird Reports (Edited by A. Wilson)
Available from A. Wilson, c/o BTO, The Nunnery, Thetford, Norfolk IP24 2PU

Norfolk Bird and Mammal Reports
Published yearly by the Norfolk and Norwich Naturalists' Society, Castle Museum, Norwich NR1 3JU.

The Birds of Cley (SJM Gantlett)
ISBN 0-9509903-0-2
Available from Sea Lawn, Coast Road, Cley-Next-The-Sea, Holt, Norfolk NR25 7RZ

The Birds Of Norfolk (Taylor, Seago, Allard, Dorling).
Published by Pica Press, ISBN 1-903206-02-2

Where To Watch Birds In East Anglia (Peter and Margaret Clarke)
Published by Helm.

USEFUL CONTACTS

WILDLIFE GROUPS

British Trust for Ornithology
The Nunnery, Thetford, Norfolk
IP24 2PU
01842 750050

Cley Bird Club
Peter Gooden, 45 Charles Road,
Holt, Norfolk,
NR25 6DA

Disabled toilets leaflet
RADAR, 12 City Forum, 250 City
Road, London EC1V 8AF
0207 125 03222

Disabled Birders Association
Bo Beolens, 18 St Mildreds Rd,
Margate, Kent CT9 2LT.
www.
disabledbirdersassociation.org.uk

English Nature
Norfolk Office,
60 Bracondale, Norwich
NR1 2BE
01603 620558
(Fax 01603 762552)
E-mail: norfolk@
english-nature.org.uk
www.english-nature.org.uk/

English Nature
Northminster House, Peterborough
PE1 1UA
01733 455000
www.english-nature.org.uk/

How Hill Trust
How Hill, Ludham, Great Yarmouth
NR29 5PG
01692 678555

The National Trust
East Anglia Regional Office,
Blickling, Norwich NR11 6NF
01263 733471
www.nationaltrust.org.uk/regions/
eastanglia/

**Norfolk and Norwich
Naturalists' Society**
Membership Secretary: SM
Livermore, 70, Naseby Way,
Dussindale,
Norwich NR7 0TP

Norfolk Bird Club
Membership Secretary: Bill
Landells, North Haven, Monks
Lane, Santon Downham, Brandon
IP27 0TG
www.norfolkbirdclub.org.uk

The Norfolk Coast Project
6 Station Road, Wells-Next-The-
Sea, Norfolk NR23 1AE
01328 711533.
www. norfolkcoastproject.org.uk

**Norfolk Ornithologists'
Association**
Holme Observatory, Broadwater
Road, Holme-Next-The-Sea,
Norfolk PE36 6LQ
01485 525406

Norfolk Wildlife Trust
Bewick House, 22 Thorpe Road,
Norwich NR1 1RY
01603 625540
e-mail: admin@nwt.cix.co.uk
www.wildlifetrust.org.uk/norfolk/

RSPB East Anglia Office
Stalham House, 65 Thorpe Road,
Norwich NR1 1UD
01603 661662

RSPB Mid-Yare Reserves
Staithes Cottage, Low Road,
Strumpshaw,
Norwich NR13 4HF
01603 715191.
E-mail: strumpshaw@rspb.org.uk

**Ted Ellis Trust
(Friends of)**
4 The Pippins, Blundeston,
Lowestoft, NR32 5AE.
www.tedellistrust.org.uk

OTHER USEFUL WILDLIFE CONTACTS

**Broadland Conservation
Centre**
Ranworth.
01603 270479

Forest Enterprise
Santon Downham, Brandon,
Suffolk IP27 0TJ
01842 810271

General Broads Authority
18 Colgate, Norwich, NR3 1BQ
01603 610734

High Lodge Forest Centre
01842 815434

**RSPB Snettisham Reserve
Office**
Snettisham Business Centre,
43a Lynn Road, Snettisham
PE31 7LR
01485 542689

BIRD NEWS, RECORDS AND INFORMATION

County Recorder
Giles Dunmore, 49 Nelson Road,
Sheringham NR25 8DA
01263 822550

Birdline East Anglia
09068 700245
(premium rate number).
Phone news to 0800 0830 803

OTHER NUMBERS

**Great Yarmouth Tourist
Information**
Marine Parade, Yarmouth.
01493 842195 (Easter –
September), or 01493 846345
(October – April).

**Hunstanton Tourist
Information**
01485 532610

**North Norfolk Tourist
Information**
North Norfolk District Council
Holt road, Cromer
01263 513811

Norwich Tourist Information
The Guildhall, Gaol Hill, Norwich.
01603 666071

Thetford Town Council
King's House, Thetford, IP24 2AP.
01842 754247

Traveline East Anglia,
0870 6082608.
www. travelineeastanglia.org.uk

INDEX

This index lists all site names, other relevant places and all birds listed in the 'target' or 'other likely species' lists in the site guide section. The number of entries listed under each species should not be seen as an indication of how common or otherwise the bird is in Norfolk.

INDEX

222

INDEX

223

INDEX